THE NEW ENGLISH HYMNAL

THE NEW ENGLISH HYMNAL

Words Edition

THE CANTERBURY PRESS NORWICH

The Canterbury Press Norwich, St Mary's Works,
St Mary's Plain, Norwich, Norfolk NR3 3BH
The Canterbury Press Norwich is a publishing imprint
of Hymns Ancient & Modern Limited

WORDS EDITION
ISBN 0 907547 49 4

First published 1986
Second impression March 1986
Third impression September 1986
Fourth impression May 1987
Fifth impression March 1988
Sixth impression February 1989
Seventh impression March 1990
Eighth impression September 1990
Ninth impression January 1991
Tenth impression November 1992
Eleventh impression November 1993

© Compilation, *The English Hymnal Company Ltd*

Music processed by Halstan & Co Ltd,
Amersham, Bucks
Filmset by Eta Services (Typesetters) Ltd,
Beccles, Suffolk
Printed and Bound in Great Britain by
The Bath Press, Avon

PREFACE

It was with an awareness that they had set themselves a daunting task that the editors undertook to produce a successor to the *English Hymnal*. Now almost eighty years old, and unrevised during that period save for a new music edition in 1933, the publication of the original book in 1906 proved to be a landmark in English hymnody. It set new standards in words and music for Anglican worship in the twentieth century.

That century is near its end. It has seen changes in theological understanding and in modes of worship which cannot but affect what is provided for the worshipper to sing. Nevertheless, it is some indication of the quality of the original book that out of 656 hymns we have felt it right to retain approximately 400 in a smaller collection. To these we have added 100 from other sources old and new, and have also provided a liturgical section of some forty items. Among these appear the plainsong sequences. Though not in common use, they are deeply valued by those who have become accustomed to them. Good choirs with some training in plainsong should be encouraged to attempt them.

A feature of the *English Hymnal* was its full provision of office hymns for Sundays and other holy days. This principle has been retained, though on a more limited scale. Except for seasons and some of the greater feasts only one office hymn rather than two is provided. This has enabled us to dispense with some of the less successful translations, and in a few places we have provided new hymns in the traditional style. The office hymn need not be limited to the choir offices; it can appropriately be used at the eucharist as an introit or gradual, so setting the theme of the day.

Ordinary hymns proper to particular saints' days have rarely been noted for their high quality and we make no

v

extravagant claims for those we have included; but we felt an obligation to provide for all the red-letter days 'to be observed'. In some instances we have greatly revised or rewritten those which appeared in the *English Hymnal*.

We have retained the general arrangement of the *English Hymnal*, based chiefly on the Church's year and her sacramental life. In a book whose primary purpose is to be an accompaniment to the liturgy there was no reason to do otherwise; but an important caveat should be borne in mind. If a hymn is placed, say, in Advent or Passiontide, that does not necessarily imply that it is unsuitable for use at other times. This will be apparent to those who consult the list of suggested hymns for Sundays and other holy days which we have provided.

In the book as a whole we have tried to include most of the great classic hymns in common use, as well as more recent hymns which have established themselves. We have also admitted a few new ones which have yet to stand the test of use. Where a well-known hymn has become wedded to a particular tune we have provided that tune, sometimes giving as an alternative the tune to which it was set in the *English Hymnal*; but tunes in the 1933 edition which have been little used are mostly omitted. Very occasionally, on the ground of widespread use in some parishes, we have admitted hymns, and sometimes tunes, which we would not otherwise have included. To meet current liturgical practice the eucharistic section has been considerably enlarged. We have also provided a number of carols, mainly, though not exclusively, for the Christmas season.

The post-war surge in hymn-writing has not been ignored, but we regard much of it as poor in quality and ephemeral in expression. In particular, while the social gospel is an important element in Christian teaching, its translation into verse can be so contemporary that it quickly becomes dated. It remains true that the offering of objective praise and worship to God, the lover of mankind, is the ultimate ground of man's love of his fellow-man. By including a section headed

'The Kingdom of God' and similar hymns elsewhere in the book, we have not overlooked the social duty of Christians, but we believe that its application to immediate needs can often be better expressed in sermon and prayers than in hymnody.

Some may be critical of revisions and alterations which we have made in original texts. We make no apology for it except where we may have done it badly; it is a process which has long been current—certainly since Charles Wesley wrote 'Hark, how all the welkin rings!' and, no doubt, before that. Our aim has been to make what is sung such that it can be sung with sincerity. Occasionally minor adjustments have been made to secure a better musical accentuation. Well-known and popular hymns have rarely been amended, though we felt it desirable to abandon the description of our Lord as 'lone and dreary'.

We have made no attempt to alter into the 'you' form hymns which use the second person singular in addressing God. As far as we are aware, congregations experience no difficulty in understanding and in using the traditional form in which most hymns have been written.

To meet the widespread and increasing use of the *Alternative Service Book*, the liturgical section supplies two simple settings for the eucharist, Merbecke for Rite B, and a new congregational setting in speech-rhythm for Rite A. We hope that the latter may fulfil a need which has frequently been expressed.

Processions in church are not as much in fashion as once they were, but we have in each section indicated hymns suitable for use in procession, and in the liturgical section have given a series of versicles, responses and collects, where their use at the close of a procession is desired.

It will be apparent from what we have written that the *New English Hymnal* is only in a very limited sense an experimental book. Its aim is to be what its predecessor claimed to be, 'a humble companion' to the common prayer and worship of the Church of England—and, it may be, of other provinces of the

Anglican Communion. As such we present our work, in the hope that it may be used to give greater glory to God in his people's offering of the sacrifice of praise.

ANTHONY CAESAR
CHRISTOPHER DEARNLEY
MARTIN DRAPER
MICHAEL FLEMING
ARTHUR HUTCHINGS
COLIN ROBERTS
GEORGE TIMMS (*Chairman*)

CONTENTS

ix

CONTENTS

ACKNOWLEDGEMENTS

The English Hymnal Company and The Canterbury Press Norwich thank the owners or controllers of copyright for permission to use the copyright material listed below. Every effort has been made to trace copyright owners, and the compilers apologize to any whose rights have inadvertently not been acknowledged.

WORDS

Numbers in italics indicate a translation

AUTHOR	PERMISSION GRANTED BY	NO. OF HYMN
Alington, C. A.	Hymns Ancient and Modern Ltd	107, 199, 265, 477
Appleford, P.	Copyright 1960. Josef Weinberger Ltd	297
Baelz, P.	Author	395
Bayly, A. F.	Oxford University Press	405
Bell, G. K. A.	Oxford University Press (from *Enlarged Songs of Praise*)	345
Bell M. F.	Oxford University Press (from *English Hymnal*)	109
Briggs, G. W.	Oxford University Press	114
,,	Oxford University Press (from *Enlarged Songs of Praise*)	279, 494
Brooks, R. T.	Copyright © 1954 Renewal 1982 by Hope Publishing Company, Carol Stream, Il. 60188, USA. All Rights Reserved	438
,,	Copyright © 1984 by Hope Publishing Company. All Rights Reserved	496
Burns, E. J.	Author	486
Carter, S.	Stainer & Bell Ltd. Further reproduction prohibited without consent of the copyright holder	375
Crum, J. M. C.	Oxford University Press	115
Dudley-Smith, T.	Author	43, 44, 186, 258, 340, 400

ACKNOWLEDGEMENTS

AUTHOR	PERMISSION GRANTED BY	NO. OF HYMN
Farjeon, Eleanor	David Higham Associated Limited (from *The Children's Bells*)	237
Foley, B	Faber Music Ltd.	140, 236
Gillett, G.	Oxford University Press (from *English Hymnal*)	212, 380, 522
Green, Fred Pratt	Stainer & Bell Ltd. Further reproduction prohibited without the consent of the copyright holder	10
Greenwood, H.	The Society of the Sacred Mission	123
Hardy, H. E.	A. R. Mowbray & Co. Ltd.	89
Herklots, Rosamond	Oxford University Press	66
Hewlett, M.	Oxford University Press (from *English Praise*)	142, 293
Hodgetts, M.	Author	266
Housman, L.	Oxford University Press (from *English Hymnal*)	38, 162, 163, 166, 174, 203, 220 (Altd)
Idle, C.	Jubilate Hymns Ltd.	363
Judd, F. A.	The Society of the Sacred Mission	192
Moore J. B.	Author	319
Morgan, E.	Hymns Ancient & Modern Ltd	487
Parsons, R. G.	Cannot trace copyright owner	310
Peacey, J. R.	The Exors. of Mrs J. R. Peacey	161, 321
Quinn SJ, James	Geoffrey Chapman, a division of Cassell Ltd	361, 513
,,	International Committee on English in the Liturgy (from *Resource Collection of Hymns and Service Music for the Liturgy* © 1981. All rights reserved.)	323
Reid, W. W. (Jr.)	Copyright © 1959 by The Hymn Society of America, Texas Christian University, Fort Worth, TX 76129, USA	370

ACKNOWLEDGEMENTS

AUTHOR	PERMISSION GRANTED BY	NO. OF HYMN
Riley, A.	Oxford University Press (from *English Hymnal*)	81, 179, 180, 190, 300, 330, 478
Riley, H.	Author	288
Roberts, R. E.	Oxford University Press (from *English Hymnal*)	136, 168 (Altd)
Rutt, C. R.	Author	512
Sparrow-Simpson, W. J.	Novello & Co. Ltd	272
Struther, Jan	Oxford University Press (from *Enlarged Songs of Praise*)	239
Timms, G. B.	Oxford University Press (from *English Praise*)	185, 275, 312, 356, 428, 446
,,	Canterbury Press Norwich	35, 45, 58, 154, 173, 176, 196, 315
Tucker, F. Bland	The Church Pension Fund, New York	284, 335
Winslow, J.	Mrs J. Tyrrell	240
Wren, B.	Oxford University Press (from *Faith Looking Forward*)	177

Extracts from *The Book of Common Prayer of 1662*, which is Crown Copyright in the United Kingdom, are reproduced by permission of Eyre & Spottiswoode (Publishers) Limited, Her Majesty's Printer, London.	Extracts appear in 504, 506, 515, 518, 525
The Scripture quotations contained herein are from the *Revised Standard Version of the Bible*, copyrighted © 1946, 1952, 1971 by the Division of Christian Education of the National Council of the Churches of Christ in the U.S.A., and are used by permission. All rights reserved.	Extracts appear in 518
The Gloria, Benedictus, Sanctus and Agnus Dei from *The Order for Holy Communion Rite A* in The Alternative Service Book 1980 are © the International Consultation on English Texts and are reproduced with permission of the Central Board of Finance of the Church of England. Other material from Holy Communion Rite A is reproduced by permission of the Central Board of Finance of the Church of England. Extracts from *The Order for Holy*	541 Rite A 542 Rite B

ACKNOWLEDGEMENTS

Communion Rite B, some of which are adapted from the Book of Common Prayer, which is Crown copyright, are also reproduced with permission.

The music for *Rite A* has been compiled by, and is the copyright of G. B. Timms and E. H. Warrell. The music for *Rite B* is an arrangement by A. J. B. Hutchings. Permission to reproduce, in both cases, should be sought from the Canterbury Press Norwich.

The following copyright texts were written by the Editors of *English Praise* and permission to reprint should be sought in the first instance from Oxford University Press.
7, 40, 108, 203, 228, 256, 257, 298, 481
The following copyright texts belong to or have been altered by the Editors and permission to reprint should be sought from The Canterbury Press Norwich.
1, 2, 8, 11, 53, 54, 96, 98, 136, 139, 156, 160, 164, 167, 168, 181, 195, 201, 211, 218, 219, 220, 221, 222, 223, 240, 316, 318, 321, 325, 327, 423, 470, 520, 528–540.

COPYRIGHT

GRANTS

Liberal grants of The New English Hymnal are made by the Publishers to help parishes in the introduction of the book or in the renewal of existing supplies. An application form for a grant can be obtained from the Canterbury Press Norwich, St Mary's Works, St Mary's Plain, Norwich, Norfolk NR3 3BH.

EXPLANATORY NOTES

In each section the Office Hymns are printed first, followed by a note suggesting hymns suitable for a procession. Thereafter, in each section the hymns appear in alphabetical order.

'Amen' is printed only at the end of hymns of which the last verse is in the form of a doxology. Even there its use may be regarded as optional, except in one or two instances where it is musically the conclusion, and in the case of the plainsong melodies of the Office Hymns, with which it should always be used.

Refrains are printed in *italic*.

The sign ⋆ indicates that the verse or verses may be omitted without injury to the sense of the hymn.

The sign † after an author's name indicates a slight alteration to the original text; the sign ‡ a more extensive alteration.

The method of singing the Responsorial Psalms is given where they appear, at page 540.

PART I

THE CHRISTIAN YEAR

1 OFFICE HYMN

Conditor alme siderum

CREATOR of the stars of night,
Thy people's everlasting light,
O Jesu, Saviour of us all,
Regard thy servants when they call.

2 Thou, grieving at the bitter cry
Of all creation doomed to die,
Didst come to save a ruined race
With healing gifts of heavenly grace.

3 Thou camest, Bridegroom of the bride,
As drew the world to evening-tide,
Proceeding from a virgin shrine,
The Son of Man, yet Lord divine.

4 At thy great name, exalted now,
All knees must bend, all hearts must bow,
And things in heaven and earth shall own
That thou art Lord and King alone.

5 To thee, O holy One, we pray,
Our judge in that tremendous day,
Preserve us, while we dwell below,
From every onslaught of the foe.

6 All praise, eternal Son, to thee,
Whose advent sets thy people free,
Whom with the Father we adore,
And Spirit blest, for evermore.   Amen.

From the Latin
Tr J. M. NEALE 1818–66
and EDITORS

2 OFFICE HYMN

Verbum supernum prodiens

O HEAVENLY Word of God on high,
Whose love has brought salvation nigh,
And from the Father's heart didst come
To save a race by sin undone.

2 Our minds enlighten from above,
And kindle with the fire of love,
That as we hear thy gospel read,
All sinful thoughts may flee in dread.

3 So, when thou comest at the last,
And earth's long history is past,
May we be set at thy right hand,
And with thine own in glory stand.

4 Grant thou thy gifts of grace below,
In heaven an endless joy bestow,
Who art our sole and sovereign Lord,
The saving judge, and saints' reward.

5   All praise, eternal Son, to thee,
    Whose advent sets thy people free,
    Whom with the Father we adore,
    And Spirit blest, for evermore.   Amen.

EDITORS, based upon the Latin,
c 10th century

3   COME, thou long-expected Jesus,
    Born to set thy people free,
    From our fears and sins release us,
    Let us find our rest in thee.

2   Israel's strength and consolation,
    Hope of all the earth thou art,
    Dear desire of every nation,
    Joy of every longing heart.

3   Born thy people to deliver,
    Born a child and yet a king,
    Born to reign in us for ever,
    Now thy gracious kingdom bring.

4   By thine own eternal Spirit,
    Rule in all our hearts alone;
    By thine all-sufficient merit
    Raise us to thy glorious throne.

CHARLES WESLEY 1707–88

4   GABRIEL'S message does away
    Satan's curse and Satan's sway,
Out of darkness brings our Day:
    So, behold,
    All the gates of heaven unfold.

2   He that comes despised shall reign;
    He that cannot die, be slain;
Death by death its death shall gain:

3   Weakness shall the strong confound;
    By the hands, in grave-clothes wound,
Adam's chains shall be unbound:

4   By the sword that was his own,
    By that sword, and that alone,
Shall Goliath be o'erthrown:

5   Art by art shall be assailed;
    To the cross shall Life be nailed;
From the grave shall hope be hailed:

Piae Cantiones 1582
Tr J. M. NEALE 1818–66

5   *Vox clara ecce intonat*

HARK! a herald voice is calling:
  'Christ is nigh,' it seems to say;
'Cast away the dreams of darkness,
  O ye children of the day!'

2 Startled at the solemn warning,
    Let the earth-bound soul arise;
Christ, her Sun, all sloth dispelling,
    Shines upon the morning skies.

3 Lo! the Lamb, so long expected,
    Comes with pardon down from heaven;
Let us haste, with tears of sorrow,
    One and all to be forgiven;

4 So when next he comes in glory,
    And earth's final hour draws near,
May he then as our defender
    On the clouds of heaven appear.

5 Honour, glory, virtue, merit,
    To the Father and the Son,
With the co-eternal Spirit,
    While unending ages run.   Amen.

From the Latin
Tr E. CASWALL 1814–78‡

6 HARK the glad sound! the Saviour comes,
    The Saviour promised long!
Let every heart prepare a throne,
    And every voice a song.

2 He comes the prisoners to release
    In Satan's bondage held;
The gates of brass before him burst,
    The iron fetters yield.

3 He comes the broken heart to bind,
  The bleeding soul to cure,
And with the treasures of his grace
  Enrich the humble poor.

4 Our glad hosannas, Prince of peace,
  Thy welcome shall proclaim,
And heaven's eternal arches ring
  With thy belovèd name.

PHILIP DODDRIDGE 1702–51†

7 HILLS of the North, rejoice,
   Echoing songs arise,
  Hail with united voice
   Him who made earth and skies:
He comes in righteousness and love,
He brings salvation from above.

2 Isles of the Southern seas,
   Sing to the listening earth,
  Carry on every breeze
   Hope of a world's new birth:
In Christ shall all be made anew,
His word is sure, his promise true.

3 Lands of the East, arise,
   He is your brightest morn,
  Greet him with joyous eyes,
   Praise shall his path adorn:
The God whom you have longed to know
In Christ draws near, and calls you now.

4   Shores of the utmost West,
       Lands of the setting sun,
    Welcome the heavenly guest
       In whom the dawn has come:
He brings a never-ending light
Who triumphed o'er our darkest night.

5   Shout, as you journey on,
       Songs be in every mouth,
    Lo, from the North they come,
       From East and West and South:
In Jesus all shall find their rest,
In him the sons of earth be blest.

EDITORS, based on
C. E. OAKLEY 1832–65

8   LIFT up your heads ye mighty gates,
    Behold the King of glory waits,
    The King of kings is drawing near,
    The Saviour of the world is here.

2   O blest the land, the city blest,
    Where Christ as ruler is confessed;
    O happy hearts and happy homes
    To whom this king in triumph comes.

3 Come then, O Saviour, and abide,
   Our hearts to thee be open wide;
May all thy inward presence feel,
   To all thy grace and love reveal.

GEORGE WEISSEL 1590–1635
Tr CATHERINE WINKWORTH 1827–78
and EDITORS

9 LO! he comes with clouds descending,
   Once for favoured sinners slain;
Thousand thousand saints attending
   Swell the triumph of his train:
     Alleluya!
   God appears, on earth to reign.

2 Every eye shall now behold him
   Robed in dreadful majesty;
Those who set at nought and sold him,
   Pierced and nailed him to the tree,
     Deeply wailing
   Shall the true Messiah see.

3 Those dear tokens of his passion
   Still his dazzling body bears,
Cause of endless exultation
   To his ransomed worshippers:
     With what rapture
   Gaze we on those glorious scars!

4 Yea, Amen! let all adore thee,
 High on thine eternal throne;
 Saviour, take the power and glory:
 Claim the kingdom for thine own:
 O come quickly!
 Alleluya! Come, Lord, come!

CHARLES WESLEY 1707–88‡

10 LONG ago, prophets knew
 Christ would come, born a Jew.
 Come to make all things new;
 Bear his People's burden,
 Freely love and pardon.
 Ring, bells, ring, ring, ring!
 Sing, choirs, sing, sing, sing!
 When he comes,
 When he comes,
 Who will make him welcome?

2 God in time, God in man,
 This is God's timeless plan:
 He will come, as a man,
 Born himself of woman,
 God divinely human.
 Ring, bells, ring, ring, ring! etc

3 Mary, hail! Though afraid,
 She believed, she obeyed.
 In her womb God is laid;
 Till the time expected
 Nurtured and protected.
 Ring, bells, ring, ring, ring! etc

4 Journey ends! Where afar
Bethlem shines, like a star,
Stable door stands ajar.
Unborn Son of Mary,
Saviour, do not tarry!
  Ring, bells, ring, ring, ring!
  Sing, choirs, sing, sing, sing!
    Jesus comes!
    Jesus comes!
  We will make him welcome!

F. PRATT GREEN b 1903

11   *Veni, veni, Emmanuel*

O COME, O come, Emmanuel!
Redeem thy captive Israel,
That into exile drear is gone
Far from the face of God's dear Son.
  Rejoice! Rejoice! Emmanuel
  Shall come to thee, O Israel.

2 O come, thou Wisdom from on high!
Who madest all in earth and sky,
Creating man from dust and clay:
To us reveal salvation's way.

3 O come, O come, Adonaï,
Who in thy glorious majesty
From Sinai's mountain, clothed with awe,
Gavest thy folk the ancient law.

4   O come, thou Root of Jesse! draw
The quarry from the lion's claw;
From those dread caverns of the grave,
From nether hell, thy people save.

5   O come, thou Lord of David's Key!
The royal door fling wide and free;
Safeguard for us the heavenward road,
And bar the way to death's abode.

6   O come, O come, thou Dayspring bright!
Pour on our souls thy healing light;
Dispel the long night's lingering gloom,
And pierce the shadows of the tomb.

7   O come, Desire of nations! show
Thy kingly reign on earth below;
Thou Corner-stone, uniting all,
Restore the ruin of our fall.

Cologne 1710, based on the
ancient Advent Antiphons
Tr T. A. LACEY 1853–1931 and EDITORS

Verse 1 may be repeated at the close

12   *Jordanis oras praevia*

ON Jordan's bank the Baptist's cry
Announces that the Lord is nigh;
Come then and hearken, for he brings
Glad tidings from the King of kings.

2 Then cleansed be every Christian breast,
And furnished for so great a guest!
Yea, let us each our hearts prepare
For Christ to come and enter there.

3 For thou art our salvation, Lord,
Our refuge and our great reward;
Without thy grace our souls must fade,
And wither like a flower decayed.

4 Stretch forth thine hand to heal our sore,
And make us rise, to fall no more;
Once more upon thy people shine,
And fill the world with love divine.

5 All praise, eternal Son, to thee
Whose advent sets thy people free,
Whom, with the Father, we adore,
And Spirit blest, for evermore.   Amen.

CHARLES COFFIN 1676–1749
Tr JOHN CHANDLER 1808–76

13 O QUICKLY come, great Judge of all;
For, awful though thine advent be,
All shadows from the truth will fall,
And falsehood die, in sight of thee:
O quickly come; for doubt and fear
Like clouds dissolve when thou art near.

2　O quickly come, great King of all;
　　　Reign all around us, and within;
　Let sin no more our souls enthral,
　　　Let pain and sorrow die with sin:
　O quickly come; for thou alone
　Canst make thy scattered people one.

3　O quickly come, true Life of all,
　　　For death is mighty all around;
　On every home his shadows fall,
　　　On every heart his mark is found:
　O quickly come; for grief and pain
　Can never cloud thy glorious reign.

4　O quickly come, sure Light of all,
　　　For gloomy night broods o'er our way,
　And weakly souls begin to fall
　　　With weary watching for the day:
　O quickly come; for round thy throne
　No eye is blind, no night is known.

LAWRENCE TUTTIET 1825–97

14　　*Instantis adventum Dei*

　　THE advent of our God
　　With eager prayers we greet,
　And singing haste upon the road
　　His glorious gift to meet.

2　　The everlasting Son
　　Scorns not the Virgin's womb;
　That we from bondage may be won
　　He bears a bondsman's doom.

3   Daughter of Sion, rise
      To meet thy lowly King;
Let not thy stubborn heart despise
      The peace he comes to bring.

4   On clouds of dazzling light,
      As Judge he comes again,
His scattered people to unite,
      With him in heaven to reign.

5   Let evil flee away,
      Ere that great hour shall dawn,
Let this old Adam day by day
      The new Man all put on.

6   Praise to the incarnate Son,
      Who comes to set us free,
With Father and with Spirit One,
      To all eternity.   Amen.

CHARLES COFFIN 1676–1749
Tr H. PUTMAN 1861–1935‡

15 THE Lord will come and not be slow,
      His footsteps cannot err;
Before him righteousness shall go,
      His royal harbinger.

2 Truth from the earth, like to a flower,
      Shall bud and blossom then;
And justice, from her heavenly bower,
      Look down on mortal men.

3 Rise, God, judge thou the earth in might,
    This wicked earth redress;
For thou art he who shalt by right
    The nations all possess.

4 The nations all whom thou hast made
    Shall come, and all shall frame
To bow them low before thee, Lord,
    And glorify thy name.

5 For great thou art, and wonders great
    By thy strong hand are done:
Thou in thy everlasting seat
    Remainest God alone.

JOHN MILTON 1608–74
cento Psalms 85, 82, 86

16   *Wachet auf*

WAKE, O wake! with tidings thrilling
The watchmen all the air are filling,
    Arise, Jerusalem, arise!
Midnight strikes! no more delaying,
'The hour has come!' we hear them saying.
        Where are ye all, ye virgins wise?
            The Bridegroom comes in sight,
            Raise high your torches bright!
                Alleluya!
            The wedding song
            Swells loud and strong:
Go forth and join the festal throng.

2 Sion hears the watchmen shouting,
   Her heart leaps up with joy undoubting,
        She stands and waits with eager eyes;
   See her Friend from heaven descending,
   Adorned with truth and grace unending!
        Her light burns clear, her star doth rise.
            Now come, thou precious Crown,
            Lord Jesu, God's own Son!
                Hosanna!
            Let us prepare
            To follow there,
   Where in thy supper we may share.

3 Every soul in thee rejoices;
   From men and from angelic voices
        Be glory given to thee alone!
   Now the gates of pearl receive us,
   Thy presence never more shall leave us,
        We stand with angels round thy throne.
            Earth cannot give below
            The bliss thou dost bestow.
                Alleluya!
            Grant us to raise,
            To length of days,
   The triumph-chorus of thy praise.

PHILIPP NICOLAI 1556–1608
Tr F. C. BURKITT 1864–1935

17 WHEN came in flesh the incarnate Word,
        The heedless world slept on,
    And only simple shepherds heard
        That God had sent his Son.

2 When comes the Saviour at the last,
    From east to west shall shine
The judgement light, and earth aghast
    Shall tremble at the sign.

3 Then shall the pure of heart be blest,
    As mild he comes to them,
As when upon the Virgin's breast
    He lay at Bethlehem:

4 As mild to meek-eyed love and faith,
    Only more strong to save;
Strengthened by having bowed to death,
    By having burst the grave.

5 Lord, who could dare see thee descend
    In state, unless he knew
Thou art the sorrowing sinner's friend,
    The gracious and the true?

6 Dwell in our hearts, O Saviour blest;
    So shall thine advent's dawn
'Twixt us and thee, our bosom-guest,
    Be but the veil withdrawn.

JOSEPH ANSTICE 1808–36†

18   YE servants of the Lord
    Each for your Master wait,
Observant of his heavenly word,
    And watchful at his gate.

2   Let all your lamps be bright,
      And trim the golden flame;
  Gird up your loins as in his sight,
      For aweful is his name.

3   Watch! 'tis your Lord's command,
      And while we speak, he's near;
  Mark the first signal of his hand,
      And ready all appear.

4   O happy servant he,
      In such a posture found!
  He shall his Lord with rapture see,
      And be with honour crowned.

5   Christ shall the banquet spread
      With his own royal hand,
  And raise that faithful servant's head
      Amidst the angelic band.

PHILIP DODDRIDGE 1702–51†

See also

501 The Advent Prose
502 The Advent Sequence
503 The Advent Antiphons
286 From glory to glory advancing
388 Jesus shall reign, where'er the sun
405 Lord of the boundless curves of space
408 Love divine, all loves excelling
466 Thou whose almighty word
483 The Church of God a kingdom is
494–500 The Kingdom of God

19   OFFICE HYMN

Veni, Redemptor gentium

Come, thou Redeemer of the earth,
And manifest thy virgin-birth:
Let every age adoring fall,
Such birth befits the God of all.

2   Begotten of no human will,
But of the Spirit, thou art still
The Word of God, in flesh arrayed,
The Saviour, now to man displayed.

3★   The virgin womb that burden gained
With virgin honour all unstained,
The banners there of virtue glow,
God in his temple dwells below.

4★   Forth from that chamber goeth he,
That royal home of purity,
A giant in twofold substance one,
Rejoicing now his course to run.

5★   From God the Father he proceeds,
To God the Father back he speeds,
Runs out his course to death and hell,
Returns on God's high throne to dwell.

6   O equal to thy Father, thou!
Gird on thy fleshly mantle now,
The weakness of our mortal state
With deathless might invigorate.

7 Thy cradle here shall glitter bright,
And darkness glow with new-born light,
No more shall night extinguish day,
Where love's bright beams their power display.

8 O Jesu, Virgin-born, to thee
Eternal praise and glory be,
Whom with the Father we adore
And Holy Spirit, evermore.   Amen.

ST AMBROSE 340–97
Tr J. M. NEALE 1818–66
and others

*Verses 4 and 5 are based upon the BCP text of Ps 19 verses 5
and 6*

20   OFFICE HYMN

A solis ortus cardine

From east to west, from shore to shore,
Let every heart awake and sing
The holy Child whom Mary bore,
The Christ, the everlasting King.

2 Behold, the world's creator wears
The form and fashion of a slave,
Our very flesh our Maker shares,
His fallen creature, man, to save.

3 For this how wondrously he wrought!
A maiden, in her lowly place,
Became, in ways beyond all thought,
The chosen vessel of his grace.

4   She bowed her to the angel's word
     Declaring what the Father willed,
     And suddenly the promised Lord
     That pure and hallowed temple filled.

5   He shrank not from the oxen's stall,
     He lay within the manger-bed,
     And he whose bounty feedeth all,
     At Mary's breast himself was fed.

6   And while the angels in the sky
     Sang praise above the silent field,
     To shepherds poor, the Lord most high,
     The one great Shepherd was revealed.

7   All glory for that blessèd morn
     To God the Father ever be,
     All praise to thee, O Virgin-born,
     And praise, blest Spirit, unto thee.   Amen.

Latin, CAELIUS SEDULIUS c 450
Tr JOHN ELLERTON 1826–93

For a procession in Christmastide see

30 O come, all ye faithful
33 Of the Father's heart begotten
34 Once in royal David's city

21 A GREAT and mighty wonder,
A full and holy cure!
The Virgin bears the Infant
With virgin-honour pure.
Repeat the hymn again!
'To God on high be glory,
And peace on earth to men!'

2 The Word becomes incarnate
And yet remains on high!
And Cherubim sing anthems
To shepherds from the sky.

3 While thus they sing your Monarch,
Those bright angelic bands,
Rejoice, ye vales and mountains,
Ye oceans clap your hands.

4 Since all he comes to ransom,
By all be he adored,
The Infant born in Bethl'em,
The Saviour and the Lord.

5 And idol forms shall perish,
And error shall decay,
And Christ shall wield his sceptre,
Our Lord and God for ay.

Greek, ST GERMANUS 634–734
Tr J. M. NEALE 1818–66
and others

22 AWAY in a manger, no crib for a bed,
The little Lord Jesus laid down his sweet head.
The stars in the bright sky looked down where
he lay,
The little Lord Jesus asleep on the hay.

2 The cattle are lowing, the baby awakes,
But little Lord Jesus no crying he makes.
I love thee, Lord Jesus! Look down from the
sky,
And stay by my side until morning is nigh.

3 Be near me, Lord Jesus; I ask thee to stay
Close by me for ever, and love me, I pray.
Bless all the dear children in thy tender care,
And fit us for heaven, to live with thee there.

ANONYMOUS
Philadelphia 1883

23 BEHOLD the great Creator makes
Himself a house of clay,
A robe of virgin flesh he takes
Which he will wear for ay.

2 Hark, hark, the wise eternal Word,
Like a weak infant cries!
In form of servant is the Lord,
And God in cradle lies.

3   This wonder struck the world amazed,
     It shook the starry frame;
   Squadrons of spirits stood and gazed,
     Then down in troops they came.

4   Glad shepherds ran to view this sight;
     A choir of angels sings,
   And eastern sages with delight
     Adore this King of kings.

5   Join then all hearts that are not stone,
     And all our voices prove,
   To celebrate this holy One,
     The God of peace and love.

THOMAS PESTEL 1584–1659

24 CHRISTIANS awake! salute the happy morn
Whereon the Saviour of the world was born;
Rise to adore the mystery of love
Which hosts of angels chanted from above;
With them the joyful tidings first begun
Of God incarnate and the Virgin's Son.

2   Then to the watchful shepherds it was told,
Who heard the angelic herald's voice, 'Behold,
I bring you tidings of a Saviour's birth
To you and all the nations on the earth:
This day hath God fulfilled his promised word,
This day is born a Saviour, Christ the Lord.'

3   He spake; and straightway that celestial choir
In hymns of joy, unknown before, conspire;
The praises of redeeming love they sang,
And heaven's whole orb with alleluyas rang:
God's highest glory was their anthem still,
Peace on the earth, and unto men goodwill.

4*   To Bethl'em straight the enlightened shepherds
     ran
To see the wonder God had wrought for man,
And found, with Joseph and the blessèd Maid,
Her Son, the Saviour, in a manger laid:
Joyful, the wondrous story they proclaim –
The first apostles of his infant fame.

5*   Like Mary let us ponder in our mind
God's wondrous love in saving lost mankind;
Trace we the Babe, who hath retrieved our loss,
From his poor manger to his bitter cross;
Then may we hope, angelic hosts among,
To sing, redeemed, a glad triumphal song.

JOHN BYROM 1691–1763‡

25 GOD rest you merry, gentlemen,
  Let nothing you dismay,
Remember Christ our Saviour
  Was born on Christmas Day,
To save us all from Satan's power
  When we were gone astray:
  O tidings of comfort and joy,
    comfort and joy!
  O tidings of comfort and joy!

2 From God our heavenly Father
  A blessèd angel came,
And unto certain shepherds
  Brought tidings of the same,
How that in Bethlehem was born
  The Son of God by name:

3 And when they came to Bethlehem
  Where our dear Saviour lay,
They found him in a manger,
  Where oxen feed on hay;
His mother Mary kneeling down,
  Unto the Lord did pray:

4 Now to the Lord sing praises,
  All you within this place,
And with true love and brotherhood
  Each other now embrace;
This holy tide of Christmas
  All other doth efface:

TRADITIONAL

26 HARK! the herald angels sing
Glory to the new-born King;
Peace on earth and mercy mild,
God and sinners reconciled:
Joyful all ye nations rise,
Join the triumph of the skies,
With the angelic host proclaim,
Christ is born in Bethlehem:
Hark! the herald angels sing
Glory to the new-born King.

2 Christ, by highest heaven adored,
Christ, the everlasting Lord,
Late in time behold him come
Offspring of a Virgin's womb!
Veiled in flesh the Godhead see,
Hail the incarnate Deity!
Pleased as man with man to dwell,
Jesus, our Emmanuel:

3 Hail the heaven-born Prince of peace!
Hail the Sun of Righteousness!
Light and life to all he brings,
Risen with healing in his wings;
Mild he lays his glory by,
Born that man no more may die,
Born to raise the sons of earth,
Born to give them second birth:

4* Come, Desire of nations, come,
   Fix in us thy humble home;
   Rise, the woman's conquering Seed,
   Bruise in us the serpent's head;
   Now display thy saving power,
   Ruined nature now restore,
   Now in mystic union join
   Thine to ours, and ours to thine:

CHARLES WESLEY 1707–88
and others

27   HOW brightly shines the Morning Star!
     The nations see and hail afar
        The Light in Judah shining.
     Thou David's son of Jacob's race,
     The Bridegroom, and the King of grace,
        For thee our hearts are pining!
           Lowly, holy,
     Great and glorious, thou victorious
           Prince of graces,
     Filling all the heavenly places!

2   Though circled by the hosts on high,
     He deigns to cast a pitying eye
        Upon his helpless creature;
     The whole creation's Head and Lord,
     By highest seraphim adored,
        Assumes our very nature.
           Jesu, grant us,
     Through thy merit, to inherit
           Thy salvation;
     Hear, O hear our supplication.

3   Rejoice, ye heav'ns; thou earth, reply;
With praise, ye sinners, fill the sky,
   For this his Incarnation.
Incarnate God, put forth thy power,
Ride on, ride on, great Conqueror,
   Till all know thy salvation.
      Amen, Amen!
Alleluya, Alleluya!
    Praise be given
Evermore by earth and heaven.

German, PHILIPP NICOLAI 1556–1608
Tr WILLIAM MERCER 1811–1873

28   IN the bleak mid-winter
    Frosty wind made moan,
Earth stood hard as iron,
    Water like a stone;
Snow had fallen, snow on snow,
    Snow on snow,
In the bleak mid winter,
    Long ago.

2   Our God, heaven cannot hold him
    Nor earth sustain;
Heaven and earth shall flee away
    When he comes to reign:
In the bleak mid-winter
    A stable place sufficed
The Lord God Almighty
    Jesus Christ.

3 Enough for him, whom cherubim
   Worship night and day,
A breastful of milk,
   And a mangerful of hay;
Enough for him, whom angels
   Fall down before,
The ox and ass and camel
   Which adore.

4 Angels and archangels
   May have gathered there,
Cherubim and Seraphim
   Thronged the air—
But only his mother
   In her maiden bliss
Worshipped the beloved
   With a kiss.

5 What can I give him
   Poor as I am?
If I were a shepherd
   I would bring a lamb;
If I were a wise man
   I would do my part;
Yet what I can I give him—
   Give my heart.

CHRISTINA ROSSETTI 1830–94

29 *Suitable also for Michaelmas*

IT came upon the midnight clear,
   That glorious song of old,
From angels bending near the earth
   To touch their harps of gold:
'Peace on the earth, good-will to men,
   From heaven's all gracious King!'
The world in solemn stillness lay
   To hear the angels sing.

2 Still through the cloven skies they come,
   With peaceful wings unfurled;
And still their heavenly music floats
   O'er all the weary world;
Above its sad and lowly plains
   They bend on hovering wing;
And ever o'er its Babel sounds
   The blessèd angels sing.

3 Yet with the woes of sin and strife
   The world has suffered long;
Beneath the angel-strain have rolled
   Two thousand years of wrong;
And man, at war with man, hears not
   The love-song which they bring:
O hush the noise, ye men of strife,
   And hear the angels sing!

4   For lo! the days are hastening on,
      By prophet bards foretold,
When, with the ever-circling years,
      Comes round the age of gold;
When peace shall over all the earth
      Its ancient splendours fling,
And the whole world give back the song
      Which now the angels sing.

EDMUND SEARS 1810–76

30   *Suitable for use in Procession*

Adeste, fideles

O COME, all ye faithful,
   Joyful and triumphant,
O come ye, O come ye to Bethlehem;
   Come and behold him
   Born the King of Angels:
      O come, let us adore him,
      O come, let us adore him,
     O come, let us adore him, Christ the Lord!

2   God of God,
      Light of Light,
Lo! he abhors not the Virgin's womb;
     Very God,
     Begotten, not created:

3*   See how the Shepherds,
     Summoned to his cradle,
Leaving their flocks, draw nigh with lowly fear;
     We too will thither
     Bend our joyful footsteps:

4*   Lo! star-led chieftains,
         Magi, Christ adoring,
Offer him incense, gold, and myrrh;
         We to the Christ Child
         Bring our heart's oblations:

5   Child, for us sinners
         Poor and in the manger,
Fain we embrace thee, with awe and love;
         Who would not love thee,
         Loving us so dearly?

6   Sing, choirs of Angels,
         Sing in exultation,
Sing, all ye citizens of heaven above;
         Glory to God
         In the Highest:

On Christmas Day

7*   Yea, Lord, we greet thee,
         Born this happy morning,
Jesu, to thee be glory given;
         Word of the Father,
         Now in flesh appearing:

Latin 18th century
Tr FREDERICK OAKELEY 1802–80
and others

31   O LITTLE One sweet, O Little One mild,
       Thy Father's purpose thou hast fulfilled;
           Thou cam'st from heaven to mortal ken,
           Equal to be with us poor men,
       O Little One sweet, O Little One mild.

2 O Little One sweet, O Little One mild,
With joy thou hast the whole world filled;
   Thou camest here from heaven's domain,
   To bring men comfort in their pain,
O Little One sweet, O Little One mild.

3 O Little One sweet, O Little One mild,
In thee Love's beauties are all distilled;
   Then light in us thy love's bright flame,
   That we may give thee back the same,
O Little One sweet, O Little One mild.

German, S. SCHEIDT 1650
Tr PERCY DEARMER 1867–1936

32 O LITTLE town of Bethlehem,
   How still we see thee lie!
Above thy deep and dreamless sleep
   The silent stars go by.
Yet in thy dark streets shineth
   The everlasting light;
The hopes and fears of all the years
   Are met in thee to-night.

2 O morning stars, together
   Proclaim the holy birth,
And praises sing to God the King,
   And peace to men on earth;
For Christ is born of Mary;
   And, gathered all above,
While mortals sleep, the angels keep
   Their watch of wondering love.

3　How silently, how silently,
　　　The wondrous gift is given!
　　So God imparts to human hearts
　　　The blessings of his heaven.
　　No ear may hear his coming;
　　　But in this world of sin,
　　Where meek souls will receive him, still
　　　The dear Christ enters in.

4*　Where children pure and happy
　　　Pray to the blessèd Child,
　　Where misery cries out to thee,
　　　Son of the mother mild;
　　Where charity stands watching
　　　And faith holds wide the door,
　　The dark night wakes, the glory breaks,
　　　And Christmas comes once more.

5　O holy Child of Bethlehem,
　　　Descend to us, we pray;
　　Cast out our sin, and enter in,
　　　Be born in us today.
　　We hear the Christmas angels
　　　The great glad tidings tell:
　　O come to us, abide with us,
　　　Our Lord Emmanuel.

PHILLIPS BROOKS 1835–93

33   *Suitable for use in Procession*

Corde natus ex parentis

OF the Father's heart begotten,
　Ere the world from chaos rose,
He is Alpha: from that Fountain
　All that is and hath been flows;
He is Omega, of all things
　Yet to come the mystic Close,
　　Evermore and evermore.

2* By his word was all created;
　He commanded and 'twas done;
Earth and sky and boundless ocean,
　Universe of three in one,
All that sees the moon's soft radiance,
　All that breathes beneath the sun,

3* He assumed this mortal body,
　Frail and feeble, doomed to die,
That the race from dust created
　Might not perish utterly,
Which the dreadful Law had sentenced
　In the depths of hell to lie,

4 O how blest that wondrous birthday,
　When the Maid the curse retrieved,
Brought to birth mankind's salvation,
　By the Holy Ghost conceived;
And the Babe, the world's Redeemer,
　In her loving arms received,

5   This is he, whom seer and sibyl
     Sang in ages long gone by;
  This is he of old revealèd
     In the page of prophecy;
  Lo! he comes, the promised Saviour;
     Let the world his praises cry!

6   Let the storm and summer sunshine,
     Gliding stream and sounding shore,
  Sea and forest, frost and zephyr,
     Day and night their Lord adore;
  Let creation join to laud thee
     Through the ages evermore,

7   Sing, ye heights of heaven, his praises;
     Angels and Archangels, sing!
  Wheresoe'er ye be, ye faithful,
     Let your joyous anthems ring,
  Every tongue his name confessing,
     Countless voices answering,

Latin, PRUDENTIUS 348–413
Tr R. F. DAVIS 1866–1937

34   ONCE in royal David's city
     Stood a lowly cattle shed,
  Where a mother laid her baby
     In a manger for his bed:
  Mary was that Mother mild,
  Jesus Christ her little Child.

2 He came down to earth from heaven
    Who is God and Lord of all,
And his shelter was a stable,
    And his cradle was a stall:
With the poor and mean and lowly,
Lived on earth our Saviour holy.

3 And through all his wondrous childhood
    Day by day like us he grew,
He was little, weak and helpless,
    Tears and smiles like us he knew:
And he feeleth for our sadness,
And he shareth in our gladness.

4 And our eyes at last shall see him
    Through his own redeeming love,
For that Child so dear and gentle,
    Is our Lord in heaven above:
And he leads his children on
To the place where he is gone.

5* Not in that poor lowly stable,
    With the oxen standing by,
We shall see him: but in heaven,
    Set at God's right hand on high,
Where like stars his children crowned,
All in white shall wait around.

MRS C. F. ALEXANDER 1818–95†

38

35 SILENT night! Holy night!
Heaven is near, earth is bright,
Angel songs are heard above
As the Child of peace and love
    Sleeps in Mary's arms,
    Sleeps in Mary's arms.

2 Silent night! Holy night!
Skies are clear, stars are bright,
Now the shepherds wend their way,
Homage to this Child to pay:
    He is Christ the Lord,
    He is Christ the Lord.

3 Silent night! Holy night!
Christ is here, all is light,
Shadows of the past are gone
With the advent of the Son,
    Born to save us all,
    Born to save us all.

G. B. TIMMS b 1910
based on J. MOHR 1792–1848

36 *Suitable also for Epiphany*

THE first Nowell the angel did say
Was to certain poor shepherds in fields as they
    lay;
In fields where they lay, keeping their sheep,
On a cold winter's night that was so deep:
    Nowell, Nowell, Nowell, Nowell,
    Born is the King of Israel.

2   They lookèd up and saw a star,
Shining in the east, beyond them far:
And to the earth it gave great light,
And so it continued both day and night:

3   And by the light of that same star,
Three Wise Men came from country far;
To seek for a king was their intent,
And to follow the star wheresoever it went:

4   This star drew nigh to the north-west;
O'er Bethlehem it took its rest,
And there it did both stop and stay
Right over the place where Jesus lay:

5   Then entered in those Wise Men three,
Full reverently upon their knee,
And offered there in his presènce
Both gold and myrrh and frankincense:

6   Then let us all with one accord
Sing praises to our heavenly Lord,
That hath made heaven and earth of naught,
And with his blood mankind hath bought:

TRADITIONAL

37   THE great God of heaven is come down to
earth,
His mother a Virgin, and sinless his birth;
The Father eternal his Father alone:
He sleeps in the manger; he reigns on the
throne:
Then let us adore him, and praise his great love:
To save us poor sinners he came from above.

2 A Babe on the breast of a Maiden he lies,
Yet sits with the Father on high in the skies;
Before him their faces the seraphim hide,
While Joseph stands waiting, unscared, by his
    side:

3 Lo! here is Emmanuel, here is the Child,
The Son that was promised to Mary so mild;
Whose power and dominion shall ever increase,
The Prince that shall rule o'er a kingdom of
    peace:

4 The Wonderful Counsellor, boundless in
    might,
The Father's own image, the beam of his light;
Behold him now wearing the likeness of man,
Weak, helpless, and speechless, in measure a
    span:

5 O wonder of wonders, which none can unfold:
The Ancient of days is an hour or two old;
The Maker of all things is made of the earth,
Man is worshipped by angels, and God comes
    to birth:

HENRY RAMSDEN BRAMLEY 1833–1917

38   THE Maker of the sun and moon,
    The Maker of the earth,
Lo! late in time, a fairer boon,
    Himself is brought to birth!

2 How blest was all creation then,
    When God so gave increase;
And Christ to heal the hearts of men,
    Brought righteousness and peace!

3 No star in all the heights of heaven
    But burned to see him go;
Yet unto earth alone was given
    His human form to know.

4 His human form, by man denied,
    Took death for human sin:
His endless love, through faith descried,
    Still lives the world to win.

5 O perfect Love, outpassing sight,
    O Light beyond our ken,
Come down through all the world to-night,
    And heal the hearts of men.

LAURENCE HOUSMAN 1865–1959

39 *Suitable also for Holy Innocents' Day*

UNTO us a boy is born!
    King of all creation,
Came he to a world forlorn,
    The Lord of every nation.

2 Cradled in a stall was he
    With sleepy cows and asses;
But the very beasts could see
    That he all men surpasses.

3 Herod then with fear was filled:
  'A prince', he said, 'in Jewry!'
And all the little boys he killed
  At Bethlem in his fury.

4 Now may Mary's son, who came
  So long ago to love us,
Lead us all with hearts aflame
  Unto the joys above us.

5 Omega and Alpha he!
  Let the organ thunder,
While the choir with peals of glee
  Doth rend the air asunder.

Latin, 15th century
Tr PERCY DEARMER 1867–1936

40 WHAT child is this, who, laid to rest
  On Mary's lap is sleeping?
Whom angels greet with anthems sweet,
  While shepherds watch are keeping?
This, this is Christ the King,
  Whom shepherds worship and angels sing:
Haste, haste to bring him praise
  The Babe, the son of Mary.

2   Why lies he in such mean estate,
     Where ox and ass are feeding?
Come, have no fear, God's son is here,
     His love all loves exceeding:
Nails, spear, shall pierce him through,
     The cross be borne for me, for you:
Hail, hail, the Saviour comes,
     The Babe, the son of Mary.

3   So bring him incense, gold and myrrh,
     All tongues and peoples own him,
The King of kings salvation brings,
     Let every heart enthrone him:
Raise, raise your song on high
     While Mary sings a lullaby,
Joy, joy, for Christ is born,
     The Babe, the son of Mary.

W. Chatterton Dix 1837–98
and Editors

41   Where is this stupendous stranger?
     Prophets, shepherds, kings, advise:
Lead me to my Master's manger,
     Show me where my Saviour lies.

2   O most mighty, O most holy,
     Far beyond the seraph's thought!
Art thou then so mean and lowly
     As unheeded prophets taught?

3   O the magnitude of meekness,
     Worth from worth immortal sprung!
  O the strength of infant weakness,
     If eternal is so young!

4   God all-bounteous, all-creative,
     Whom no ills from good dissuade,
  Is incarnate—and a native
     Of the very world he made.

CHRISTOPHER SMART 1722–71

42 WHILE shepherds watched their flocks by night,
     All seated on the ground,
  The angel of the Lord came down,
     And glory shone around.

2   'Fear not,' said he (for mighty dread
     Had seized their troubled mind);
  'Glad tidings of great joy I bring
     To you and all mankind.

3   'To you in David's town this day
     Is born of David's line
  A Saviour, who is Christ the Lord;
     And this shall be the sign:

4   'The heavenly Babe you there shall find
     To human view displayed,
  All meanly wrapped in swathing bands,
     And in a manger laid.'

5   Thus spake the seraph; and forthwith
        Appeared a shining throng
  Of angels praising God, who thus
        Addressed their joyful song:

6   'All glory be to God on high,
        And on the earth be peace;
  Good-will henceforth from heaven to men
        Begin and never cease.'

NAHUM TATE 1652–1715

SUNDAYS AFTER CHRISTMAS

43   CHILD of the stable's secret birth,
    The Lord by right of the lords of earth,
    Let angels sing of a King new-born—
    The world is weaving a crown of thorn:
      A crown of thorn for that infant head
      Cradled soft in the manger bed.

2   Eyes that shine in the lantern's ray;
    A face so small in its nest of hay—
    Face of a Child who is born to scan
    The world of men through the eyes of man:
      And from that face in the final day
      Earth and heaven shall flee away.

3   Voice that rang through the courts on high
    Contracted now to a wordless cry,
    A voice to master the wind and wave,
    The human heart and the hungry grave:
      The voice of God through the cedar trees
      Rolling forth as the sound of seas.

4 Infant hands in a mother's hand,
For none but Mary may understand
Whose are the hands and the fingers curled
But his who fashioned and made our world;
    And through these hands in the hour of
        death
    Nails shall strike to the wood beneath.

5 Child of the stable's secret birth,
The Father's gift to a wayward earth,
To drain the cup in a few short years
Of all our sorrows, our sins and tears—
    Ours the prize for the road he trod:
    Risen with Christ; at peace with God.

TIMOTHY DUDLEY-SMITH b 1926

44   *Nunc dimittis*

FAITHFUL vigil ended,
Watching, waiting cease;
Master, grant thy servant
His discharge in peace.

2 All thy Spirit promised,
All the Father willed;
Now these eyes behold it
Perfectly fulfilled.

3 This thy great deliverance
Sets thy people free;
Christ, their light, uplifted
All the nations see.

47

4   Christ, thy people's glory!
Watching, doubting, cease:
Grant to us thy servants
Our discharge in peace.

TIMOTHY DUDLEY-SMITH b 1926

45   *The Boyhood of Christ*

THE growing limbs of God the Son,
The Father's sole-begotten One,
Prepare him for his work on earth,
Who for mankind took human birth.

2   In wisdom and in grace he grows,
Each step of human life he knows,
In all save sin, like us was made,
To be a fallen people's aid.

3   His Father's house he enters in,
Where rabbis teach their cure for sin,
While in his heart he hears the call
Which through his cross won life for all.

4   And he who rules angelic bands,
Who high in heavenly glory stands,
Now yields him to his mother's will,
A boy's obedience to fulfil.

5   He all his radiant splendour hides,
And he who made the stars abides
With Joseph and the Mother blest,
In form of servant manifest.

6   To him, the Father's only Son,
     Let praise and honour now be done,
     Who by the Holy Spirit's grace
     Took flesh to save our human race.

G. B. Timms b 1910
in part based upon
Divine crescebas puer
J. B. de Santeuil 1630-97

46   Office Hymn   (Epiphany and the Sunday
              following)

Hostis Herodes impie

WHY, impious Herod, shouldst thou fear
Because the Christ is come so near?
He who doth heavenly kingdoms grant
Thine earthly realm can never want.

2   Lo, sages from the East are gone
     To where the star hath newly shone:
     Led on by light to Light they press,
     And by their gifts their God confess.

3   The Lamb of God is manifest
     Again in Jordan's water blest,
     And he who sin had never known
     By washing hath our sins undone.

4 Yet he that ruleth everything
Can change the nature of the spring,
And gives at Cana this for sign—
The water reddens into wine.

5 Then glory, Lord, to thee we pay
For thine Epiphany to-day;
All glory through eternity
To Father, Son, and Spirit be.   Amen.

Latin, CAELIUS SEDULIUS c 450
Tr PERCY DEARMER 1867–1936

For an Epiphany procession see

30 O come, all ye faithful
50 From the eastern mountains

47 AS with gladness men of old
Did the guiding star behold,
As with joy they hailed its light,
Leading onward, beaming bright,
So, most gracious God, may we
Evermore be led to thee.

2 As with joyful steps they sped,
To that lowly manger-bed,
There to bend the knee before
Him whom heaven and earth adore,
So may we with willing feet
Ever seek thy mercy-seat.

3   As they offered gifts most rare
      At that manger rude and bare,
      So may we with holy joy,
      Pure, and free from sin's alloy,
      All our costliest treasures bring,
      Christ, to thee our heavenly King.

4   Holy Jesu, every day
      Keep us in the narrow way;
      And, when earthly things are past,
      Bring our ransomed souls at last
      Where they need no star to guide,
      Where no clouds thy glory hide.

5   In the heavenly country bright
      Need they no created light;
      Thou its Light, its Joy, its Crown,
      Thou its Sun which goes not down:
      There for ever may we sing
      Alleluyas to our King.

W. CHATTERTON DIX 1837–98

48   *O sola magnarum urbium*

    BETHLEHEM, of noblest cities
      None can once with thee compare;
    Thou alone the Lord from heaven
      Didst for us incarnate bear.

2   Fairer than the sun at morning
      Was the star that told his birth;
    To the lands their God announcing,
      Seen in fleshly form on earth.

3   By its lambent beauty guided
     See the eastern kings appear;
  See them bend, their gifts to offer,
     Gifts of incense, gold and myrrh.

4   Solemn things of mystic meaning:
     Incense doth the God disclose,
  Gold a royal child proclaimeth,
     Myrrh a future tomb foreshows.

5   Holy Jesu, in thy brightness
     To the Gentile world displayed,
  With the Father and the Spirit
     Endless praise to thee be paid.   Amen.

Latin, PRUDENTIUS 348–410
Tr EDWARD CASWALL 1814–78

49   BRIGHTEST and best of the sons of the
     morning,
     Dawn on our darkness and lend us thine aid;
  Star of the East, the horizon adorning,
     Guide where our infant Redeemer is laid.

2   Cold on his cradle the dew-drops are shining,
     Low lies his head with the beasts of the stall:
  Angels adore him in slumber reclining,
     Maker and Monarch and Saviour of all.

3   Say, shall we yield him, in costly devotion,
     Odours of Edom and offerings divine?
  Gems of the mountain and pearls of the ocean,
     Myrrh from the forest or gold from the mine?

4   Vainly we offer each ample oblation,
     Vainly with gifts would his favour secure;
  Richer by far is the heart's adoration,
     Dearer to God are the prayers of the poor.

5   Brightest and best of the sons of the morning,
     Dawn on our darkness and lend us thine aid;
  Star of the East, the horizon adorning,
     Guide where our infant Redeemer is laid.

REGINALD HEBER 1783–1826

50   *Suitable for use in Procession*

FROM the eastern mountains
    Pressing on they come,
Wise men in their wisdom,
    To his humble home;
Stirred by deep devotion,
    Hasting from afar,
Ever journeying onward,
    Guided by a star.

2   There their Lord and Saviour
    As an infant lay,
Wondrous light that led them
    Onward on their way,
Ever now to lighten
    Nations from afar,
As they journey homeward
    By that guiding star.

3 Thou who in a manger
  Once hast lowly lain,
Who dost now in glory
  O'er all kingdoms reign,
Gather in the peoples,
  Who in lands afar
Ne'er have seen the brightness
  Of thy guiding star.

4 Gather in the outcasts,
  All who've gone astray,
Throw thy radiance o'er them,
  Guide them on their way;
Those who never knew thee,
  Those who've wandered far,
Guide them by the brightness
  Of thy guiding star.

5 Onward through the darkness
  Of the lonely night,
Shining still before them
  With thy kindly light,
Guide them, Jew and Gentile,
  Homeward from afar,
Young and old together,
  By thy guiding star.

6 Until every nation,
    Whether bond or free,
'Neath thy star-lit banner,
    Jesu, follows thee,
O'er the distant mountains
    To that heavenly home
Where nor sin nor sorrow
    Evermore shall come.

GODFREY THRING 1823–1903

51 HAIL, thou Source of every blessing,
    Sovereign Father of mankind!
Gentiles now, thy grace possessing,
    In thy courts admission find.

2 Once far off, but now invited,
    We approach thy sacred throne;
In thy covenant united,
    Reconciled, redeemed, made one.

3 Now revealed to eastern sages,
    See the Star of mercy shine,
Mystery hid in former ages,
    Mystery great of love divine.

4   Hail, thou universal Saviour!
      Gentiles now their offerings bring,
  In thy temple seek thy favour,
      Jesu Christ, our Lord and King.

BASIL WOODD 1760–1831

52 O WORSHIP the Lord in the beauty of
        holiness!
    Bow down before him, his glory proclaim;
  With gold of obedience, and incense of
        lowliness,
    Kneel and adore him, the Lord is his name!

2 Low at his feet lay thy burden of carefulness,
    High on his heart he will bear it for thee,
  Comfort thy sorrows, and answer thy
      prayerfulness,
    Guiding thy steps as may best for thee be.

3 Fear not to enter his courts in the slenderness
    Of the poor wealth thou wouldst reckon as
      thine:
  Truth in its beauty, and love in its tenderness,
    These are the offerings to lay on his shrine.

4 These, though we bring them in trembling and
      fearfulness,
    He will accept for the name that is dear;
  Mornings of joy give for evenings of tearfulness,
    Trust for our trembling and hope for our fear.

5 O worship the Lord in the beauty of holiness!
     Bow down before him, his glory proclaim;
   With gold of obedience, and incense of
       lowliness,
     Kneel and adore him, the Lord is his name!

J. S. B. MONSELL 1811–75

See also

23 Behold, the great creator makes
36 The first Nowell the angel did say
40 What child is this, who, laid to rest

53 OFFICE HYMN   Sunday morning

   THIS day the first of days was made,
   When God in light the world arrayed,
   And on this day gave life to men,
   When Christ our Sun arose again.

2 O Jesu, King of wondrous might,
   O Victor, glorious from the fight,
   Sweetness that may not be exprest,
   And altogether loveliest!

3 Remain with us, dear Lord, this day,
   And in our hearts thy grace display,
   That now the shades of night are fled,
   On thee our spirits may be fed.

4 Thou bread of God, and vine of heaven,
   To us let all thy grace be given,
   That when is run our earthly race,
   We may at length behold thy face.

5 O Jesu, Virgin-born, to thee
   Eternal praise and glory be,
   Whom with the Father we adore
   And Holy Spirit, evermore.   Amen.

EDITORS

54 OFFICE HYMN   Sunday evening

O Lux beata Trinitas

O TRINITY of blessèd light,
O Unity of primal might,
The fiery sun now goes his way,
Shed thou within our hearts thy ray.

2 To thee our morning song of praise,
   To thee our evening prayer we raise,
   Thy glory, suppliant, we adore,
   For ever and for evermore.

3 O Trinity, O Unity,
   Thou help of man's infirmity,
   Protect us through the hours of night,
   Who art our everlasting light.

4 To God the Father, God the Son,
   And God the Spirit, Three in One,
   Let glory, praise and worship be
   From age to age eternally.   Amen.

From the Latin
Tr J. M. NEALE 1818–66
and EDITORS

55   HAIL to the Lord's Anointed!
            Great David's greater Son;
         Hail, in the time appointed,
            His reign on earth begun!
         He comes to break oppression,
            To set the captive free;
         To take away transgression,
            And rule in equity.

2   He comes with succour speedy
        To those who suffer wrong;
    To help the poor and needy,
        And bid the weak be strong;
    To give them songs for sighing,
        Their darkness turn to light,
    Whose souls, condemned and dying,
        Were precious in his sight.

3   He shall come down like showers
     Upon the fruitful earth,
  And love, joy, hope, like flowers,
     Spring in his path to birth:
  Before him on the mountains
     Shall peace the herald go;
  And righteousness in fountains
     From hill to valley flow.

4   Kings shall fall down before him,
     And gold and incense bring;
  All nations shall adore him,
     His praise all people sing;
  To him shall prayer unceasing
     And daily vows ascend;
  His kingdom still increasing,
     A kingdom without end.

5   O'er every foe victorious,
     He on his throne shall rest,
  From age to age more glorious,
     All-blessing and all-blest:
  The tide of time shall never
     His covenant remove;
  His name shall stand for ever;
     That name to us is Love.

JAMES MONTGOMERY 1771–1854
based on Psalm 72

56 SONGS of thankfulness and praise,
Jesu, Lord, to thee we raise,
Manifested by the star
To the sages from afar;
Branch of royal David's stem
In thy birth at Bethlehem;
Anthems be to thee addrest,
God in Man made manifest.

2 Manifest at Jordan's stream,
Prophet, Priest, and King supreme;
And at Cana wedding-guest
In thy Godhead manifest;
Manifest in power divine,
Changing water into wine;
Anthems be to thee addrest,
God in Man made manifest.

3 Manifest in making whole
Palsied limbs and fainting soul;
Manifest in valiant fight,
Quelling all the devil's might;
Manifest in gracious will,
Ever bringing good from ill;
Anthems be to thee addrest,
God in Man made manifest.

4* Sun and moon shall darkened be,
Stars shall fall, the heavens shall flee;
Christ will then like lightning shine,
All will see his glorious sign;
All will then the trumpet hear,
All will see the Judge appear;
Thou by all wilt be confest,
God in Man made manifest.

5 Grant us grace to see thee, Lord,
Mirrored in thy holy word;
May we imitate thee now,
And be pure, as pure art thou;
That we like to thee may be
At thy great Epiphany,
And may praise thee, ever blest,
God in Man made manifest.

CHRISTOPHER WORDSWORTH 1807–85

57 THE race that long in darkness pined
Have seen a glorious light;
The people dwell in day, who dwelt
In death's surrounding night.

2 To hail thy rise, thou better Sun,
The gathering nations come,
Joyous as when the reapers bear
The harvest-treasures home.

3 To us a Child of hope is born,
To us a Son is given;
Him shall the tribes of earth obey,
Him all the hosts of heaven.

4 His name shall be the Prince of Peace,
For evermore adored;
The Wonderful, the Counsellor,
The great and mighty Lord.

5   His power increasing still shall spread;
        His reign no end shall know:
     Justice shall guard his throne above,
        And peace abound below.

JOHN MORISON 1750–98
based on ISAIAH 9. 2–7

58   *The Baptism of Christ*

Suitable also for Adult Baptism and Confirmation

     THE sinless one to Jordan came
     To share our fallen nature's blame;
     God's righteousness he thus fulfilled
     And chose the path his Father willed.

2   Uprising from the waters there,
     The voice from heaven did witness bear
     That he, the Son of God, had come
     To lead his scattered people home.

3   Above him see the heavenly Dove,
     The sign of God the Father's love,
     Now by the Holy Spirit shed
     Upon the Son's anointed head.

4   How blest that mission then begun
     To heal and save a race undone;
     Straight to the wilderness he goes
     To wrestle with his people's foes.

63

5   Dear Lord, let those baptized from sin
Go forth with you, a world to win,
And send the Holy Spirit's power
To shield them in temptation's hour.

6   On you shall all your people feed
And know you are the Bread indeed,
Who gives eternal life to those
That with you died, and with you rose.

G. B. TIMMS b 1910

LENT

59 OFFICE HYMN

Ecce tempus idoneum

NOW is the healing time decreed
For sins of heart and word and deed,
When we in humble fear record
The wrong that we have done the Lord:

2   Who, always merciful and good,
Has borne so long our wayward mood,
Nor cut us off unsparingly
In our so great iniquity.

3   Therefore with fasting and with prayer,
Our secret sorrow we declare,
With all good striving seek his face,
And lowly-hearted plead for grace.

4   Cleanse us, O Lord, from every stain,
    Help us the gifts of grace to gain,
    Till with the angels, linked in love,
    Joyful we tread thy courts above.

5   We pray thee, holy Trinity,
    One God, unchanging Unity,
    That we from this our abstinence
    May reap the fruits of penitence.   Amen.

                    Latin, *Tr* T. A. LACEY 1853–1931

60   OFFICE HYMN

         Audi benigne Conditor

    O KIND Creator, bow thine ear
    To mark the cry, to know the tear
    Before thy throne of mercy spent
    In this thy holy fast of Lent.

2   Our hearts are open, Lord, to thee:
    Thou knowest our infirmity;
    Pour out on all who seek thy face
    Abundance of thy pardoning grace.

3   Our sins are many, this we know;
    Spare us, good Lord, thy mercy show;
    And for the honour of thy name
    Our fainting souls to life reclaim.

4   Give us the self-control that springs
     From discipline of outward things,
     That fasting inward secretly
     The soul may purely dwell with thee.

5   We pray thee, holy Trinity,
     One God, unchanging Unity,
     That we from this our abstinence
     May reap the fruits of penitence.   Amen.

                  Latin, ascribed to ST GREGORY 540–604
                            Tr T. A. LACEY 1853–1931

61   OFFICE HYMN COMPLINE

         Christe qui lux es et dies

     O CHRIST, who art the Light and Day,
     Thou drivest darksome night away!
     We know thee as the Light of light,
     Illuminating mortal sight.

2   All-holy Lord, we pray to thee,
     Keep us to-night from danger free;
     Grant us, dear Lord, in thee to rest,
     So be our sleep in quiet blest.

3   And while the eyes soft slumber take,
     Still be the heart to thee awake;
     Be thy right hand upheld above
     Thy servants resting in thy love.

4　O strong defender, be thou nigh
　　To bid the powers of darkness fly;
　　Keep us from sin, and guide for good
　　Thy servants purchased by thy blood.

5　Remember us, dear Lord, we pray
　　While in this mortal flesh we stay:
　　'Tis thou who dost the soul defend—
　　Be present with us to the end.

6　Blest Three in One and One in Three,
　　Almighty God, we pray to thee
　　That thou wouldst now vouchsafe to bless
　　Our fast with fruits of righteousness.　　Amen.

6th century Latin
Tr WILLIAM COPELAND 1804–85
and others

62　AH, holy Jesu, how hast thou offended,
　　That man to judge thee hath in hate pretended?
　　By foes derided, by thine own rejected,
　　　　O most afflicted.

2　Who was the guilty? Who brought this upon
　　　　thee?
　　Alas, my treason, Jesu, hath undone thee.
　　'Twas I, Lord Jesu, I it was denied thee:
　　　　I crucified thee.

3 Lo, the good Shepherd for the sheep is
    offered;
  The slave hath sinnèd, and the Son hath
    suffered;
  For man's atonement, while he nothing
    heedeth,
        God intercedeth.

4 For me, kind Jesu, was thy incarnation,
  Thy mortal sorrow, and thy life's oblation;
  Thy death of anguish and thy bitter passion,
        For my salvation.

5 Therefore, kind Jesu, since I cannot pay thee,
  I do adore thee, and will ever pray thee,
  Think on thy pity and thy love unswerving,
        Not my deserving.

ROBERT BRIDGES 1844–1930
from J. HEERMANN 1585–1647
based on an 11th century
Latin meditation

63   *Quicumque certum quaeritis*

ALL ye who seek a comfort sure
  In trouble and distress,
Whatever sorrow vex the mind,
  Or guilt the soul oppress,

2 Jesus, who gave himself for you
  Upon the cross to die,
Opens to you his sacred heart;
  O to that heart draw nigh.

3   Ye hear how kindly he invites;
        Ye hear his words so blest—
    'All ye that labour come to me,
        And I will give you rest.'

4   O Jesus, joy of saints on high,
        Thou hope of sinners here,
    Attracted by those loving words
        To thee I lift my prayer.

5   Wash thou my wounds in that dear blood
        Which forth from thee doth flow;
    New grace, new hope inspire, a new
        And better heart bestow.

18th century Latin
Tr EDWARD CASWALL 1814–78

64   BE thou my guardian and my guide,
        And hear me when I call;
    Let not my slippery footsteps slide,
        And hold me lest I fall.

2   The world, the flesh, and Satan dwell
        Around the path I tread;
    O, save me from the snares of hell,
        Thou quickener of the dead.

3   And if I tempted am to sin,
        And outward things are strong,
    Do thou, O Lord, keep watch within,
        And save my soul from wrong.

4   Still let me ever watch and pray,
       And feel that I am frail;
     That if the tempter cross my way,
       Yet he may not prevail.

ISAAC WILLIAMS 1802–65

65   CHRISTIAN, dost thou see them
       On the holy ground,
     How the troops of Midian
       Prowl and prowl around?
     Christian, up and smite them,
       Counting gain but loss;
     Smite them by the merit
       Of the holy Cross.

2   Christian, dost thou feel them,
       How they work within,
     Striving, tempting, luring,
       Goading into sin?
     Christian, never tremble;
       Never be down-cast;
     Smite them by the virtue
       Of the Lenten fast.

3   Christian, dost thou hear them,
       How they speak thee fair?
     'Always fast and vigil?
       Always watch and prayer?'
     Christian, answer boldly,
       'While I breathe, I pray:'
     Peace shall follow battle,
       Night shall end in day.

4　'Well I know thy trouble,
　　　O my servant true;
　　Thou art very weary—
　　　I was weary too;
　　But that toil shall make thee
　　　Some day all mine own,
　　And the end of sorrow
　　　Shall be near my throne.'

J. M. NEALE 1818–66

66　'FORGIVE our sins as we forgive'
　　　You taught us, Lord, to pray;
　　But you alone can grant us grace
　　　To live the words we say.

2　How can your pardon reach and bless
　　　The unforgiving heart
　　That broods on wrongs, and will not let
　　　Old bitterness depart?

3　In blazing light your Cross reveals
　　　The truth we dimly knew,
　　How small the debts men owe to us,
　　　How great our debt to you.

4　Lord, cleanse the depths within our souls,
　　　And bid resentment cease;
　　Then, reconciled to God and man,
　　　Our lives will spread your peace.

ROSAMOND HERKLOTS 1905–87

67   FORTY days and forty nights
      Thou wast fasting in the wild,
Forty days and forty nights
      Tempted and yet undefiled.

2   Sunbeams scorching all the day,
      Chilly dewdrops nightly shed,
Prowling beasts about thy way,
      Stones thy pillow, earth thy bed.

3   Let us thine endurance share,
      And awhile from joys abstain,
With thee watching unto prayer,
      Strong with thee to suffer pain.

4   And if Satan, vexing sore,
      Flesh or spirit should assail,
Thou, his vanquisher before,
      Grant we may not faint nor fail.

5   So shall we have peace divine,
      Holier gladness ours shall be,
Round us too shall angels shine,
      Such as ministered to thee.

6   Keep, O keep us, Saviour dear,
      Ever constant by thy side,
That with thee we may appear
      At the eternal Eastertide.

G. H. SMYTTAN 1822–70
and FRANCIS POTT 1832–1909‡

68 JESU, Lord of life and glory,
  Bend from heaven thy gracious ear;
While our waiting souls adore thee,
  Friend of helpless sinners, hear:
    By thy mercy,
    O deliver us, good Lord.

2 From the depth of nature's blindness,
  From the hardening power of sin,
From all malice and unkindness,
  From the pride that lurks within:
    By thy mercy,
    O deliver us, good Lord.

3 When temptation sorely presses,
  In the day of Satan's power,
In our times of deep distresses,
  In each dark and trying hour:
    By thy mercy,
    O deliver us, good Lord.

4 In the weary hours of sickness,
  In the times of grief and pain,
When we feel our mortal weakness,
  When the creature's help is vain:
    By thy mercy,
    O deliver us, good Lord.

5 In the solemn hour of dying,
  In the face of judgement day,
May our souls, on thee relying,
  Find thee still our rock and stay:
    By thy mercy,
    O deliver us, good Lord.

6   Jesu, may thy promised blessing
      Comfort to our souls afford;
May we now, thy love possessing,
    And at length our full reward,
      Ever praise thee,
    Good and ever-glorious Lord.

JOHN CUMMINS 1795–1867†

69   LORD, in this thy mercy's day,
    Ere it pass for ay away,
    On our knees we fall and pray.

2   Lord, on us thy Spirit pour,
    Kneeling lowly at the door,
    Lest it close for evermore.

3   By thy night of agony,
    By thy supplicating cry,
    By thy willingness to die.

4   By thy tears of bitter woe,
    For Jerusalem below,
    Let us not thy love forgo.

5   Grant us 'neath thy wings a place,
    Lest we lose the day of grace,
    Ere we shall behold thy face.

ISAAC WILLIAMS 1802–65†

70   LORD Jesus, think on me,
      And purge away my sin;
From earthborn passions set me free,
      And make me pure within.

2   Lord Jesus, think on me,
      With care and woe opprest;
Let me thy loving servant be,
      And taste thy promised rest.

3   Lord Jesus, think on me,
      Amid the battle's strife;
In all my pain and misery
      Be thou my health and life.

4   Lord Jesus, think on me,
      Nor let me go astray;
Through darkness and perplexity
      Point thou the heavenly way.

5   Lord Jesus, think on me,
      When flows the tempest high:
When on doth rush the enemy
      O Saviour, be thou nigh.

6   Lord Jesus, think on me,
      That, when the flood is past,
I may the eternal brightness see,
      And share thy joy at last.

Greek, SYNESIUS OF CYRENE 375–430
Tr A. W. CHATFIELD 1808–96

71   *Te laeta, mundi Conditor*

MAKER of earth, to thee alone
   Perpetual rest belongs;
And those bright choirs around thy throne
   May pour their endless songs.

2 But we—ah, holy now no more!
   Are doomed to toil and pain;
Yet exiles on an alien shore
   May sing their country's strain.

3 Father, whose promise binds thee still
   To heal the suppliant throng,
Grant us to mourn the deeds of ill
   That banish us so long;

4 And, while we mourn, in faith to rest
   Upon thy love and care,
Till thou restore us with the blest
   The song of heaven to share.

5 O God the Father, God the Son,
   And God the Holy Ghost,
To thee be praise, great Three in One,
   From thy created host.   Amen.

Latin, CHARLES COFFIN 1676–1749
Tr J. M. NEALE 1818–66

72 MY faith looks up to thee,
Thou Lamb of Calvary,
  Saviour divine!
Now hear me while I pray,
Take all my guilt away,
O let me from this day
  Be wholly thine.

2 May thy rich grace impart
Strength to my fainting heart,
  My zeal inspire;
As thou hast died for me,
O may my love to thee
Pure, warm, and changeless be,
  A living fire.

3 While life's dark maze I tread,
And griefs around me spread,
  Be thou my guide;
Bid darkness turn to day,
Wipe sorrow's tears away,
Nor let me ever stray
  From thee aside.

4 When ends life's transient dream,
When death's cold sullen stream
  Shall o'er me roll,
Blest Saviour, then in love
Fear and distrust remove;
O bear me safe above,
  A ransomed soul.

RAY PALMER 1808–87

73   *O Deus, ego amo te*

MY God, I love thee; not because
   I hope for heaven thereby,
Nor yet because who love thee not
   Are lost eternally.

2   Thou, O my Jesus, thou didst me
     Upon the Cross embrace;
   For me didst bear the nails and spear,
     And manifold disgrace,

3   And griefs and torments numberless,
     And sweat of agony;
   E'en death itself; and all for one
     Who was thine enemy.

4   Then why, O blessèd Jesu Christ,
     Should I not love thee well,
   Not for the sake of winning heaven,
     Or of escaping hell;

5   Not with the hope of gaining aught,
     Not seeking a reward;
   But as thyself hast lovèd me,
     O ever-loving Lord!

6   E'en so I love thee, and will love,
     And in thy praise will sing,
   Solely because thou art my God,
     And my eternal King.

17th century Latin
Tr EDWARD CASWALL 1814–78

74 O FOR a heart to praise my God,
    A heart from sin set free;
A heart that always feels thy blood
    So freely spilt for me:

2 A heart resigned, submissive, meek,
    My dear Redeemer's throne;
Where only Christ is heard to speak,
    Where Jesus reigns alone:

3 A humble, lowly, contrite heart,
    Believing, true, and clean,
Which neither life nor death can part
    From him that dwells within:

4 A heart in every thought renewed,
    And full of love divine;
Perfect and right and pure and good,
    A copy, Lord, of thine.

5 My heart, thou know'st, can never rest
    Till thou create my peace;
Till of mine Eden repossest,
    From self, and sin, I cease.

6 Thy nature, gracious Lord, impart,
    Come quickly from above;
Write thy new name upon my heart,
    Thy new best name of love.

CHARLES WESLEY 1707–88

75　　*Summi largitor praemii*

O THOU who dost accord us
　　The highest prize and guerdon,
　　　　Thou hope of all our race,
Jesu, do thou afford us
　　The gift we ask of pardon
　　　　For all who humbly seek thy face.

2　With whispered accusation
　　　Our conscience tells of sinning
　　　　　In thought and word and deed;
　　Thine is the restoration,
　　　The work of grace beginning
　　　　　For souls from every burden freed.

3　For who, if thou reject us,
　　　Shall raise the fainting spirit?
　　　　　'Tis thine alone to spare:
　　That thou to life elect us
　　　Through our Redeemer's merit,
　　　　　Shall be thy people's lowly prayer.

4　O Trinity most glorious,
　　　Thy pardon free bestowing,
　　　　　Defend us evermore;
　　That in thy courts victorious,
　　　Thy love more truly knowing,
　　　　　We may with all thy saints adore.

From the Latin
Tr based on that of J. W. HEWETT 1859

76 TAKE up thy cross, the Saviour said,
  If thou wouldst my disciple be;
Deny thyself, the world forsake,
  And humbly follow after me.

2 Take up thy cross; let not its weight
  Fill thy weak spirit with alarm;
His strength shall bear thy spirit up,
  And brace thy heart, and nerve thine arm.

3* Take up thy cross, nor heed the shame,
  Nor let thy foolish pride rebel;
The Lord for thee the Cross endured,
  To save thy soul from death and hell.

4 Take up thy cross then in his strength,
  And calmly every danger brave;
'Twill guide thee to a better home,
  And lead to victory o'er the grave.

5 Take up thy cross, and follow Christ,
  Nor think till death to lay it down;
For only he who bears the cross
  May hope to wear the glorious crown.

6 To thee, great Lord, the One in Three,
  All praise for evermore ascend;
O grant us in our home to see
  The heavenly life that knows no end.

CHARLES EVEREST 1814–77

See also

507 The Lent Prose
333 All my hope on God is founded
337 As pants the hart for cooling streams

and some of the hymns for Passiontide

REFRESHMENT SUNDAY

77   THE God of love my Shepherd is,
    And he that doth me feed;
While he is mine and I am his,
    What can I want or need?

2   He leads me to the tender grass,
    Where I both feed and rest;
Then to the streams that gently pass:
    In both I have the best.

3   Or if I stray, he doth convert,
    And bring my mind in frame,
And all this not for my desert,
    But for his holy name.

4   Yea, in death's shady black abode
    Well may I walk, not fear;
For thou art with me, and thy rod
    To guide, thy staff to bear.

5 Surely thy sweet and wondrous love
   Shall measure all my days;
And as it never shall remove
   So neither shall my praise.

GEORGE HERBERT 1593–1633

See also for Mothering Sunday

78 OFFICE HYMN

Pangue lingua gloriosi proelium certaminis

SING, my tongue, the glorious battle,
   Sing the ending of the fray,
O'er the Cross, the victor's trophy,
   Sound the loud triumphant lay:
Tell how Christ, the world's Redeemer,
   As a Victim won the day.

2 God in pity saw man fallen,
   Shamed and sunk in misery,
When he fell on death by tasting
   Fruit of the forbidden tree:
Then another tree was chosen
   Which the world from death should free.

3 Therefore when the appointed fulness
   Of the holy time was come,
He was sent who maketh all things
   Forth from God's eternal home:
Thus he came to earth, incarnate,
   Offspring of a maiden's womb.

4 Thirty years among us dwelling,
   Now at length his hour fulfilled,
Born for this, he meets his Passion,
   For that this he freely willed,
On the Cross the Lamb is lifted,
   Where his life-blood shall be spilled.

5 To the Trinity be glory,
   To the Father and the Son,
With the co-eternal Spirit,
   Ever Three and ever One,
One in love and one in splendour,
   While unending ages run.   Amen.

Latin, VENANTIUS FORTUNATUS 530–609
Tr mainly by PERCY DEARMER 1867–1936

A longer version of this hymn will be found at 517

79 OFFICE HYMN

Vexilla Regis prodeunt

THE royal banners forward go,
The Cross shines forth in mystic glow,
Where he in flesh, our flesh who made,
Our sentence bore, our ransom paid.

2 Where deep for us the spear was dyed,
Life's torrent rushing from his side,
To wash us in that precious flood,
Where mingled water flowed, and blood.

3 Fulfilled is all that David told
In true prophetic song of old,
The universal Lord is he,
Who reigns and triumphs from the tree.

4 O Tree of beauty, Tree of light,
O Tree with royal purple dight,
Elect on whose triumphal breast
Those holy limbs should find their rest!

5 On whose dear arms, so widely flung,
The weight of this world's ransom hung,
The price of humankind to pay
And spoil the spoiler of his prey.

6 O Cross, our one reliance, hail!
So may thy power with us prevail
To give new virtue to the saint,
And pardon to the penitent.

7   To thee, eternal Three in One,
Let homage meet by all be done:
Whom by thy Cross thou dost restore,
Preserve and govern evermore.   Amen.

Latin, VENANTIUS FORTUNATUS 530–609
Tr J. M. NEALE 1818–66†

Verse 3 is based upon Ps 96 verse 10

80   OFFICE HYMN COMPLINE

Cultor Dei, memento

SERVANT of God, remember
    The stream thy soul bedewing,
The grace that came upon thee
    Anointing and renewing.

2   When kindly slumber calls thee,
        Upon thy bed reclining,
Trace thou the Cross of Jesus,
        Thy heart and forehead signing.

3   The Cross dissolves the darkness,
        And drives away temptation;
It calms the wavering spirit
        By quiet consecration.

4* Begone, begone, the terrors
        Of vague and formless dreaming;
Begone, thou fell deceiver,
        With all thy boasted scheming.

5* Begone, thou crookèd serpent,
    Who, twisting and pursuing,
By fraud and lie preparest
    The simple soul's undoing;

6* Tremble, for Christ is near us,
    Depart, for here he dwelleth,
And this, the Sign thou knowest,
    Thy strong battalions quelleth.

7 Then while the weary body
    Its rest in sleep is nearing,
The heart will muse in silence
    On Christ and his appearing.

8 To God, eternal Father,
    To Christ, our King, be glory,
And to the Holy Spirit,
    In never-ending story.   Amen.

Latin, PRUDENTIUS 348–413
Tr T. A. LACEY 1853–1931

81   *The Crown of Thorns*

DOST thou truly seek renown
    Christ his glory sharing?
Wouldst thou win the heavenly crown
    Victor's garland bearing?
Tread the path the Saviour trod,
Look upon the crown of God,
    See what he is wearing.

2   This the king of heaven bore
       In that sore contending,
This his sacred temples wore,
       Honour to it lending,
In this helmet faced the foe,
On the rood he laid him low,
       Satan's kingdom ending.

3   Christ upon the tree of scorn
       In salvation's hour,
Turned to gold these pricks of thorn
       By his passion's power:
So on sinners, who had earned
Endless death, from sin returned,
       Endless blessings shower.

4   When in death's embrace we lie,
       Then, good Lord, be near us,
With thy presence fortify,
       And with victory cheer us,
Turn our erring hearts to thee,
That we crowned for ay may be:
       O good Jesu, hear us!

13th century Latin
Tr ATHELSTAN RILEY 1858–1945†

82   DROP, drop, slow tears,
       And bathe those beauteous feet,
Which brought from heaven
       The news and Prince of peace.

2   Cease not, wet eyes,
         His mercies to entreat;
    To cry for vengeance
         Sin doth never cease.

3   In your deep floods
         Drown all my faults and fears;
    Nor let his eye
         See sin, but through my tears.

PHINEAS FLETCHER 1582–1650

83 GLORY be to Jesus,
            Who, in bitter pains,
        Poured for me the life-blood
            From his sacred veins.

2   Grace and life eternal
         In that Blood I find;
    Blest be his compassion,
         Infinitely kind.

3   Blest through endless ages
         Be the precious stream,
    Which from endless torment
         Doth the world redeem.

4   Abel's blood for vengeance
         Pleaded to the skies;
    But the Blood of Jesus
         For our pardon cries.

5 Oft as it is sprinkled
   On our guilty hearts,
Satan in confusion
   Terror-struck departs.

6 Oft as earth exulting
   Wafts its praise on high,
Hell with terror trembles,
   Heaven is filled with joy.

7 Lift ye then your voices;
   Swell the mighty flood;
Louder still and louder
   Praise the precious Blood.

Italian (author unknown)
Tr EDWARD CASWALL 1814-78

84 IT is a thing most wonderful,
   Almost too wonderful to be,
That God's own Son should come from heaven,
   And die to save a child like me.

2 And yet I know that it is true:
   He chose a poor and humble lot,
And wept, and toiled, and mourned, and died
   For love of those who loved him not.

3 But even could I see him die,
    I could but see a little part
Of that great love, which, like a fire,
    Is always burning in his heart.

4 It is most wonderful to know
    His love for me so free and sure;
But 'tis more wonderful to see
    My love for him so faint and poor.

5 And yet I want to love thee, Lord;
    O light the flame within my heart,
And I will love thee more and more,
    Until I see thee as thou art.

W. WALSHAM HOW 1823–97

85 JESU, meek and lowly,
    Saviour pure and holy,
    On thy love relying
    Hear me humbly crying.

2 Prince of life and power,
    My salvation's tower,
    On the Cross I view thee
    Calling sinners to thee.

3 There behold me gazing
    At the sight amazing;
    Bending low before thee,
    Helpless I adore thee.

4 By thy red wounds streaming,
With thy life-blood gleaming,
Blood for sinners flowing,
Pardon free bestowing;

5 By that fount of blessing,
Thy dear love expressing,
All my aching sadness
Turn thou into gladness.

6 Lord in mercy guide me,
Be thou e'er beside me;
In thy ways direct me,
'Neath thy wings protect me.

HENRY COLLINS 1827–1919

86 MY song is love unknown,
My Saviour's love to me,
Love to the loveless shown,
That they might lovely be.
O, who am I,
That for my sake
My Lord should take
Frail flesh, and die?

2 He came from his blest throne,
Salvation to bestow:
But men made strange, and none
The longed-for Christ would know.
But O, my Friend,
My Friend indeed,
Who at my need
His life did spend!

3   Sometimes they strew his way,
        And his sweet praises sing;
    Resounding all the day
        Hosannas to their King.
            Then 'Crucify!'
                Is all their breath,
                And for his death
            They thirst and cry.

4* Why, what hath my Lord done?
        What makes this rage and spite?
    He made the lame to run,
        He gave the blind their sight.
            Sweet injuries!
                Yet they at these
                Themselves displease,
            And 'gainst him rise.

5   They rise, and needs will have
        My dear Lord made away;
    A murderer they save,
        The Prince of Life they slay.
            Yet cheerful he
                To suffering goes,
                That he his foes
            From thence might free.

6* In life no house, no home,
        My Lord on earth might have;
    In death no friendly tomb,
        But what a stranger gave.
            What may I say?
                Heav'n was his home;
                But mine the tomb
            Wherein he lay.

7   Here might I stay and sing,
    No story so divine;
Never was love, dear King,
    Never was grief like thine!
      This is my Friend,
        In whose sweet praise
      I all my days
    Could gladly spend.

SAMUEL CROSSMAN 1624–83

87   NATURE with open volume stands
    To spread her Maker's praise abroad,
And every labour of his hands
    Shows something worthy of a God.

2   But in the grace that rescued man
    His brightest form of glory shines;
Here on the Cross 'tis fairest drawn
    In precious blood and crimson lines.

3   Here his whole Name appears complete;
    Nor wit can guess, nor reason prove
Which of the letters best is writ,
    The Power, the Wisdom, or the Love.

4   O the sweet wonders of that Cross
    Where Christ our Saviour loved, and died!
Her noblest life my spirit draws
    From his dear wounds and stricken side.

5   I would for ever speak his Name
     In sounds to mortal ears unknown,
With angels join to praise the Lamb,
     And worship at his Father's throne.

ISAAC WATTS 1674–1748

88   *Prome vocem, mens, canoram.*

NOW my soul, thy voice upraising,
    Tell in sweet and mournful strain
How the Crucified, enduring
    Grief and wounds, and dying pain,
Freely of his love was offered,
    Sinless was for sinners slain.

2   See, his hands and feet are fastened!
    So he makes his people free;
Not a wound whence Blood is flowing
    But a fount of grace shall be;
Yea, the very nails which nail him
    Nail us also to the Tree.

3   Jesu, may those precious fountains
    Drink to thirsting souls afford;
Let them be our cup and healing,
    And at length our full reward:
So a ransomed world shall ever
    Praise thee, its redeeming Lord.

Latin, CLAUDE DE SANTEUIL 1628–84
Tr H. W. BAKER 1821–77

89 O DEAREST Lord, thy sacred head
   With thorns was pierced for me;
  O pour thy blessing on my head
   That I may think for thee.

2 O dearest Lord, thy sacred hands
   With nails were pierced for me;
  O shed thy blessing on my hands
   That they may work for thee.

3 O dearest Lord, thy sacred feet
   With nails were pierced for me;
  O pour thy blessing on my feet
   That they may follow thee.

4 O dearest Lord, thy sacred heart
   With spear was pierced for me;
  O pour thy Spirit in my heart
   That I may live for thee.

FATHER ANDREW S.D.C. 1869–1946

90 O SACRED head, sore wounded,
   Defiled and put to scorn;
  O kingly head, surrounded
   With mocking crown of thorn:
  What sorrow mars thy grandeur?
   Can death thy bloom deflower?
  O countenance whose splendour
   The hosts of heaven adore.

2★ Thy beauty, long-desirèd,
    Hath vanished from our sight;
Thy power is all expirèd,
    And quenched the light of light.
Ah me! for whom thou diest,
    Hide not so far thy grace:
Show me, O Love most highest,
    The brightness of thy face.

3★ I pray thee, Jesus, own me,
    Me, Shepherd good, for thine;
Who to thy fold hast won me,
    And fed with truth divine.
Me guilty, me refuse not,
    Incline thy face to me,
This comfort that I lose not,
    On earth to comfort thee.

4 In thy most bitter passion
    My heart to share doth cry,
With thee for my salvation
    Upon the Cross to die.
Ah, keep my heart thus movèd
    To stand thy Cross beneath,
To mourn thee, well-belovèd,
    Yet thank thee for thy death.

5 My days are few, O fail not,
    With thine immortal power,
To hold me that I quail not
    In death's most fearful hour:
That I may fight befriended,
    And see in my last strife
To me thine arms extended
    Upon the Cross of life.

PAUL GERHARDT 1607–76 from
a 14th century Latin hymn
Tr ROBERT BRIDGES 1844–1930

91 SWEET the moments, rich in blessing,
    Which before the Cross I spend,
Life, and health, and peace possessing
    From the sinner's dying friend.

2 Here I stay, for ever viewing
    Mercy streaming in his blood;
Precious drops, my soul bedewing,
    Plead and claim my peace with God.

3 Truly blessèd is this station,
    Low before his Cross to lie,
While I see divine compassion
    Floating in his languid eye.

4   Lord, in ceaseless contemplation
      Fix our hearts and eyes on thee,
   Till we taste thy full salvation,
      And unveiled thy glories see.

WILLIAM SHIRLEY 1725–86
and others

92   THERE is a green hill far away,
      Without a city wall,
   Where the dear Lord was crucified
      Who died to save us all.

2   We may not know, we cannot tell,
      What pains he had to bear,
   But we believe it was for us
      He hung and suffered there.

3   He died that we might be forgiven,
      He died to make us good;
   That we might go at last to heaven,
      Saved by his precious blood.

4   There was no other good enough
      To pay the price of sin;
   He only could unlock the gate
      Of heaven, and let us in.

5   O, dearly, dearly has he loved,
      And we must love him too,
   And trust in his redeeming blood,
      And try his works to do.

MRS C. F. ALEXANDER 1818–95

93   WERE you there when they crucified my Lord?
Were you there when they crucified my Lord?
Oh, sometimes it causes me to tremble, tremble,
    tremble;
Were you there when they crucified my Lord?

2   Were you there when they nailed him to the tree?
Were you there when they nailed him to the tree?
Oh, sometimes it causes me to tremble, tremble,
    tremble;
Were you there when they nailed him to the tree?

3   Were you there when they pierced him in the
    side?
Were you there when they pierced him in the
    side?
Oh, sometimes it causes me to tremble, tremble,
    tremble;
Were you there when they pierced him in the
    side?

4   Were you there when the sun refused to shine?
Were you there when the sun refused to shine?
Oh, sometimes it causes me to tremble, tremble,
    tremble;
Were you there when the sun refused to shine?

5   Were you there when they laid him in the tomb?
Were you there when they laid him in the tomb?
Oh, sometimes it causes me to tremble, tremble,
    tremble;
Were you there when they laid him in the tomb?

6   Were you there when he rose from out the tomb?
    Were you there when he rose from out the tomb?
    Oh, sometimes it causes me to tremble, tremble,
       tremble;
    Were you there when he rose from out the tomb?

Negro Spiritual

94   WE sing the praise of him who died,
    Of him who died upon the Cross;
  The sinner's hope let men deride,
    For this we count the world but loss.

2   Inscribed upon the Cross we see
    In shining letters, 'God is Love';
  He bears our sins upon the Tree;
    He brings us mercy from above.

3   The Cross! it takes our guilt away;
    It holds the fainting spirit up;
  It cheers with hope the gloomy day,
    And sweetens ev'ry bitter cup.

4   It makes the coward spirit brave,
    And nerves the feeble arm for fight;
  It takes its terror from the grave,
    And gilds the bed of death with light;

5   The balm of life, the cure of woe,
    The measure and the pledge of love,
  The sinner's refuge here below,
    The angels' theme in heaven above.

THOMAS KELLY 1769–1854

95 WHEN I survey the wondrous Cross,
   On which the Prince of glory died,
My richest gain I count but loss,
   And pour contempt on all my pride.

2 Forbid it, Lord, that I should boast
   Save in the death of Christ my God;
All the vain things that charm me most,
   I sacrifice them to his blood.

3 See from his head, his hands, his feet,
   Sorrow and love flow mingled down;
Did e'er such love and sorrow meet,
   Or thorns compose so rich a crown?

4 His dying crimson like a robe,
   Spreads o'er his body on the Tree;
Then am I dead to all the globe,
   And all the globe is dead to me.

5 Were the whole realm of nature mine,
   That were a present far too small;
Love so amazing, so divine,
   Demands my soul, my life, my all.

ISAAC WATTS 1674–1748

See also

379 In the cross of Christ I glory
445 Rock of ages, cleft for me

Passiontide Office Hymns until Wednesday. No Office Hymns on Thursday, Friday or Saturday.

For the Liturgical Ceremonies of Palm Sunday, Maundy Thursday and Good Friday, see 508–517.

The following are suitable where the Devotion of the Seven Words is used on Good Friday:

First Word	66	Forgive our sins, as we forgive
Second Word	391	King of glory, King of peace
Third Word	97	At the cross, her station keeping
Fourth Word	85	Jesu, meek and lowly
Fifth Word	292	Jesu, thou joy of loving hearts
Sixth Word	95	When I survey the wondrous cross
Seventh Word	380	It is finished! Christ hath known

96   O THOU who through this holy week
　　　　The path of suffering trod,
　　Our sins to heal, our souls to seek,
　　　　And bring us to our God.

2　　We cannot comprehend the woe
　　　　Thy love was pleased to bear;
　　O Saviour Christ, we only know
　　　　That all our hopes are there.

3　　Then grant us, Lord, this week to trace
　　　　Thy passion and thy love,
　　And by thine all-inspiring grace
　　　　Uplift our hearts above:

4   Beyond the pain, beyond the cross,
     The Christ of glory see,
And count the things of earth but loss
     To gain our heaven in thee.

J. M. NEALE 1818–66
and EDITORS

GOOD FRIDAY

97   *Stabat mater dolorosa*

AT the Cross her station keeping,
Stood the mournful Mother weeping,
    Close to Jesus at the last.
Through her soul, of joy bereavèd,
Bowed with anguish, deeply grievèd,
    Now at length the sword hath passed.

2* O, that blessèd one, grief-laden,
Blessèd Mother, blessèd Maiden,
    Mother of the all-holy One;
O that silent, ceaseless mourning,
O those dim eyes, never turning
    From that wondrous, suffering Son.

3 Who on Christ's dear Mother gazing,
In her trouble so amazing,
    Born of woman, would not weep?
Who on Christ's dear Mother thinking,
Such a cup of sorrow drinking,
    Would not share her sorrow deep?

4 For his people's sins, in anguish,
    There she saw the victim languish,
      Bleed in torments, bleed and die:
    Saw the Lord's anointed taken;
    Saw her Child in death forsaken,
      Heard his last expiring cry.

5 In the Passion of my Maker,
    Be my sinful soul partaker,
      May I bear with her my part;
    Of his Passion bear the token,
    In a spirit bowed and broken
      Bear his death within my heart.

6* May his wounds both wound and heal me,
    He enkindle, cleanse, anneal me,
      Be his Cross my hope and stay.
    May he, when the mountains quiver,
    From that flame which burns for ever
      Shield me on the judgement day.

7 Jesu, may thy Cross defend me,
    And thy saving death befriend me,
      Cherished by thy deathless grace:
    When to dust my dust returneth,
    Grant a soul that to thee yearneth
      In thy Paradise a place.

13th century Latin
Tr by various hands

98   O COME and stand beneath the cross,
     Come, and be at the Saviour's side,
With sword-pierced Mary and with John,
     Jesus, our Love, is crucified.

2   'Could ye not watch with me one hour?'
     Peter, his Lord has thrice denied;
The rest have fled in frightened grief;
     Jesus, their Lord, is crucified.

3   'If thou be Christ, then save us now';
     Blame not the pain-racked thief who cried:
He saves us all, this Lamb of God,
     Who for our sins was crucified.

4   Pierced by the spear, from thence there flow
     Water and blood from out his side:
Baptise me in that cleansing stream,
     Jesus, my Lord, the crucified.

5   'All is accomplished'—hear his word
     Who on that wondrous cross has died:
The travail of his soul is done;
     Victor, he reigns, the crucified.

6   Rent is the veil, the way revealed,
     Where heaven's gate he opens wide
Through death to life his own shall rise,
     Through him, their Lord, once crucified.

EDITORS

99 IT is finished! Blessèd Jesus,
    Thou hast breathed thy latest sigh,
Teaching us the sons of Adam
    How the Son of God can die.

2 Lifeless lies the piercèd Body,
    Resting in its rocky bed;
Thou hast left the Cross of anguish
    For the mansions of the dead.

3 In the hidden realms of darkness
    Shines a light unseen before,
When the Lord of dead and living
    Enters at the lowly door.

4 Lo, in spirit, rich in mercy
    Comes he from the world above,
Preaching to the souls in prison
    Tidings of his dying love.

5 Lo, the heavenly light around him,
    As he draws his people near;
All amazed they come rejoicing
    At the gracious words they hear.

6 Patriarch and priest and prophet
    Gather round him as he stands,
In adoring faith and gladness
    Hearing of the piercèd hands.

7 There in lowliest joy and wonder
    Stands the robber by his side,
Reaping now the blessèd promise
    Spoken by the Crucified.

8   Jesus, Lord of our salvation,
     Let thy mercy rest on me;
    Grant me too, when life is finished,
     Rest in Paradise with thee.

WILLIAM MACLAGAN 1826–1910

EASTERTIDE

100   OFFICE HYMN

Aurora lucis rutilat

THE day draws on with golden light,
Glad songs go echoing through the height,
The broad earth lifts an answering cheer,
And hell makes moan with wailing fear.

2   For lo, he comes, the mighty King,
   To take from death his power and sting,
   To trample down his gloomy reign,
   And break the weary prisoner's chain.

3   Enclosed he lay in rocky cell,
   With guard of armèd sentinel;
   But thence returning, strong and free,
   He comes in might of victory.

4   The sad Apostles mourn him slain,
   Nor hope to see their Lord again,
   When, to their very eyes restored,
   They look upon the risen Lord.

EASTERTIDE

5* Those wounds before their eyes displayed
They see in heavenly light arrayed,
And what they see they testify
In open witness fearlessly.

6* O Christ, the King of gentleness,
Thy people's hearts do thou possess,
That we may render all our days
An endless sacrifice of praise.

7 Maker of all, to thee we pray,
Fulfil in us thy joy today;
When death assails, grant, Lord, that we
May share thy Paschal victory.

8 To thee who, dead, again dost live,
All glory, Lord, thy people give,
All glory to the Father be
And Spirit blest, eternally.   Amen.

Latin, probably 4th century
Tr T. A. LACEY 1853–1931‡

101 OFFICE HYMN

Ad cenam Agni providi

THE Lamb's high banquet we await
In snow-white robes of royal state,
And now, the Red Sea's channel past,
To Christ our Prince we sing at last.

2　Upon the altar of the Cross
　　His Body has redeemed our loss,
　　And tasting of his precious Blood,
　　Our life is hid with Christ in God.

3　That Paschal eve God's arm was bared,
　　The devastating angel spared;
　　By strength of hand our hosts went free
　　From Pharoah's ruthless tyranny.

4　Now Christ our Passover is slain,
　　The Lamb of God that knows no stain,
　　And he, the true unleavened Bread,
　　Is truly our oblation made.

5*　O thou from whom hell's monarch flies,
　　O great, O very Sacrifice,
　　Thy captive people are set free,
　　And endless life restored in thee.

6*　For Christ, arising from the dead,
　　From conquered hell victorious sped,
　　He thrusts the tyrant down to chains,
　　And Paradise for man regains.

7　Maker of all, to thee we pray,
　　Fulfil in us thy joy today;
　　When death assails, grant, Lord, that we
　　May share thy Paschal victory.

8   To thee who, dead, again dost live,
All glory, Lord, thy people give,
All glory to the Father be
And Spirit blest, eternally.   Amen.

Latin, probably 7th century
Tr J. M. NEALE 1818–1866‡

For a procession in Eastertide see

109 Hail thee, festival day!
125 Ye sons and daughters of the King

102   A BRIGHTER dawn is breaking,
And earth with praise is waking;
For thou, O King most highest,
The power of death defiest;

2   And thou hast come victorious,
With risen Body glorious,
Who now for ever livest,
And life abundant givest.

3   O free the world from blindness,
And fill the world with kindness,
Give sinners resurrection,
Bring striving to perfection;

4   In sickness give us healing,
In doubt thy clear revealing,
That praise to thee be given
In earth as in thy heaven.

PERCY DEARMER 1867–1936

103   ALLELUYA! Alleluya!
Hearts to heaven and voices raise;
Sing to God a hymn of gladness,
Sing to God a hymn of praise;
He who on the Cross a victim
For the world's salvation bled,
Jesus Christ, the King of glory,
Now is risen from the dead.

2   Christ is risen, Christ the first-fruits
Of the holy harvest field,
Which will all its full abundance
At his second coming yield;
Then the golden ears of harvest
Will their heads before him wave,
Ripened by his glorious sunshine
From the furrows of the grave.

3   Christ is risen, we are risen;
Shed upon us heavenly grace,
Rain, and dew, and gleams of glory
From the brightness of thy face;
That we, Lord, with hearts in heaven
Here on earth may fruitful be,
And by angel-hands be gathered,
And be ever safe with thee.

4   Alleluya! Alleluya!
        Glory be to God on high;
    To the Father, and the Saviour,
        Who has gained the victory;
    Glory to the Holy Spirit,
        Fount of love and sanctity;
    Alleluya! Alleluya!
        To the Triune Majesty.   Amen.

CHRISTOPHER WORDSWORTH 1807–85

104 AT the Lamb's high feast we sing
     Praise to our victorious King:
     Who hath washed us in the tide
     Flowing from his piercèd side;
     Praise we him whose love divine
     Gives the guests his blood for wine,
     Gives his body for the feast,
     Love the Victim, Love the Priest.

2*   Where the Paschal blood is poured,
     Death's dark angel sheathes his sword;
     Israel's hosts triumphant go
     Through the wave that drowns the foe.
     Christ, the Lamb whose blood was shed,
     Paschal victim, Paschal bread!
     With sincerity and love
     Eat we Manna from above.

3 Mighty Victim from on high,
Powers of hell beneath thee lie;
Death is broken in the fight,
Thou hast brought us life and light.
Now thy banner thou dost wave,
Conquering Satan and the grave.
See the prince of darkness quelled;
Heaven's bright gates are open held.

4 Paschal triumph, Paschal joy,
Only sin can this destroy;
From sin's death do thou set free,
Souls re-born, dear Lord, in thee.
Hymns of glory, songs of praise,
Father, unto thee we raise.
Risen Lord, all praise to thee,
Ever with the Spirit be.

From a Latin Breviary hymn
Tr ROBERT CAMPBELL 1814–68

105 CHRIST the Lord is risen again!
Christ hath broken every chain!
Hark, the angels shout for joy,
Singing evermore on high,

Alleluya!

2 He who gave for us his life,
Who for us endured the strife,
Is our Paschal Lamb to-day!
We too sing for joy, and say

Alleluya!

3 He who bore all pain and loss
Comfortless upon the Cross,
Lives in glory now on high,
Pleads for us, and hears our cry.
Alleluya!

4 He whose path no records tell,
Who descended into hell;
Who the strong man armed hath bound,
Now in highest heaven is crowned.
Alleluya!

5 Now he bids us tell abroad
How the lost may be restored,
How the penitent forgiven,
How we too may enter heaven.
Alleluya!

6 Thou, our Paschal Lamb indeed,
Christ, to-day thy people feed;
Take our sins and guilt away,
That we all may sing for ay,
Alleluya!

German, MICHAEL WEISSE c 1480–1534
Tr CATHERINE WINKWORTH 1827–78

106 COME, ye faithful, raise the strain
　　　Of triumphant gladness;
　　God hath brought his Israel
　　　Into joy from sadness;
　　Loosed from Pharaoh's bitter yoke
　　　Jacob's sons and daughters;
　　Led them with unmoistened foot
　　　Through the Red Sea waters.

2　'Tis the spring of souls to-day;
　　　Christ hath burst his prison,
　　And from three days' sleep in death
　　　As a sun hath risen;
　　All the winter of our sins,
　　　Long and dark, is flying
　　From his light, to whom we give
　　　Laud and praise undying.

3　Now the queen of seasons, bright
　　　With the day of splendour,
　　With the royal feast of feasts,
　　　Comes its joy to render;
　　Comes to glad Jerusalem,
　　　Who with true affection
　　Welcomes in unwearied strains
　　　Jesu's Resurrection.

4 Neither might the gates of death,
  Nor the tomb's dark portal,
 Nor the watchers, nor the seal,
  Hold thee as a mortal;
 But today amidst thine own
  Thou didst stand, bestowing
 That thy peace which evermore
  Passeth human knowing.

Greek, St John of Damascus c 750
Tr J. M. Neale 1816–66†

107 GOOD Christian men, rejoice and sing!
 Now is the triumph of our King:
 To all the world glad news we bring:
     Alleluya!

2 The Lord of Life is risen for ay:
 Bring flowers of song to strew his way;
 Let all mankind rejoice and say:
     Alleluya!

3 Praise we in songs of victory
 That Love, that Life, which cannot die,
 And sing with hearts uplifted high:
     Alleluya!

4 Thy name we bless, O risen Lord,
 And sing today with one accord
 The life laid down, the life restored:
     Alleluya!

Cyril Alington 1872–1955

108 HAIL, Easter bright, in glory dight!
    Ye heavens, laugh and sing:
Since Christ our light uprose by night,
    Let carols greet the King.

2 The work of death has been reversed
    By Jesus' victory;
And mortals from their prison burst
    To his new life, and free.

3 Was ever such a battle won?
    By loss, the victor's gain:
And he who held the reed of scorn,
    A sceptre doth obtain.

4 Then sing of him who rose from death,
    Sing forth with heart and voice!
In Christ, our sun, our life, our light,
    Let earth and heaven rejoice.

DANIEL'S *Thesaurus Hymnologicus* c 1530
Tr G. R. WOODWARD 1848–1934 and EDITORS

109 *Suitable for use in Procession at Easter and Ascension*

Salve, festa dies

Easter

Hail thee, Festival Day, blest day that art hallowed for ever;
Day wherein Christ arose, breaking the kingdom of death.

Ascension

*Hail thee, Festival Day, blest day that art
    hallowed for ever;*
*Day when the Lord ascends, high in the heavens to
    reign.*

Easter and Ascension:

2 Lo, the fair beauty of earth, from the death of
      the winter arising,
   Every good gift of the year, now with its Master
      returns.

3 Daily the loveliness grows, adorned with the
      glory of blossom;
   Green is the woodland with leaves, bright are
      the meadows with flowers.

4 He who was nailed to the cross is Lord and
      the ruler of all things;
   All things created on earth, worship the Maker
      of all.

_____

Easter only:

5 Ill it beseemeth that thou, by whose hand all
      things are encompassed,
   Captive and bound should remain, deep in the
      gloom of the rock.

6 Rise now, O Lord from the grave, and cast off
      the shroud that enwrapped thee;
   Leaving the caverns of death, show us the light
      of thy face.

7   God of all pity and power, let thy word be
        assured to the doubting;
    Lo, he breaks forth from the tomb! See, he
        appears to his own!

Ascension only:

5   He who has conquered the grave now rises to
        heavenly splendour;
    Fitly the light gives him praise—meadows and
        ocean and sky.

6   Christ, in thy triumph ascend: thou hast led
        captivity captive;
    Heaven her gates unbars, flinging her increase of
        light.

7   Thence shall the Spirit descend on them that
        await his appearing;
    Flame from the heart of our God, life-giving
        Spirit of peace.

Easter and Ascension:

8   Jesus, thou Health of the world, enlighten our
        minds, O Redeemer,
    Son of the Father supreme, only-begotten of
        God.

9   So shalt thou bear in thine arms an immaculate
        people to heaven,
    Bearing them pure unto God, pledge of thy
        victory here.

10 Equal art thou, co-eternal, in fellowship One
    with the Father,
And with the Spirit of truth, God evermore to
    be blest!

Editors and others, based on the Latin of
VENANTIUS FORTUNATUS 530–609

110 JESUS Christ is risen to-day,   Alleluya!
Our triumphant holy day,   Alleluya!
Who did once, upon the Cross,   Alleluya!
Suffer to redeem our loss.   Alleluya!

2 Hymns of praise then let us sing,   Alleluya!
Unto Christ, our heavenly King,   Alleluya!
Who endured the Cross and grave,   Alleluya!
Sinners to redeem and save.   Alleluya!

3 But the pains that he endured   Alleluya!
Our salvation have procured;   Alleluya!
Now above the sky he's King,   Alleluya!
Where the angels ever sing.   Alleluya!

Lyra Davidica 1708

111 JESUS Christ is risen:
The feast, good Christians, therefore keep;
The Lamb has bled to save the sheep,
Christ innocent, our ransom paid,
Mankind and God at one hath made:
    Alleluya, Alleluya.

2   Jesus Christ is risen:
    Speak, Mary Magdalen, and say
    What sawest thou upon the way?
    'I saw the grave, and there adored
    The glory of the risen Lord':

3   Jesus Christ is risen:
    'Within the grave on either hand
    I saw a white-robed angel stand;
    My Saviour Christ, my hope, my stay,
    Hath risen from the tomb today':

4   Jesus Christ is risen:
    We know for certain, truth to tell,
    That Christ arose from death and hell;
    And while thy Paschal song we sing,
    Have pity on us, Victor-king:

G. R. WOODWARD 1848–1934
based on *Victimae Paschali*

112   JESUS lives! thy terrors now
    Can, O Death, no more appal us;
  Jesus lives! by this we know
    Thou, O grave, canst not enthral us.
      Alleluya!

2   Jesus lives! henceforth is death
    But the gate of life immortal;
  This shall calm our trembling breath,
    When we pass its gloomy portal.
      Alleluya!

3 Jesus lives! for us he died;
  Then, alone to Jesus living,
Pure in heart may we abide,
  Glory to our Saviour giving.
                    Alleluya!

4 Jesus lives! our hearts know well
  Nought from us his love shall sever;
Life, nor death, nor powers of hell
  Tear us from his keeping ever.
                    Alleluya!

5 Jesus lives! to him the throne
  Over all the world is given;
May we go where he is gone,
  Rest and reign with him in heaven.
                    Alleluya!

CHRISTIAN GELLERT 1715–69
Tr FRANCES COX 1812–97†

113 LOVE'S redeeming work is done;
  Fought the fight, the battle won:
  Lo, our Sun's eclipse is o'er!
  Lo, he sets in blood no more!

2 Vain the stone, the watch, the seal,
  Christ has burst the gates of hell;
  Death in vain forbids his rise;
  Christ has opened Paradise.

123

3 Lives again our glorious King;
Where, O Death, is now thy sting?
Dying once, he all doth save;
Where thy victory, O grave?

4 Soar we now where Christ has led,
Following our exalted Head;
Made like him, like him we rise;
Ours the cross, the grave, the skies.

5 Hail the Lord of earth and heaven!
Praise to thee by both be given:
Thee we greet triumphant now;
Hail, the Resurrection thou!

CHARLES WESLEY 1707–88

114 *Suitable also for Adult Baptism*

NOW is eternal life,
   If risen with Christ we stand,
In him to life reborn,
   And holden in his hand;
No more we fear death's ancient dread,
In Christ arisen from the dead.

2 For God, the living God,
   Stooped down to man's estate;
By death destroying death,
   Christ opened wide life's gate:
He lives, who died; he reigns on high;
Who lives in him shall never die.

3   Unfathomed love divine,
     Reign thou within my heart;
  From thee nor depth nor height,
     Nor life nor death can part;
  Our life is hid with God in thee,
  Now and through all eternity.

G. W. BRIGGS 1875–1959†

115   NOW the green blade riseth from the buried
      grain,
  Wheat that in dark earth many days has lain;
  Love lives again, that with the dead has been:
    Love is come again,
    Like wheat that springeth green.

2   In the grave they laid him, Love whom men
      had slain,
  Thinking that never he would wake again,
  Laid in the earth like grain that sleeps unseen:

3   Forth he came at Easter, like the risen grain,
  He that for three days in the grave had lain,
  Quick from the dead, my risen Lord is seen:

4   When our hearts are wintry, grieving, or in
      pain,
  Thy touch can call us back to life again,
  Fields of our hearts, that dead and bare have
      been:

J. M. C. CRUM 1872–1958

116 *Suitable at the Easter Vigil*

O PRAISE our great and glorious Lord,
   And call upon his name,
To strains of joy tune every chord,
   His mighty acts proclaim:
Tell how he freed his chosen race
   From Pharaoh's heavy hand,
And led them by his sovereign grace
   To seek the promised land.

2 He gave the shadowing cloud by day,
   The moving fire by night,
To guide his people on their way,
   And make their darkness light:
To us, the light of Christ our Lord
   Illumines all our ways;
He leads us by his gospel word,
   And turns our sighs to praise.

3 We too have manna from on high,
   The bread that came from heaven,
And he who brought salvation nigh
   Has living water given:
A rock is ours, from whence the spring
   In rich abundance flows,
And Christ that rock, our priest and king,
   Both life and health bestows.

4   Come, let us prize this heavenly food,
    And trust our heavenly guide,
So shall we find death's fearful flood
    Serene as Jordan's tide;
So safely reach th'eternal shore
    No more by ills opprest;
Where saints their Lord and God adore,
    And in his glory, rest.

EDITORS, based upon verses by
HARRIET AUBER 1773–1862

117   THE Day of Resurrection!
    Earth, tell it out abroad;
The Passover of gladness,
    The Passover of God!
From death to life eternal,
    From earth unto the sky,
Our Christ hath brought us over
    With hymns of victory.

2   Our hearts be pure from evil,
    That we may see aright
The Lord in rays eternal
    Of resurrection-light;
And, listening to his accents,
    May hear so calm and plain
His own 'All hail,' and, hearing,
    May raise the victor strain.

3 Now let the heavens be joyful,
    And earth her song begin,
The round world keep high triumph,
    And all that is therein;
Let all things seen and unseen
    Their notes of gladness blend,
For Christ the Lord hath risen,
    Our joy that hath no end.

Greek, ST JOHN OF DAMASCUS c 750
Tr J. M. NEALE 1816–66‡

118 THE Lord is risen indeed!
    Now is his work performed;
Now is the mighty Captive freed,
    And death's strong castle stormed.

2 The Lord is risen indeed!
    Then hell has lost his prey;
With him is risen the ransomed seed
    To reign in endless day.

3 The Lord is risen indeed!
    He lives, to die no more;
He lives, the sinner's cause to plead,
    Whose curse and shame he bore.

THOMAS KELLY 1769–1855

119   *Finita jam sunt proelia*

THE strife is o'er, the battle done;
Now is the Victor's triumph won;
O let the song of praise be sung.

Alleluya!

2   Death's mightiest powers have done their
        worst,
And Jesus hath his foes dispersed;
Let shouts of praise and joy outburst.

3   On the third morn he rose again
Glorious in majesty to reign;
O let us swell the joyful strain.

4★ He brake the age-bound chains of hell;
The bars from heaven's high portals fell;
Let hymns of praise his triumph tell.

5★ Lord, by the stripes which wounded thee
From death's dread sting thy servants free,
That we may live, and sing to thee.

Latin 17th century
Tr FRANCIS POTT 1832–1909

120   *A toi la gloire, O Ressuscité*

THINE be the glory, risen, conquering Son,
Endless is the victory thou o'er death hast won;
Angels in bright raiment rolled the stone away,
Kept the folded grave-clothes where thy body
    lay.
  Thine be the glory, risen, conquering Son,
  Endless is the vict'ry thou o'er death hast won.

2 Lo, Jesus meets us, risen from the tomb;
  Lovingly he greets us, scatters fear and gloom;
  Let the Church with gladness hymns of
    triumph sing,
  For her Lord now liveth, death hath lost its
    sting:

3 No more we doubt thee, glorious Prince of
    Life;
  Life is nought without thee: aid us in our
    strife,
  Make us more than conquerors through thy
    deathless love;
  Bring us safe through Jordan to thy home
    above:

French, EDMOND BUDRY 1854–1932
Tr RICHARD HOYLE 1875–1939

121 THIS joyful Eastertide,
　　Away with sin and sorrow.
My Love, the Crucified,
　　Hath sprung to life this morrow:

Had Christ, that once was slain,
*　　Ne'er burst his three-day prison,*
Our faith had been in vain:
*　　But now hath Christ arisen.*

2　My flesh in hope shall rest,
　　And for a season slumber:
Till trump from east to west
　　Shall wake the dead in number:

3　Death's flood hath lost his chill,
　　Since Jesus crossed the river:
Lover of souls, from ill
　　My passing soul deliver:

G. R. WOODWARD 1848–1934

122 THOU hallowed chosen morn of praise,
　　That best and greatest shinest:
Lady and queen and day of days,
　　Of things divine, divinest!
On thee our praises Christ adore
For ever and for evermore.

2　Come, let us taste the Vine's new fruit,
　　For heavenly joy preparing;
To-day the branches with the Root
　　In Resurrection sharing:
Whom as true God our hymns adore
For ever and for evermore.

131

3 Rise, Sion, rise! and looking forth,
   Behold thy children round thee!
From east and west, from south and north,
   Thy scattered sons have found thee;
And in thy bosom Christ adore
For ever and for evermore.

4 O Father, O co-equal Son,
   O co-eternal Spirit,
In persons Three, in Godhead One,
   And One in power and merit;
In thee baptized, we thee adore
For ever and for evermore.   Amen.

Greek, St John of Damascus c 750
Tr J. M. Neale 1818–66

123 WALKING in a garden
   At the close of day,
Adam tried to hide him
   When he heard God say:
'Why are you so frightened,
   Why are you afraid?
You have brought the winter in,
   Made the flowers fade.'

2 Walking in a garden
   Where the Lord had gone,
Three of the disciples,
   Peter, James, and John;
They were very weary,
   Could not keep awake,
While the Lord was kneeling there,
   Praying for their sake.

3   Walking in a garden
        At the break of day,
    Mary asked the gardener
        Where the body lay;
    But he turned towards her,
        Smiled at her and said:
    'Mary, spring is here to stay,
        Only death is dead.'

HILARY GREENWOOD b 1929

124   *Chorus novae Jerusalem*

    YE choirs of new Jerusalem,
        Your sweetest notes employ,
    The Paschal victory to hymn
        In strains of holy joy.

2   How Judah's Lion burst his chains,
        And crushed the serpent's head;
    And brought with him, from death's domains,
        The long-imprisoned dead.

3   From hell's devouring jaws the prey
        Alone our Leader bore;
    His ransomed hosts pursue their way
        Where he hath gone before.

4   Triumphant in his glory now
        His sceptre ruleth all,
    Earth, heaven, and hell before him bow,
        And at his footstool fall.

5 While joyful thus his praise we sing,
   His mercy we implore,
Into his palace bright to bring
   And keep us evermore.

6 All glory to the Father be,
   All glory to the Son,
All glory, Holy Ghost, to thee,
   While endless ages run.   Alleluya!   Amen.

ST FULBERT OF CHARTRES d 1028
Tr ROBERT CAMPBELL 1814–68

125   *Suitable for use in Procession*

O filii et filiae

ALLELUYA! Alleluya! Alleluya!
Ye sons and daughters of the King,
Whom heavenly hosts in glory sing,
To-day the grave hath lost its sting.
           Alleluya!

2 On that first morning of the week,
Before the day began to break,
The Marys went their Lord to seek.

3 An Angel bade their sorrow flee,
For thus he spake unto the three:
'Your Lord is gone to Galilee.'

4 That night the Apostles met in fear,
Amidst them came their Lord most dear,
And said: 'Peace be unto you here!'

5 When Thomas afterwards had heard
That Jesus had fulfilled his word,
He doubted if it were the Lord.

6 'Thomas, behold my side,' saith he,
'My hands, my feet, my body see;
'And doubt not, but believe in me.'

7 No longer Thomas then denied;
He saw the feet, the hands, the side;
'Thou art my Lord and God,' he cried.

8 Blessèd are they that have not seen,
And yet whose faith hath constant been,
In life eternal they shall reign.

9* On this most holy day of days,
To God your hearts and voices raise
In laud, and jubilee, and praise.

10* And we with Holy Church unite,
As evermore is just and right,
In glory to the King of Light.

Latin, JEAN TISSERAND d 1419
Tr J. M. NEALE 1818–66

See also

519 The Easter Sequence
296 Lord, enthroned in heavenly splendour
351 Come, ye faithful, raise the anthem
375 I danced in the morning
446 Sing Alleluya forth ye saints on high

126 LORD, in thy name thy servants plead,
    And thou hast sworn to hear;
Thine is the harvest, thine the seed,
    The fresh and fading year.

2 Our hope, when autumn winds blew wild,
    We trusted, Lord, with thee;
And still, now spring has on us smiled,
    We wait on thy decree.

3 The former and the latter rain,
    The summer sun and air,
The green ear, and the golden grain,
    All thine, are ours by prayer.

4 Thine too by right, and ours by grace,
    The wondrous growth unseen,
The hopes that soothe, the fears that brace,
    The love that shines serene.

5 So grant the precious things brought forth
    By sun and moon below,
That thee in thy new heaven and earth
    We never may forgo.

JOHN KEBLE 1792–1866

127 TO thee our God we fly
    For mercy and for grace;
O hear our lowly cry,
    And hide not thou thy face.
    O Lord, stretch forth thy mighty hand,
    And guard and bless our native land.

2 Arise, O Lord of hosts!
    Be jealous for thy name,
And drive from out our coasts
    The sins that put to shame.

3 Thy best gifts from on high
    In rich abundance pour,
That we may magnify
    And praise thee evermore.

4 The powers ordained by thee
    With heavenly wisdom bless;
May they thy servants be,
    And rule in righteousness.

5 Give peace, Lord, in our time,
    O let no foe draw nigh,
Nor lawless deeds of crime
    Insult thy majesty.

6 The Church of thy dear Son
    Inflame with love's pure fire,
Bind her once more in one;
    With life and truth inspire.

W. WALSHAM HOW 1823–97

See also

262 We plough the fields and scatter
263 All creatures of our God and King
267 The spacious firmament on high
416 O God of Bethel, by whose hand
490 Judge eternal, throned in splendour
493 Rejoice, O land, in God thy might
    The Litany may be sung in procession.

128 OFFICE HYMN

Aeterne Rex altissime

ETERNAL Monarch, King most high,
Whose blood hath brought redemption nigh,
By whom the death of Death was wrought
And conquering grace's battle fought:

2   Ascending to the throne of might,
And seated at the Father's right,
All power in heaven is Jesu's own,
That here his manhood had not known.

3   Yea, angels tremble when they see
How changed is our humanity;
For flesh hath purged what flesh had stained,
And God, the flesh of God, hath reigned.

4   Be thou our joy and strong defence,
Who art our future recompense:
So shall the light that springs from thee
Be ours through all eternity.

5   O risen Christ, ascended Lord,
All praise to thee let earth accord,
Who art, while endless ages run,
With Father and with Spirit One.   Amen.

Latin c 5th century
Tr J. M. NEALE 1818–66

For a procession in Ascensiontide see

109 Hail thee, festival day!
130 Hail the day that sees him rise

129 OFFICE HYMN COMPLINE

Jesu nostra redemptio

O CHRIST, our hope, our hearts' desire,
Redemption's only spring;
Creator of the world art thou,
Its Saviour and its King.

2 How vast the mercy and the love
Which laid our sins on thee,
And led thee to a cruel death
To set thy people free.

3 But now the bonds of death are burst,
The ransom has been paid;
And thou art on thy Father's throne
In glorious robes arrayed.

4 O may thy mighty love prevail
Our sinful souls to spare;
O may we come before thy throne,
And find acceptance there!

5 O Christ, be thou our present joy,
Our future great reward;
Our only glory may it be
To glory in the Lord.

6 All praise to thee, ascended Lord;
All glory ever be
To Father, Son, and Holy Ghost,
Through all eternity.   Amen.

Latin c 8th century
Tr JOHN CHANDLER 1806–76

130   *Suitable for use in Procession*

HAIL the day that sees him rise   Alleluya!
Glorious to his native skies;   Alleluya!
Christ, awhile to mortals given,   Alleluya!
Enters now the highest heaven!   Alleluya!

2   There the glorious triumph waits;   Alleluya!
Lift your heads, eternal gates!   Alleluya!
Christ hath vanquished death and sin;
      Alleluya!
Take the King of glory in.   Alleluya!

3*   See! the heaven its Lord receives,   Alleluya!
Yet he loves the earth he leaves: Alleluya!
Though returning to his throne,   Alleluya!
Still he calls mankind his own.   Alleluya!

4*   See! he lifts his hands above;   Alleluya!
See! he shows the prints of love: Alleluya!
Hark! his gracious lips bestow   Alleluya!
Blessings on his Church below.   Alleluya!

5*   Still for us he intercedes;   Alleluya!
His prevailing death he pleads;   Alleluya!
Near himself prepares our place,   Alleluya!
Harbinger of human race.   Alleluya!

6   Lord, though parted from our sight,
      Alleluya!
Far above yon azure height,   Alleluya!
Grant our hearts may thither rise,   Alleluya!
Seeking thee beyond the skies.   Alleluya!

7 There we shall with thee remain,   Alleluya!
   Partners of thine endless reign;   Alleluya!
   There thy face unclouded see,   Alleluya!
   Find our heaven of heavens in thee.   Alleluya!

CHARLES WESLEY 1707–88 and
THOMAS COTTERILL 1779–1823

When the tune 'Chislehurst' is used Alleluya *is omitted in the
third line and sung three times in the fourth line*

131   *Supreme Rector coelitum*

O KING most high of earth and sky
   On prostrate death thou treadest,
And with thy blood dost mark the road
   Whereby to heaven thou leadest.

2 O Christ, behold thine orphaned fold,
     Which thou hast borne with anguish,
   Steeped in the tide from thy rent side;
     O leave us not to languish!

3 The glorious gain of all thy pain
     Henceforth dost thou inherit;
   Now comes the hour—then gently shower
     On us thy promised Spirit!

Latin Breviary hymn 17th century
Tr WILLIAM BLEW 1808–94

132 SEE the Conqueror mounts in triumph,
    See the King in royal state
Riding on the clouds his chariot
    To his heavenly palace gate;
Hark! the choirs of angel voices
    Joyful alleluyas sing,
And the portals high are lifted
    To receive their heavenly King.

2 Who is this that comes in glory,
    With the trump of jubilee?
Lord of battles, God of armies,
    He has gained the victory;
He who on the cross did suffer,
    He who from the grave arose,
He has vanquished sin and Satan,
    He by death has spoiled his foes.

3 Thou hast raised our human nature
    In the clouds to God's right hand;
There we sit in heavenly places,
    There with thee in glory stand;
Jesus reigns, adored by angels;
    Man with God is on the throne;
Mighty Lord, in thine ascension
    We by faith behold our own.

4 Glory be to God the Father;
    Glory be to God the Son,
Dying, risen, ascending for us,
    Who the heavenly realm has won;
Glory to the Holy Spirit;
    To One God in persons Three;
Glory both in earth and heaven,
    Glory, endless glory be.   Amen.

CHRISTOPHER WORDSWORTH 1807–85

133 THE eternal gates lift up their heads,
    The doors are opened wide,
The King of glory is gone up
    Unto his Father's side.

2 And ever on our earthly path
    A gleam of glory lies,
A light still breaks behind the cloud
    That veils thee from our eyes.

3 Lift up our hearts, lift up our minds,
    And let thy grace be given,
That, while we live on earth below,
    Our treasure be in heaven;

4 That, where thou art at God's right hand,
    Our hope, our love may be:
Dwell in us now, that we may dwell
    For evermore in thee.

MRS C. F. ALEXANDER 1818–95

134   THE head that once was crowned with thorns
       Is crowned with glory now:
A royal diadem adorns
       The mighty victor's brow.

2   The highest place that heaven affords
       Is his, is his by right,
The King of kings and Lord of lords,
       And heaven's eternal light;

3   The joy of all who dwell above,
       The joy of all below,
To whom he manifests his love,
       And grants his name to know.

4   To them the cross, with all its shame.
       With all its grace is given:
Their name an everlasting name,
       Their joy the joy of heaven.

5   They suffer with their Lord below,
       They reign with him above,
Their profit and their joy to know
       The mystery of his love.

6   The cross he bore is life and health,
       Though shame and death to him;
His people's hope, his people's wealth,
       Their everlasting theme.

THOMAS KELLY 1769–1854

135   THE Lord ascendeth up on high,
    Loud anthems round him swelling;
The Lord hath triumphed gloriously,
    In power and might excelling:
Hell and the grave are captive led;
Lo, he returns, our glorious Head,
    To his eternal dwelling.

2   The heavens with joy receive their Lord;
    O day of exultation!
By saints, by angel-hosts adored
    For his so great salvation:
O earth, adore thy glorious King,
His rising, his ascension sing
    With grateful adoration.

3   By saints in earth and saints in heaven,
    With songs for ever blended,
All praise to Christ our King be given,
    Who hath to heaven ascended:
To Father, Son, and Holy Ghost,
The God of heaven's resplendent host,
    In bright array extended.

ARTHUR RUSSELL 1806–74
and others

See also

109 Hail thee, Festival Day!
271 Alleluya, sing to Jesus
332 All hail the power of Jesu's name

PENTECOST or WHITSUNDAY

136 OFFICE HYMN

Beata nobis gaudia

REJOICE, the year upon its way
Has brought again that blessèd day
When on the Church by Christ our Lord
The Holy Spirit was outpoured.

2 From out the heavens a rushing noise
Came like the tempest's sudden voice,
And mingled with the Apostles' prayer,
Proclaiming loud that God was there.

3 Like quivering tongues of light and flame,
Upon each one the Spirit came:
Tongues, that the earth might hear their call,
And fire, that love might burn in all.

4 And so to all were spread abroad
The wonders of the works of God;
They knew the prophet's word fulfilled,
And owned the gift which God had willed.

5   Look down, most gracious God, this day
Upon thy people as they pray;
And Christ the Lord upon us pour
The Spirit's gift for evermore.   Amen.

EDITORS, based upon the Latin,
c 4th century

For a Whitsuntide procession see

139 Come, thou Holy Spirit, come
142 Sing to him in whom creation

137   COME down, O Love divine,
Seek thou this soul of mine,
And visit it with thine own ardour glowing;
O Comforter, draw near,
Within my heart appear,
And kindle it, thy holy flame bestowing.

2   O let it freely burn,
Till earthly passions turn
To dust and ashes in its heat consuming;
And let thy glorious light
Shine ever on my sight,
And clothe me round, the while my path
illuming.

3   Let holy charity
Mine outward vesture be,
And lowliness become mine inner clothing;
True lowliness of heart,
Which takes the humbler part,
And o'er its own shortcomings weeps with
loathing.

4   And so the yearning strong,
       With which the soul will long,
Shall far outpass the power of human telling;
     For none can guess its grace,
       Till he become the place
Wherein the Holy Spirit makes his dwelling.

Italian, BIANCO DA SIENA d 1434
Tr R. F. LITTLEDALE 1833–90

138   COME, Holy Ghost, our souls inspire,
       And lighten with celestial fire;
       Thou the anointing Spirit art,
       Who dost thy sevenfold gifts impart:

2   Thy blessèd unction from above
     Is comfort, life, and fire of love;
     Enable with perpetual light
     The dullness of our blinded sight:

3   Anoint and cheer our soilèd face
     With the abundance of thy grace:
     Keep far our foes, give peace at home;
     Where thou art guide no ill can come.

4 Teach us to know the Father, Son,
And thee, of Both, to be but One;
That through the ages all along
This may be our endless song,

Praise to thy eternal merit,
Father, Son, and Holy Spirit.   Amen.

JOHN COSIN 1594–1672
based on *Veni, creator Spiritus*

139 *Suitable for use in Procession*

Veni, sancte Spiritus

COME, thou Holy Spirit, come,
And from thy celestial home
   Shed thy light and brilliancy:
Father of the poor, draw near,
Giver of all gifts, be here,
   Come, the soul's true radiancy.

2 Come, of comforters the best,
Of the soul the sweetest guest,
   Come in toil refreshingly:
Thou in labour rest most sweet,
Thou art shadow from the heat,
   Comfort in adversity.

3 O thou Light most pure and blest,
Shine within the inmost breast
   Of thy faithful company:
Where thou art not, man has nought,
Every holy deed and thought
   Comes from thy divinity.

4 Sinful hearts do thou make whole,
Bring to life the arid soul,
   Guide the feet that go astray:
Make the stubborn heart unbend,
To the faint, new hope extend,
   Wounded souls, their hurt allay.

5 Fill the faithful, who confide
In thy power to guard and guide,
   With thy sevenfold mystery:
Here thy grace and virtue send,
Grant salvation in the end,
   And in heaven felicity.

Latin, STEPHEN LANGTON d 1228
Tr J. M. NEALE 1818–66
and EDITORS

The plainsong melody for this hymn, The Golden Sequence,
will be found at 520

140 HOLY Spirit, come, confirm us
   In the truth that Christ makes known;
We have faith and understanding
   Through your promised light alone.

2 Holy Spirit, come, console us,
   Come as Advocate to plead,
Loving Spirit from the Father,
   Grant in Christ the help we need.

3   Holy Spirit, come, renew us,
       Come yourself to make us live,
    Holy through your loving presence,
       Holy through the gifts you give.

4   Holy Spirit, come, possess us,
       You the love of Three in One,
    Holy Spirit of the Father,
       Holy Spirit of the Son.

BRIAN FOLEY b 1919

141   HOLY Spirit, ever dwelling
             In the holiest realms of light;
          Holy Spirit, ever brooding
             O'er a world of gloom and night;
          Holy Spirit, ever raising
             Sons of earth to thrones on high;
          Living, life-imparting Spirit,
             Thee we praise and magnify.

   2   Holy Spirit, ever living
          As the Church's very life;
       Holy Spirit, ever striving
          Through her in a ceaseless strife;
       Holy Spirit ever forming
          In the Church the mind of Christ;
       Thee we praise with endless worship
          For thy fruit and gifts unpriced.

3   Holy Spirit, ever working
         Through the Church's ministry;
     Quickening, strengthening, and absolving,
         Setting captive sinners free;
     Holy Spirit, ever binding
         Age to age, and soul to soul,
     In a fellowship unending—
         Thee we worship and extol.

TIMOTHY REES 1874–1939

142   *Suitable for use in Procession*

      SING to him in whom creation
          Found its shape and origin;
      Spirit, moving on the waters,
          Troubled by the God within;
      Source of breath to all things breathing,
          Life in whom all lives begin.

2   Sing to God, the close companion
         Of our inmost thoughts and ways;
     Who, in showing us his wonders,
         Is himself the power to gaze;
     And his will, to those who listen,
         By a still small voice conveys.

3   Holy men, both priest and prophet,
         Caught his accents, spoke his word;
     His the truth behind the wisdoms
         Which as yet know not our Lord;
     He the love of God eternal,
         Which in Christ was seen and heard.

4   Tell of how the ascended Jesus
     Armed a people for his own;
  How a hundred men and women
     Turned the known world upside down,
  To its dark and furthest corners
     By the Wind of Whitsun blown.

5   Pray we then, O Lord the Spirit,
     On our lives descend in might;
  Let thy flame break out within us,
     Fire our hearts and clear our sight,
  Till, white-hot in thy possession,
     We, too, set the world alight.

6   Praise, O praise the Holy Spirit,
     Praise the Father, praise the Word,
  Source, and Truth, and Inspiration,
     Trinity in deep accord:
  Through thy Voice which speaks within us
     We thy creatures own thee Lord.

MICHAEL HEWLETT b 1916

143   *Suitable for a gradual*

    SPIRIT of mercy, truth and love,
    Shed thy blest influence from above,
    And still from age to age convey
    The wonders of this sacred day.

2   In every clime, by every tongue,
    Be God's eternal praises sung;
    Let all the listening earth be taught
    The acts our great Redeemer wrought.

3 Unfailing comfort, heavenly guide,
Still o'er thy holy Church preside;
Still let mankind thy blessings prove,
Spirit of mercy, truth and love.

Foundling Hospital Collection 1774

See also

342 Breathe on me, Breath of God
347 Come, gracious Spirit, heavenly Dove
348 Come, Holy Ghost, our hearts inspire
367 Gracious Spirit, Holy Ghost
409 Love of the Father, Love of God the Son
419 O Holy Spirit, Lord of grace
421 O King, enthroned on high

TRINITY SUNDAY

144 OFFICE HYMN

O Pater sancte

FATHER most holy, merciful and tender;
Jesus our Saviour, with the Father reigning;
Spirit all-kindly, Advocate, Defender,
    Light never waning;

2 Trinity sacred, Unity unshaken;
    Deity perfect, giving and forgiving,
Light of the angels, Life of the forsaken,
    Hope of all living;

3 Maker of all things, all thy creatures praise
thee;
Lo, all things serve thee through thy whole
creation:
Hear us, Almighty, hear us as we raise thee
Heart's adoration.

4 To the all-ruling triune God be glory:
Highest and greatest, help thou our
endeavour,
We too would praise thee, giving honour
worthy,
Now and for ever.   Amen.

Latin c 10th century
Tr PERCY DEARMER 1867–1936

For a procession at Trị̣ *see*

148 The God of Abraham praise
159 I bind unto myself today

145   *Ave colenda Trinitas*

ALL hail, adorèd Trinity;
All hail, eternal Unity;
O God the Father, God the Son,
And God the Spirit, ever One.

2 Three Persons praise we evermore,
One only God our hearts adore;
In thy sweet mercy ever kind
May we our sure protection find.

3 O Trinity, O Unity,
  Be present as we worship thee;
  And with the songs that angels sing
  Unite the hymns of praise we bring.

Latin, c 10th century
Tr JOHN CHAMBERS 1805–93

146 HOLY, Holy, Holy! Lord God Almighty!
  Early in the morning our song shall rise to
    thee;
  Holy, Holy, Holy! Merciful and mighty!
  God in three Persons, blessèd Trinity!

2 Holy, Holy, Holy! all the saints adore thee,
  Casting down their golden crowns around the
    glassy sea;
  Cherubim and seraphim falling down before
    thee,
  Which wert, and art, and evermore shalt be.

3 Holy, Holy, Holy! though the darkness hide
    thee,
  Though the eye of sinful man thy glory may
    not see,
  Only thou art holy, there is none beside thee
  Perfect in power, in love, and purity.

4   Holy, Holy, Holy! Lord God Almighty!
      All thy works shall praise thy name, in earth,
        and sky, and sea;
    Holy, Holy, Holy! Merciful and mighty!
      God in three Persons, blessèd Trinity!

REGINALD HEBER 1783–1826

147   MOST ancient of all mysteries,
        Before thy throne we lie;
      Have mercy now, most merciful,
        Most holy Trinity.

2   When heaven and earth were yet unmade,
      When time was yet unknown,
    Thou in thy bliss and majesty
      Didst live and love alone.

3   Thou wert not born; there was no fount
      From which thy Being flowed;
    There is no end which thou canst reach;
      But thou art simply God.

4   How wonderful creation is,
      The work which thou didst bless,
    And O, what then must thou be like,
      Eternal loveliness!

5   Most ancient of all mysteries,
      Before thy throne we lie;
    Have mercy now, most merciful,
      Most holy Trinity.

F. W. FABER 1814–63

148   *Suitable for use in Procession*

THE God of Abraham praise
Who reigns enthroned above,
Ancient of everlasting days,
    And God of love:
To him uplift your voice,
    At whose supreme command
From earth we rise and seek the joys
    At his right hand.

2*   Though nature's strength decay,
    And earth and hell withstand,
To Canaan's bounds we urge our way
    At his command.
The watery deep we pass,
    With Jesus in our view,
And through the howling wilderness
    Our way pursue.

3*   The goodly land we see,
    With peace and plenty blest,
A land of sacred liberty
    And endless rest;
There milk and honey flow,
    And oil and wine abound,
And trees of life for ever grow
    With mercy crowned.

4   There dwells the Lord our King,
        The Lord our Righteousness,
  Triumphant o'er the world and sin,
        The Prince of Peace:
      On Sion's sacred height
      His kingdom he maintains,
  And glorious with his saints in light
        For ever reigns.

5*   Before the Saviour's face
        The ransomed nations bow,
  O'erwhelmed at his almighty grace
        For ever new:
      He shows the prints of love—
      They kindle to a flame,
  And sound through all the worlds above
        The slaughtered Lamb.

6   Before the great Three-One
        They all exulting stand,
  And tell the wonders he has done
        Throughout the land:
      The listening spheres attend,
      And swell the growing fame,
  And sing in songs which never end
        The wondrous name.

7   The God who reigns on high
        The great archangels sing,
  And 'Holy, holy, holy' cry
        'Almighty King!
      Who was, and is the same,
      And evermore shall be:
  Eternal Father, great I AM,
        We worship thee.'

8   The whole triumphant host
Give thanks to God on high:
'Hail, Father, Son and Holy Ghost'
    They ever cry:
Hail, Abraham's God and mine!
(I join the heavenly lays)
All might and majesty are thine,
    And endless praise.

THOMAS OLIVERS 1725–99
based on the Hebrew *Yigdal*

See also

CORPUS CHRISTI

or

THANKSGIVING FOR HOLY COMMUNION

Thursday after Trinity Sunday

OFFICE HYMNS 268, 269 and see other hymns under
Holy Communion 270–315

EMBER DAYS

See

FROM TRINITY SUNDAY TO ADVENT

149 OFFICE HYMN   Sunday morning

Nocte surgentes

FATHER, we praise thee, now the night is over,
Active and watchful, stand we all before thee;
Singing we offer prayer and meditation:
> Thus we adore thee.

2 Monarch of all things, fit us for thy mansions;
Banish our weakness, health and wholeness
> sending;
Bring us to heaven, where thy saints united
> Joy without ending.

3 All-holy Father, Son and equal Spirit,
Trinity blessèd, send us thy salvation;
Thine is the glory, gleaming and resounding
> Through all creation.   Amen.

Latin, 10th century or earlier
Tr PERCY DEARMER 1867–1936

150 Office Hymn   Sunday evening

Creator lucis optime

O BLEST Creator of the light,
Who makest day with radiance bright,
And o'er the forming world didst call
The light from chaos first of all;

2   Whose wisdom joined in meet array
The morn and eve, and named them Day:
Night comes with all its darkling fears;
Regard thy people's prayers and tears:

3   Lest, sunk in sin and whelm'd with strife,
They lose the gift of endless life;
While, thinking but the thoughts of time,
They weave them chains of guilt and crime.

4   But grant them grace that they may strain
The heavenly gate and prize to gain:
Each harmful lure aside to cast,
And purge away each error past.

5   O Father, that we ask be done,
Through Jesus Christ, thine only Son,
Who with the Spirit and with thee
Doth live and reign eternally.   Amen.

Latin, 8th century or earlier

151   OFFICE HYMN   Weekday mornings

Jam lucis orto sidere

NOW that the daylight fills the sky,
We lift our hearts to God on high,
That he, in all we do or say,
Would keep us free from harm to-day:

2   Would guard our hearts and tongues from
        strife;
From anger's din would hide our life;
From all ill sights would turn our eyes;
Would close our ears from vanities:

3   Would keep our inmost conscience pure;
Our souls from folly would secure;
Would bid us check the pride of sense
With due and holy abstinence.

4   So we, when this new day is gone,
And night in turn is drawing on,
With conscience by the world unstained
Shall praise his name for victory gained.

5   O God the Father, unto thee
Let everlasting glory be;
And glory to thine only Son,
With God the Spirit, ever One.   Amen.

Latin, 8th century or earlier
Tr J. M. NEALE 1818–66

152   OFFICE HYMN   Weekday evenings

Deus Creator omnium

CREATOR of the earth and sky,
Ruling the firmament on high,
Clothing the day with robes of light,
Blessing with gracious sleep the night,

2   That rest may comfort weary men,
And brace to useful toil again,
And soothe awhile the harassed mind,
And sorrow's heavy load unbind:

3   Day sinks; we thank thee for thy gift;
Night comes; and once again we lift
Our prayer and vows and hymns that we
Against all ills may shielded be.

4   That when black darkness closes day,
And shadows thicken round our way,
Faith may no darkness know, and night
From faith's clear beam may borrow light.

5   Pray we the Father and the Son,
And Holy Spirit, Three in One;
Blest Trinity, whom all obey,
Guard thou thy sheep by night and day.

Amen.

Latin, ST AMBROSE 340–97
Tr CHARLES BIGG 1840–1908

THE NAMING OF JESUS

or

The Circumcision of Christ

January 1st

153 OFFICE HYMN

Exultet cor praecordiis

O LET the heart beat high with bliss,
  Yea, let it triumph at the sound
Of Jesus' name, so sweet it is,
  For every joy therein is found.

2 The name that comforteth in woe,
    The name of Jesus healing sin,
  The name that curbs the powers below
    And drives away the death within:

3 The name that soundeth ever sweet
    In speech or verse or holy song,
  And bids us run with willing feet,
    Consoled, and comforted, and strong.

4 Then let the name of Jesus ring
    With lofty praise in every place;
  Let heart and voice together sing—
    That name shall every ill efface.

5 Ah! Jesus, health of sinful men,
    Give ear unto our loving prayer;
  Guide thou our wandering feet again,
    And hold our doings in thy care.

6   O Jesus, of the Virgin born,
      Immortal honour be to thee;
  Praise to the Father infinite,
      And Holy Ghost eternally.   Amen.

Latin, 15th century
Tr PERCY DEARMER 1867–1936

Or the Christmas Office Hymns may be used

See also

291 The Rosy Sequence
332 All hail the power of Jesu's name
374 How sweet the name of Jesus sounds
386 Jesu, the very thought of thee
470 To the name that brings salvation

THE CONVERSION OF ST PAUL

January 25th

154 OFFICE HYMN

A heavenly splendour from on high,
A light too great for mortal eye,
Deprives the hunter of his prey
And turns his threatening wrath away.

2   In darkened eyes, an inward light
  Begins to shine upon his sight,
  As in his heart he hears the call
  To follow, and surrender all.

3 The Christ, for sinners crucified,
   Whose risen power he had denied,
   Now claims this servant for his own,
   And bids him make the gospel known.

4 The nations listen to his voice,
   And in the peace of Christ rejoice;
   The Church on earth his praises sing,
   Who led the Gentiles to their King.

5 Blest Paul, the convert of the Lord,
   May heaven's light to us afford
   A blindness to the lures of sin,
   That we with thee a crown may win.

6 To God the Father, God the Son,
   And God the Spirit, Three in One,
   From saints on earth and saints in heaven,
   Let everlasting praise be given.   Amen.

G. B. TIMMS b 1910

155 WE sing the glorious conquest
         Before Damascus' gate,
      When Saul, the Church's spoiler,
         Came breathing threats and hate;
      The ravening wolf rushed forward
         Full early to the prey;
      But lo! the Shepherd met him,
         And bound him fast to-day!

2 O Glory most excelling
    That smote across his path!
O Light that pierced and blinded
    The zealot in his wrath!
O Voice that spake within him
    The calm reproving word!
O Love that sought and held him
    The bondman of his Lord!

3 O Wisdom, ordering all things
    In order strong and sweet,
What nobler spoil was ever
    Cast at the Victor's feet?
What wiser master-builder
    E'er wrought at thine employ,
Than he, till now so furious
    Thy building to destroy?

4 Lord, teach thy Church the lesson,
    Still in her darkest hour
Of weakness and of danger
    To trust thy hidden power.
Thy grace by ways mysterious
    The wrath of man can bind,
And in thy boldest foeman
    Thy chosen saint can find!

JOHN ELLERTON 1826–93

See also

51 Hail, thou source of every blessing
216 Disposer supreme, and judge of the earth

THE PRESENTATION OF CHRIST
IN THE TEMPLE
February 2nd

156 OFFICE HYMN

Quod chorus vatum

Sing how the age-long promise of a Saviour
Spoken through lips of prophets by the Spirit,
In blessèd Mary, Mother of the Christ-child,
　　　　Finds its fulfilment.

2　Virgin most pure, and wondrously
　　　　conceiving,
　Bearing incarnate God in awed obedience,
　Now she presents him for a spotless offering
　　　　Unto his Father.

3　In God's high temple, Simeon the righteous
　Takes to his loving arms with holy rapture
　That One for whom his longing eyes had
　　　　waited,
　　　　　　Jesus, Messiah.

4　Where now his Mother next her Son is seated,
　In those fair mansions of the heavenly kingdom,
　May Christ our Saviour grant to us his servants
　　　　Life everlasting.

5　Father eternal, Son, and Holy Spirit,
　Trinity blessed, Maker and Redeemer,
　Giver of life, and Author of salvation,
　　　　Thine be the glory.　Amen.

EDITORS, based on the
Latin c 9th century

157 HAIL to the Lord who comes,
 Comes to his temple gate!
Not with his angel host,
 Not in his kingly state;
No shouts proclaim him nigh,
 No crowds his coming wait;

2 But borne upon the throne
 Of Mary's gentle breast,
Watched by her duteous love,
 In her fond arms at rest;
Thus to his Father's house
 He comes, the heavenly guest.

3 There Joseph at her side
 In reverent wonder stands;
And, filled with holy joy,
 Old Simeon in his hands
Takes up the promised Child,
 The glory of all lands.

4 Hail to the great First-born
 Whose ransom-price they pay!
The Son before all worlds,
 The Child of man to-day,
That he might ransom us
 Who still in bondage lay.

5 O Light of all the earth,
  Thy children wait for thee!
Come to thy temples here,
  That we, from sin set free,
Before thy Father's face
  May all presented be!

JOHN ELLERTON 1826–93

For the Candlemas ceremony see 506

See also

ST DAVID

Patron of Wales

March 1st

158 *Office Hymn 221*

WE praise thy name, all-holy Lord,
  For him, the beacon-light
That shone beside our western sea
  Through mists of ancient night;
Who sent to Ireland's fainting Church
  New tidings of thy word:
For David, prince of Cambrian saints,
  We praise thee, holy Lord.

2 For all the saintly band whose prayers
    Still gird our land about,
Of whom, lest men disdain their praise,
    The voiceless stones cry out;
Our hills and vales on every hand
    Their names and deeds record:
For these, thy ancient hero host,
    We praise thee, holy Lord.

3 Grant us but half their burning zeal,
    But half their iron faith,
But half their charity of heart,
    And fortitude to death;
That we with them and all thy saints
    May in thy truth accord,
And ever in thy holy Church
    May praise thee, holy Lord.

EBENEZER NEWELL 1853–1916

See also

479 Faith of our fathers, taught of old

ST PATRICK
Patron of Ireland
March 17th

159 *Office Hymn 221*

St Patrick's Breastplate

I BIND unto myself today
    The strong name of the Trinity,
By invocation of the same,
    The Three in One, and One in Three.

2 I bind this day to me for ever,
     By power of faith, Christ's Incarnation;
  His baptism in Jordan river;
     His death on Cross for my salvation;
  His bursting from the spicèd tomb;
     His riding up the heavenly way;
  His coming at the day of doom;
     I bind unto myself today.

3 I bind unto myself the power
     Of the great love of Cherubim;
  The sweet 'Well done' in judgement hour;
     The service of the Seraphim,
  Confessors' faith, Apostles' word,
     The Patriarchs' prayers, the Prophets'
       scrolls,
  All good deeds done unto the Lord,
     And purity of virgin souls.

4 I bind unto myself today
     The virtues of the star-lit heaven,
  The glorious sun's life-giving ray,
     The whiteness of the moon at even,
  The flashing of the lightning free,
     The whirling wind's tempestuous shocks,
  The stable earth, the deep salt sea,
     Around the old eternal rocks.

5 I bind unto myself today
     The power of God to hold and lead,
  His eye to watch, his might to stay,
     His ear to hearken to my need.
  The wisdom of my God to teach,
     His hand to guide, his shield to ward;
  The word of God to give me speech,
     His heavenly host to be my guard.

6   I bind unto myself the name,
     The strong name of the Trinity;
  By invocation of the same,
     The Three in One, and One in Three.
  Of whom all nature hath creation;
     Eternal Father, Spirit, Word:
  Praise to the Lord of my salvation,
     Salvation is of Christ the Lord.

St Patrick 372–466
Tr Mrs C. F. Alexander 1818–95

Hymn 278 may be inserted after verse 5 if desired

ST JOSEPH OF NAZARETH
March 19th

160   Office Hymn

LORD, hear the praises of thy faithful people
Gathered to honour, on this holy feast-day,
Joseph thy servant, guardian of the Christ-
    child,
       Husband of Mary.

2   Second in honour to the Virgin Mother,
Gladly he yielded to his high vocation,
When in a vision he was told the story
       Of her conceiving.

3   And when the Saviour, whom prophetic voices
Long had predicted, lay within the manger,
Mother and Infant, by his strong protection,
       Rested securely.

4 May his example give to us thy servants
Love of Christ Jesus, bringer of salvation,
That with Saint Joseph we at length may praise
thee
In life eternal.

5 Almighty Father, unto thee be glory,
With Christ our Saviour and the Holy Spirit,
From all thy people, here and in thy heaven,
Now and for ever.   Amen.

EDITORS

See also

37 The great God of heaven is come down to earth
187 Virgin-born, we bow before thee

THE ANNUNCIATION

March 25th

161 *Office Hymns 180, 181*

FOR Mary, Mother of the Lord
God's holy name be praised,
Who first the Son of God adored
As on her child she gazed.

2 The angel Gabriel brought the word
She should Christ's mother be;
Our Lady, handmaid of the Lord,
Made answer willingly.

3 The heavenly call she thus obeyed,
And so God's will was done;
The second Eve love's answer made
Which our redemption won.

4 She gave her body for God's shrine,
  Her heart to piercing pain,
And knew the cost of love divine
  When Jesus Christ was slain.

5 Dear Mary, from your lowliness
  And home in Galilee,
There comes a joy and holiness
  To every family.

6 Hail, Mary, you are full of grace,
  Above all women blest;
Blest in your Son, whom your embrace
  In birth and death confessed.

J. R. Peacey 1896–1971‡

See also
The Blessed Virgin Mary 182–188

st george
Patron of England
April 23rd

162 *Office Hymns 217, 218*

LORD God of Hosts, within whose hand
Dominion rests on sea and land,
Before whose word of life or death
The strength of nations is but breath:
O King, enthroned all thrones above,
Give strength unto the land we love.

2 Thou Breath of Life since time began,
Breathing upon the lips of man,
Hast taught each kindred race to raise
United word to sound thy praise:
So, in this land, join, we beseech,
All hearts and lips in single speech.

3 To George our Saint thou gavest grace
Without one fear all foes to face,
And to confess by faithful death
That Word of Life which was his breath.
O help us, Helper of Saint George,
To fear no bonds that man can forge.

4 Arm us like him, who in thy trust
Beat down the dragon to the dust;
So that we too may tread down sin
And with thy saints a crown may win.
Help us, O God, that we may be
A land acceptable to thee.

LAURENCE HOUSMAN 1865–1959

See also
National 488–493

ST MARK
April 25th

163 *Office Hymns 213, 214*

THE Saint who first found grace to pen
The Life which was the Life of men,
And shed abroad the Gospel's ray,
His fame we celebrate to-day.

2 Lo, drawn by Pentecostal fire,
His heart conceived its great desire,
When pure of mind, inspired, he heard
And with his hand set forth the Word.

3 Then, clearly writ, the Godhead shone
Serene and fair to look upon;
And through that record still comes power
To lighten souls in death's dark hour.

4 O holy mind, for wisdom fit
Wherein that Life of lives stood writ,
May we through minds of like accord
Show forth the pattern of our Lord.

5 And so may all whose minds are dark
Be led to truth by good Saint Mark,
And after this our earthly strife
Stand written in the Book of Life.

LAURENCE HOUSMAN 1865–1959

ST PHILIP AND ST JAMES
May 1st

164 *Office Hymns 213, 214*

Caelestis aulae principes

TWIN princes of the courts of heaven,
To you by Christ our Lord was given
With all the apostolic band,
A place of honour at his hand.

2 For he who would the Father see
Shall there behold him gloriously,
And who was least on earth below
Shall there the highest glories know.

3 On earth you bore the gospel light
And shed its rays o'er man's dark night,
That Christ, our life, our truth, our way,
Might bring us to eternal day.

4 No arts of subtle speech were heard
When, preaching Christ, you spoke his word:
Proclaiming faith in him who died,
You led disciples to his side.

5 In faith you yielded up your breath
To him the victor over death,
And found in him, the risen Lord,
Salvation and a full reward.

6 To God the Father glory be,
And praise, O Jesu Christ, to thee,
Whom with the Spirit we adore,
One Lord, one God, for evermore.   Amen.

EDITORS, partly based on the
Latin of J. B. DE SANTEUIL 1630–97

*Verse 2 relates to Philip ('Lord, show us the Father') and to
James the Less*

See also

464 Thou art the Way: by thee alone

ST MATTHIAS
May 14th

165 *Office Hymns 213, 214*

THE highest and the holiest place
  Guards not the heart from sin;
The Church that safest seems without
  May harbour foes within.

2 Within that small and chosen band
  Beloved above the rest,
One fell from his apostleship,
  A traitor soul unblest.

3 But ne'er the great designs of God
  Man's sin shall overthrow;
A better witness to the truth
  Forth to the lands shall go.

4 Matthias was the chosen one—
  God's purpose cannot fail—
The word of grace no less shall sound,
  The truth no less prevail.

5 Righteous, O Lord, are all thy ways:
  Long as the worlds endure,
From foes without and foes within
  Preserve thy Church secure.

HENRY ALFORD 1810–71‡

THE VISITATION
May 31st

166 OFFICE HYMN

Festum Matris gloriosae

NOW in holy celebration
 Sing we of that Mother blest,
In whose flesh for our salvation
 God incarnate deigned to rest,
When her cousin's salutation
 Named in faith the mystic guest.

2* Lo, the advent Word confessing,
 Spake for joy the voice yet dumb,
Through his mother's lips addressing
 Her, of motherhood the sum,
Bower of beauty, blest and blessing,
 Crowned with fruit of life to come.

3 'Whence,' she cried, at that fair meeting,
 'Comes to me this great reward?
For when first I heard the greeting
 Of the Mother of my Lord,
In my womb, the joy repeating,
 Leapt my babe in sweet accord!'

4 Lo, at that glad commendation
 Joy found voice in Mary's breast
While in holy exultation
 She her Maker's power confessed,
At whose word each generation
 Now henceforward names her blest.

5   Triune Godhead, health supplying,
    Ruler of eternity,
On the fount of grace relying,
    We uplift our hearts to thee,
Praying that in realms undying
    We at one with Life may be.   Amen.

Latin, 15th century
Tr LAURENCE HOUSMAN 1865–1959

See also

186 Tell out my soul, the greatness of the Lord
and other hymns of the Blessed Virgin Mary 180–188

ST BARNABAS

June 11th

167   *Office Hymns 213, 214*

THE 'Son of Consolation',
    Saint Barnabas the good,
Filled with the Holy Spirit
    And faith in Christ the Lord,
In lowly self-oblation,
    To make an offering meet,
Laid down his earthly riches
    At the Apostles' feet.

2   The Son of Consolation,
    In following his Lord
Attained the martyr's glory,
    And entered his reward:
With him is faith now ended,
    For ever lost in sight,
Where love made perfect fills him
    With praise and joy and light.

3 All sons of consolation,
    How great their joys will be
When Christ the King shall tell them
    'You did it unto me':
The merciful and loving
    The loving Lord shall own,
And set them as his jewels
    Around the Father's throne.

MAUD COOTE 1852–1935
and EDITORS

See Acts 11.24 'he was a good man, full of the Holy Spirit and of faith.'

BIRTH OF ST JOHN THE BAPTIST
June 24th

168 OFFICE HYMN

ON this high feast day honour we the Baptist,
Greatest and last of Israel's line of prophets,
Kinsman of Jesus, herald of salvation,
    Chosen forerunner.

2 Lo, from the heavens Gabriel descending,
Brings to thy father tidings of thy coming,
Telling thy name, and all thy life's high calling
    Duly announcing.

3 When Zechariah doubted what was told him,
Dumbness assailed him, sealing firm the
    promise,
Till, at thy naming, lo, his voice resounded
    Loud in God's praises.

4 Greater art thou than all the sons of Adam,
   Lowly in spirit, faithfully proclaiming
   Israel's Messiah, Jesus our Redeemer,
      Thus we exalt thee.

5 Father eternal, Son, and Holy Spirit,
   God everlasting, hear thy people's praises;
   Let saints on earth with all the saints in glory,
      Ever adore thee. Amen.

      EDITORS, based on the Latin
      of PAUL THE DEACON 730–99

169   HAIL, harbinger of morn:
    Thou that art this day born,
   And heraldest the Word with clarion voice!
    Ye faithful ones, in him
    Behold the dawning dim
   Of the bright day, and let your hearts rejoice.

2   John;—by that chosen name
    To call him, Gabriel came
   By God's appointment from his home on high:
    What deeds that babe should do
    To manhood when he grew,
   God sent his angel forth to testify.

3   There is none greater, none,
    Than Zechariah's son;
   Than this no mightier prophet hath been born:
    Of prophets he may claim
    More than a prophet's fame;
   Sublimer deeds than theirs his brow adorn.

4   'Lo, to prepare thy way,'
       Did God the Father say,
   'Before thy face my messenger I send,
       Thy coming to forerun;
       As on the orient sun
   Doth the bright daystar morn by morn attend.'

5   Praise therefore God most high;
       Praise him who came to die
   For us, his Son that liveth evermore;
       And to the Spirit raise,
       The Comforter, like praise,
   While time endureth, and when time is o'er.

                    Latin, THE VENERABLE BEDE 673–735
                        Tr CHARLES CALVERLEY 1831–84

170   LO, in the wilderness a voice
           'Make straight the way' is crying:
       When men are turning from the light,
           And hope and love seem dying,
       The prophet comes to make us clean:
       'There standeth one you have not seen,
           Whose voice you are denying.'

   2   God give us grace to hearken now
           To those who come to warn us,
       Give sight and strength, that we may kill
           The vices that have torn us,
       Lest love professed should disappear
       In creeds of hate, contempt, and fear,
           That crush and overturn us.

3 When from the vineyard cruel men
  Cast out the heavenly powers
And Christendom denies its Lord,
  The world in ruin cowers.
Now come, O God, in thy great might!
Unchanged, unchanging is thy right,
  Unswayed thy justice towers.

PERCY DEARMER 1867–1936

See also

12 On Jordan's bank the Baptist's cry

ST PETER AND ST PAUL
June 29th

171 *Office Hymns 213, 214*

Aurea luce

WITH golden splendour and with roseate hues
  of morn,
O gracious Saviour, Light of light, this day
  adorn,
Which brings to ransomed sinners hopes of that
  far home
Where saints and angels sing the praise of
  martyrdom.

2 Peter Keybearer, Paul the Teacher of mankind,
Lights of the world and judges sent to loose and
  bind,
Alike triumphant or by cross and sword-stroke
  found,
In life's high senate stand with victor's laurel
  crowned.

3   Good Shepherd, Peter, unto whom the charge
      was given
    To close or open ways of pilgrimage to heaven,
    In sin's hard bondage held may we have grace
      to know
    The full remission thou wast granted to bestow.

4   O noble Teacher, Paul, we trust to learn of thee
    Both earthly converse and the flight of ecstasy;
    Till from the fading truths that now we know
      in part
    We pass to fullness of delight for mind and
      heart.

5* Twin olive branches, pouring oil of gladness
      forth,
    Your prayers shall aid us, that for all our little
      worth,
    Believing, hoping, loving, we for whom ye
      plead,
    This body dying, may attain to life indeed.

6   Now to the glorious Trinity be duly paid
    Worship and honour, praise and service
      unafraid,
    Who in unchanging Unity, one Lord sublime,
    Hath ever lived as now and to unending time.
                         Amen.

Latin c 6th century
Tr T. A. LACEY 1853–1931

172   *For St Peter only*

'THOU art the Christ, O Lord,
　The Son of God most high!'
For ever be adored
　That name in earth and sky,
In which, though mortal strength may fail,
The saints of God at last prevail.

2　　O surely he was blest
　　With blessedness unpriced,
　Who, taught of God, confessed
　　The Godhead in the Christ;
For of thy Church, Lord, thou didst own
Thy saint a true foundation-stone.

3　　Thrice fallen, thrice restored,
　　The bitter lesson learnt,
　That heart for thee, O Lord,
　　With triple ardour burnt.
The cross he took he laid not down
Until he grasped the martyr's crown.

4　　O bright triumphant faith,
　　O courage void of fears,
　O love most strong in death,
　　O penitential tears!
By these, Lord, keep us lest we fall,
And make us go where thou shalt call.

W. WALSHAM HOW 1823–97

ST THOMAS
July 3rd

173 *Office Hymns 213, 214*

BLESSED Thomas, doubt no longer,
  See the wounds in hand and side,
Now behold the risen Saviour
  Who for thee has bled and died,
And from death's dark pit arising,
  Lives in body glorified.

2 Here behold the love victorious,
    Over death triumphant now,
  See the feet where nails were driven,
    And thy faith in him avow:
  For he lives, the world's redeemer,
    Unto whom all knees shall bow.

3 Thomas looked upon the Master:
    Was it then indeed the Lord?
  Were those wounds no phantom tokens?
    Did the sight with truth accord?
  Scarce believing, joy unbounded,
    Leapt to greet the Saviour's word.

4 Prostrate falling, Thomas worshipped:
    'O my Master, Lord and God',
  Here in truth was Christ the Saviour
    Who the path of suffering trod,
  And, to ransom souls unnumbered,
    Broke in pieces Satan's rod.

5 Thomas, sight has now convinced thee,
   Faith within thy heart has stirred;
Blessèd more those faithful servants,
   Trusting in the Saviour's word,
Who, though vision is denied them,
   Still believe, and own him Lord.

6 Grant, O Father, that among them
   We thy servants may be known,
And the ground be ever fruitful
   Where the seed of faith was sown,
Till at length in heaven's glory,
   Faith and vision are but one.

G. B. TIMMS b 1910

See also

125 Ye sons and daughters of the King
455 Strong Son of God, immortal Love

ST MARY MAGDALENE
July 22nd

174 OFFICE HYMN

O Maria, noli flere

MARY, weep not, weep no longer,
   Now thy heart hath gained its goal;
Here, in truth, the Gardener standeth,
   But the Gardener of thy soul,
Who within thy spirit's garden
   By his love hath made thee whole.

2   Now from grief and lamentation
     Lift thy drooping heart with cheer;
While for love of him thou mournest,
     Lo, thy Lord regained is here!
Fainting for him, thou hast found him;
     All unknown, behold him near!

3* Whence thy sorrow, whence thy weeping,
     Since with thee true bliss abides?
In thy heart, though undiscovered,
     Balm of consolation hides:
Holding all, thou canst no longer
     Lack the cure that Health provides.

4   Nay, no wonder if she knows not
     Till the Sower's seed be sown,
Till from him, the Word eternal,
     Light within her heart is thrown.
Now he calls her, and 'Rabboni,'
     She in turn her Lord doth own.

5   Faith that washed the feet of Jesus,
     Fed with dew the Fount of Grace,
Win for us a like compassion,
     That, with all the ransomed race,
At the glory of his rising
     We may see him face to face.

6 Glory be to God and honour,
   Who, preferring sacrifice,
Far above the rich man's bounty,
   Sweetness found in Mary's sighs,
Who for all, his love foretasting,
   Spreads the banquet of the skies. Amen.

Latin, 13th century
Tr LAURENCE HOUSMAN 1865–1959

See also

123 Walking in a garden
519 The Easter Sequence

ST JAMES THE GREAT

July 25th

175 *Office Hymns 213, 214*

LORD, who shall sit beside thee,
   Enthroned on either hand,
When clouds no longer hide thee,
   'Mid all thy faithful band?

2 Who drinks the cup of sorrow
   Thy Father gave to thee
'Neath shadows of the morrow
   In dark Gethsemane;

3 Who on thy Passion thinking
   Can find in loss a gain,
And dare to meet unshrinking
   Thy baptism of pain.

4 O Jesu, form within us
    Thy likeness clear and true;
By thine example win us
    To suffer or to do.

5 This law itself fulfilleth,—
    Christlike to Christ is nigh,
And, where the Father willeth,
    Shall sit with Christ on high.

WILLIAM ROMANIS 1824–99

THE TRANSFIGURATION
August 6th

176 OFFICE HYMN

O VISION blest of heavenly light,
Which meets the three disciples' sight,
When on the holy mount they see
Their Lord's transfigured majesty.

2 More bright than day his raiment shone;
The Father's voice proclaimed the Son
Belov'd before the worlds were made,
For us in mortal flesh arrayed.

3 And with him there on either hand
Lo, Moses and Elijah stand,
To show how Christ, to those who see,
Fulfils both law and prophecy.

4 O Light from light, by love inclined,
Jesu, redeemer of mankind,
Accept thy people's prayer and praise
Which on the mount to thee they raise.

5 Be with us, Lord, as we descend
   To walk with thee to journey's end,
   That through thy cross we too may rise,
   And share thy triumph in the skies.

6 To thee, O Father; Christ, to thee,
   Let praise and endless glory be,
   Whom with the Spirit we adore,
   One Lord, one God, for evermore.   Amen.

G. B. TIMMS b 1910

177 CHRIST, upon the mountain peak
   Stands alone in glory blazing.
   Let us, if we dare to speak,
   With the saints and angels praise him—
   Alleluya!

2 Trembling at his feet we saw
   Moses and Elijah speaking.
   All the prophets and the Law
   Shout through them their joyful greeting.—
   Alleluya!

3 Swift the cloud of glory came,
   God proclaiming in its thunder
   Jesus as his Son by name!
   Nations, cry aloud in wonder!—
   Alleluya!

4 This is God's beloved Son!
   Law and prophets fade before him;
   First and last, and only One,
   Let Creation now adore him:
   Alleluya!

BRIAN WREN b 1936

178   'TIS good, Lord, to be here!
          Thy glory fills the night;
     Thy face and garments, like the sun,
          Shine with unborrowed light.

2   'Tis good, Lord, to be here,
          Thy beauty to behold,
     Where Moses and Elijah stand,
          Thy messengers of old.

3   Fulfiller of the past,
          Promise of things to be,
     We hail thy Body glorified,
          And our redemption see.

4   Before we taste of death,
          We see thy kingdom come;
     We fain would hold the vision bright,
          And make this hill our home.

5   'Tis good, Lord, to be here!
          Yet we may not remain;
     But since thou bidst us leave the mount
          Come with us to the plain.

J. ARMITAGE ROBINSON 1858–1933

See also

234 Christ, whose glory fills the skies
286 From glory to glory advancing
389 Jesus, these eyes have never seen
399 Light of the lonely pilgrim's heart

ST BARTHOLOMEW
August 24th

179 *Office Hymns 213, 214*

SAINTS of God! Lo, Jesu's people
  Age to age your glory tell;
In his name for us ye laboured,
  Now in bliss eternal dwell.

2 Twelve poor men, by Christ anointed,
    Braved the rich, the wise, the great,
  All the world counts dear rejecting,
    Rapt in their apostolate.

3 Thus the earth their death-wounds purchased,
    Hallowed by the blood therefrom,
  On her bosom bore the nations,
    Laved, illumined,—Christendom.

4 On this feast, almighty Father,
    May we praise thee with the Son,
  Evermore his love confessing,
    Who from Both with Both is One.   Amen.

ATHELSTAN RILEY 1858–1945

This hymn is an acrostic on the name
SAINT BARTHOLOMEW. Nevertheless, it is
appropriate for a feast of any of the Twelve.

THE BLESSED VIRGIN MARY
September 8th

180 OFFICE HYMN

Ave, maris Stella

HAIL, O Star that pointest
   Towards the port of heaven,
Thou to whom as maiden
   God for Son was given.

2 When the salutation
   Gabriel had spoken,
Peace was shed upon us,
   Eva's bonds were broken.

3 Bound by Satan's fetters,
   Health and vision needing,
God will aid and light us
   At thy gentle pleading.

4 Jesu's tender Mother,
   Make thy supplication
Unto him who chose thee
   At his Incarnation;

5 That, O matchless Maiden,
   Passing meek and lowly,
Thy dear Son may make us
   Blameless, chaste and holy.

6 So, as now we journey,
   Aid our weak endeavour.
Till we gaze on Jesus,
   And rejoice for ever.

7   Father, Son and Spirit,
    Three in One confessing,
  Give we equal glory,
    Equal praise and blessing.   Amen.

Latin, c 9th century
Tr ATHELSTAN RILEY 1858–1945

181   OFFICE HYMN

Quem terra, pontus, aethera

THE Lord whom earth and sea and sky
Adore and praise and magnify,
Who o'er their threefold fabric reigns,
The Virgin's spotless womb contains.

2   And he whose will is ever done
By moon and seas, by stars and sun,
Is borne upon a maiden's breast,
Whom God's foreseeing grace possessed.

3   How blest that Mother, in whose shrine
The very Word of God divine,
The maker of the earth and sky,
Was pleased in fleshly form to lie.

4   Blest in the message Gabriel brought,
Blest in the work the Spirit wrought,
Blest evermore, who brought to birth
The long-Desired of all the earth.

5 O Jesu, Virgin-born, to thee
Eternal praise and glory be,
Whom with the Father we adore
And Holy Spirit, evermore.   Amen.

Latin, VENANTIUS FORTUNATUS 530–609
Tr J. M. NEALE 1818–66
and EDITORS

For a procession on feasts of the Blessed Virgin see

185 Sing we of the blessed Mother
188 Ye who own the faith of Jesus

182   HER Virgin eyes saw God incarnate born,
When she to Bethl'em came that happy morn;
How high her raptures then began to swell,
None but her own omniscient Son can tell.

2   As Eve when she her fontal sin reviewed,
Wept for herself and all she should include,
Blest Mary with man's Saviour in embrace
Joyed for herself and for all human race.

3   All saints are by her Son's dear influence blest,
She kept the very Fountain at her breast;
The Son adored and nursed by the sweet Maid
A thousandfold of love for love repaid.

4   Heaven with transcendent joys her entrance
graced,
Next to his throne her Son his Mother placed;
And here below, now she's of heaven possest,
All generations are to call her blest.

THOMAS KEN 1637–1711

183   *O gloriosa femina*

O GLORIOUS Maid, exalted far
Beyond the light of burning star,
From him who made thee thou hast won
Grace to be Mother of his Son.

2 That which was lost in hapless Eve
   Thy holy offspring did retrieve;
   The tear-worn sons of Adam's race
   Through thee have seen the heavenly place.

3 Thou wast the gate of heaven's high Lord,
   The door through which the light hath poured.
   Christians rejoice, for through a Maid
   To all mankind is life conveyed.

4 O Jesu, Virgin-born, to thee
   Eternal praise and glory be,
   Whom with the Father we adore
   And Holy Spirit, evermore.   Amen.

Latin, VENANTIUS FORTUNATUS 530–609
Tr PERCY DEARMER 1867–1936

184   SHALL we not love thee, Mother dear,
                Whom Jesus loves so well,
            And to his glory year by year
                Thy praise and honour tell?

2   Thee did he choose from whom to take
         True flesh, his flesh to be;
     In it to suffer for our sake,
         And by it make us free.

3 O wondrous depth of love divine,
    That he should bend so low;
And, Mary, O what joy was thine
    The Saviour's love to know.

4 Joy to be Mother of the Lord,
    Yet thine the truer bliss,
In every thought and deed and word
    To be for ever his.

5 Now in the realm of life above
    Close to thy Son thou art,
While on thy soul glad streams of love
    Flow from his sacred heart.

6 Jesu, the Virgin's holy Son,
    Praise we thy Mother blest;
Grant when our earthly course is run,
    Life with the saints at rest.

H. W. BAKER 1821–77
and EDITORS

185 SING we of the blessèd Mother
    Who received the angel's word,
And obedient to his summons
    Bore in love the infant Lord;
Sing we of the joys of Mary
    At whose breast that child was fed
Who is Son of God eternal
    And the everlasting Bread.

2   Sing we, too, of Mary's sorrows,
      Of the sword that pierced her through,
  When beneath the cross of Jesus
      She his weight of suffering knew,
  Looked upon her Son and Saviour
      Reigning high on Calvary's tree,
  Saw the price of man's redemption
      Paid to set the sinner free.

3   Sing again the joys of Mary
      When she saw the risen Lord,
  And in prayer with Christ's apostles,
      Waited on his promised word:
  From on high the blazing glory
      Of the Spirit's presence came,
  Heavenly breath of God's own being,
      Manifest through wind and flame.

4   Sing the chiefest joy of Mary
      When on earth her work was done,
  And the Lord of all creation
      Brought her to his heavenly home:
  Virgin Mother, Mary blessèd,
      Raised on high and crowned with grace,
  May your Son, the world's redeemer,
      Grant us all to see his face.

G. B. TIMMS b 1910

186 *Magnificat*

TELL out, my soul, the greatness of the Lord:
  Unnumbered blessings, give my spirit voice;
Tender to me the promise of his word;
  In God my Saviour shall my heart rejoice.

2 Tell out, my soul, the greatness of his name:
  Make known his might, the deeds his arm has
    done;
His mercy sure, from age to age the same;
  His holy name, the Lord, the Mighty One.

3 Tell out, my soul, the greatness of his might:
  Powers and dominions lay their glory by;
Proud hearts and stubborn wills are put to flight,
  The hungry fed, the humble lifted high.

4 Tell out, my soul, the glories of his word:
  Firm is his promise, and his mercy sure.
Tell out, my soul, the greatness of the Lord
  To children's children and for evermore.

TIMOTHY DUDLEY-SMITH b 1926
based on ST LUKE 1. 46–55 in
the *New English Bible*

187 VIRGIN-BORN, we bow before thee:
  Blessèd was the womb that bore thee;
    Mary, Mother meek and mild,
    Blessèd was she in her Child.
  Blessèd was the breast that fed thee;
  Blessèd was the hand that led thee;
    Blessèd was the parent's eye
    That watched thy slumbering infancy.

2   Blessèd she by all creation,
Who brought forth the world's salvation,
    And blessèd they—for ever blest,
    Who love thee most and serve thee best.
Virgin-born, we bow before thee:
Blessèd was the womb that bore thee;
    Mary, Mother meek and mild,
    Blessèd was she in her Child.

REGINALD HEBER 1783–1826

188   *Suitable for use in Procession*

YE who own the faith of Jesus
    Sing the wonders that were done,
When the love of God the Father
    O'er our sin the victory won,
When he made the Virgin Mary
    Mother of his only Son.
Hail Mary, full of grace.

2   Blessèd were the chosen people
    Out of whom the Lord did come,
Blessèd was the land of promise
    Fashioned for his earthly home;
But more blessèd far the Mother
    She who bare him in her womb.

3   Wherefore let all faithful people
    Tell the honour of her name,
Let the Church in her foreshadowed
    Part in her thanksgiving claim;
What Christ's Mother sang in gladness
    Let Christ's people sing the same.

4 Let us weave our supplications,
    She with us and we with her,
For the advancement of the faithful,
    For each faithful worshipper,
For the doubting, for the sinful,
    For each heedless wanderer.

5* May the Mother's intercessions
    On our homes a blessing win,
That the children all be prospered,
    Strong and fair and pure within,
Following our Lord's own footsteps,
    Firm in faith and free from sin.

6* For the sick and for the agèd,
    For our dear ones far away,
For the hearts that mourn in secret,
    All who need our prayers today,
For the faithful gone before us,
    May the holy Virgin pray.

7 Praise, O Mary, praise the Father,
    Praise thy Saviour and thy Son,
Praise the everlasting Spirit,
    Who hath made thee ark and throne;
O'er all creatures high exalted,
    Lowly praise the Three in One.

V. S. STUCKEY COLES 1845–1929

See also

161 For Mary, Mother of the Lord

ST MATTHEW
September 21st

189 *Office Hymns 213, 214*

HE sat to watch o'er customs paid,
A man of scorned and hardening trade,
Alike the symbol and the tool
Of foreign masters' hated rule.

2 But grace within his breast had stirred;
There needed but the timely word:
It came, true Lord of souls, from thee,
That royal summons, 'Follow me.'

3 Enough, when thou wast passing by,
To hear thy voice, to meet thine eye:
He rose, responsive to the call,
And left his task, his gains, his all.

4 O wise exchange! with these to part,
And lay up treasure in the heart—
Who now with crown of light doth shine
Among the apostolic line.

5 Come, Saviour, as in days of old;
Pass where the world has strongest hold,
And faithless care and selfish greed
Are thorns which choke the holy seed.

6 Who keep thy gifts, O bid them claim
The steward's, not the owner's name;
Who yield up all for thy dear sake,
Let them of Matthew's wealth partake.

WILLIAM BRIGHT 1824–1901†

MICHAELMAS
September 29th

190 OFFICE HYMN

Christe, sanctorum decus angelorum

CHRIST, the fair glory of the holy angels,
Thou who hast made us, thou who o'er us rulest,
Grant of thy mercy unto us thy servants
    Steps up to heaven.

2 Send thy archangel, Michael, to our succour;
Peacemaker blessèd, may he banish from us
Striving and hatred, so that for the peaceful
    All things may prosper.

3 Send thy archangel, Gabriel, the mighty;
Herald of heaven, may he from us mortals
Spurn the old serpent, watching o'er the temples
    Where thou art worshipped.

4 Send thy archangel, Raphael, the restorer
Of the misguided ways of men who wander,
Who at thy bidding strengthens soul and body
    With thine anointing.

5 May the blest Mother of our God and Saviour,
May the assembly of the saints in glory,
May the celestial companies of angels
    Ever assist us.

6 Father almighty, Son and Holy Spirit,
God ever blessèd, be thou our preserver;
Thine is the glory which the angels worship,
          Veiling their faces.   Amen.

Latin, 9th century
Tr ATHELSTAN RILEY 1858–1945

For a procession at Michaelmas see
192 Sons of the Holy One
193 Stars of the morning

191   AROUND the throne of God a band
Of glorious angels ever stand;
Bright things they see, sweet harps they hold,
And on their heads are crowns of gold.

2   Some wait around him, ready still
To sing his praise and do his will;
And some when he commands them, go
To guard his servants here below.

3   Lord, give thy angels every day
Command to guide us on our way,
And bid them every evening keep
Their watch around us while we sleep.

4   So shall no evil thing draw near,
To do us harm or cause us fear;
And we shall dwell, when life is past,
With angels round thy throne at last.

J. M. NEALE 1818–66†

192 *Suitable for use in Procession*

SONS of the Holy One bright with his
    splendour,
  Wakened to life at creation's new day,
First to uplift in the joy of surrender
  Spirits to worship and wills to obey.

2 Armies of Michael, a heavenly wonder,
    Crashed to the onset with evil on high,
Till the proud angel, o'ercome by their thunder,
  Dropped on his darkening wings from the sky.

3 Stars of the morn, for creation returning
    Praise to the wisdom ordaining the whole,
Hushed their glad songs, in amazement
    discerning
  God's very likeness in man's living soul.

4 Sentries of Paradise, knew ye no sorrow,
    Guarding the way with a flame of the sword?
Visioned ye not on a glorious morrow
  Man by a tree to his Eden restored?

5 Gabriel came with his high salutation,
    Burning with ardour and eager in flight.
'Ave Maria!' The dawn of salvation
  Rose at its music and banished our night.

6 See, then, my soul, on a stairway all golden
    Angels ascending, descending again!
Sion is here, if our eyes were not holden,
  Praise would not fail for their service to men.

7   Praise God for Michael, in strife our defender,
     Praise him for Raphael, our healer and guide,
  Praise him for guardians, watchful and tender,
     True to their charges in need at their side.

8   Laud to thee, Father of spirits supernal!
     We with the angels adore thee, O Son!
  Comforter holy, proceeding, eternal,
     In thee be glory to God, Three in One.

                               Amen.

                           F. A. JUDD

193   STARS of the morning, so gloriously bright,
      Filled with celestial resplendence and light,
      These that, where night never followeth day,
      Raise the Trisagion ever and ay:

2   These are thy counsellors, these dost thou own,
     Lord God of Sabaoth, nearest thy throne;
  These are thy ministers, these dost thou send,
     Help of the helpless ones, man to defend.

3   These keep the guard amid Salem's dear
       bowers;
  Thrones, Principalities, Virtues, and Powers;
  Where, with the Living Ones, mystical Four,
  Cherubim, Seraphim bow and adore.

4* 'Who like the Lord?' thunders Michael the
      Chief;
  Raphael, 'the Cure of God,' comforteth grief;
  And, as at Nazareth, prophet of peace,
  Gabriel, 'the Light of God,' bringeth release.

5   Then, when the earth was first poised in mid
       space,
  Then, when the planets first sped on their race,
  Then, when were ended the six days' employ,
  Then all the Sons of God shouted for joy.

6   Still let them succour us; still let them fight,
  Lord of angelic hosts, battling for right;
  Till, where their anthems they ceaselessly pour,
  We with the angels may bow and adore.

J. M. NEALE 1818–66
from the Greek

The Trisagion is a hymn to the thrice-holy God

See also

29 It came upon the midnight clear
336 Angel voices, ever singing
343 Bright the vision that delighted
475 Ye holy angels bright
478 Ye watchers and ye holy ones

ST LUKE

October 18th

194   *Office Hymns 213, 214*

SAVIOUR, who didst healing give,
  Still in power go before us;
Thou through death didst bid men live,
  Unto fuller life restore us;
Strength from thee the fainting found,
  Deaf men heard, the blind went seeing;
At thy touch was banished sickness,
  And the leper felt new being.

2 Thou didst work thy deeds of old
      Through the loving hands of others;
   Still thy mercies manifold
      Bless men by the hands of brothers;
   Angels still before thy face
      Go, sweet health to brothers bringing;
   Still, hearts glow to tell his praises
      With whose name the Church is ringing.

3 Loved physician! for his word
      Lo, the gospel page burns brighter,
   Mission servant of the Lord,
      Painter true, and perfect writer;
   Saviour, of thy bounty send
      Such as Luke of gospel story,
   Friends to all in body's prison
      Till the sufferers see thy glory.

H. D. RAWNSLEY 1851–1920

See also

ST SIMON AND ST JUDE
October 28th

195 *Office Hymns 213, 214*

LORD of all the saints, we praise thee
  For those two apostles blest,
Whom this day thy people honour,
  Who on earth thy name confest:
Serving here the Christ who called them
  They have gained the promised rest.

2 Unto heaven's splendour raisèd,
    There made perfect by thy grace,
  They, by angel hosts surrounded,
    Ever see their Father's face,
  Where the songs of exultation
    Sound from all the ransomed race.

3 Simon, may thy zeal inflame us
    Christ our Lord to serve with might;
  Blessèd Jude, thou true disciple,
    We thy faithfulness recite:
  May God grant us grace to follow
    Till, with thee, faith ends in light.

4 Glory be to God the Father,
    Glory be to God the Son,
  Glory be to God the Spirit,
    Ever Three and ever One,
  One in love and one in splendour,
    While unending ages run.   Amen.

EDITORS

Verse 3 refers to St Luke 6.15 'Simon who was called the Zealot'
and St John 14.22 'Judas (not Iscariot) said to him'

ALL SAINTS

November 1st

196 OFFICE HYMN

FATHER, in whom thy saints are one,
Bought by the blood of thy dear Son,
We praise thee for thy hallowing grace
In those who now behold thy face.

2 For they have gained eternal rest,
And in the heavenly mansions blest
They dwell among the angelic throng,
And hear the one unending song.

3 The patriarchs and prophets old
The heavenly splendour now behold;
The Baptist, herald of thy Son,
Enjoys the fruit of labour done.

4 But first among the saintly band,
The Mother, at her Son's right hand,
Adores the Saviour's endless love,
In that eternal home above.

5 The Twelve now see the Father's face,
While all who've run their earthly race
In one glad company rejoice
To hear the heavenly bridegroom's voice.

6 Father of all, to thee we pray,
Keep us for ever in the way
That leads us to the heavenly rest
Among the glories of the blest.

7 To God the Father, God the Son,
And God the Spirit, Three in One,
All worship, love and honour be,
Both now and in eternity.   Amen.

G. B. TIMMS b 1910
freely based on Latin hymns
for *All Saints*

For a procession on feasts of the Saints see

197 For all the saints who from their labours rest
231 Who are these like stars appearing

197 FOR all the saints who from their labours rest,
Who | thee by faith before the world confest,
Thy | name, O Jesu, be for ever blest.
Alleluya!

2 Thou wast their rock, their fortress, and their
      might;
Thou, Lord, their Captain in the well-fought
      fight;
Thou in the darkness drear their one true Light.

3 O may thy soldiers, faithful, true, and bold,
Fight as the saints who nobly fought of old,
And | win, with them, the victor's crown of gold.

4 O blest communion! fellowship divine!
We feebly struggle, they in glory shine;
Yet | all are one in thee, for all are thine.

5 And when the strife is fierce, the warfare long,
Steals on the ear the distant triumph-song,
And | hearts are brave again, and arms are stron

6 The golden evening brightens in the west;
Soon, soon to faithful warriors cometh rest:
Sweet is the calm of Paradise the blest.

7 But lo! there breaks a yet more glorious day;
The | saints triumphant rise in bright array:
The | King of glory passes on his way.

8 From earth's wide bounds, from ocean's farthest
coast,
Through | gates of pearl streams in the countles
host,
Singing to Father, Son, and Holy Ghost.

Alleluya!

W. WALSHAM HOW 1823–97

*In verses 1, 3, 4, 5, 7 and 8 the word before the barline
is sung to the same note as the previous word*

198 THE Church triumphant in thy love,
Their mighty joys we know;
They sing the Lamb in hymns above,
And we in hymns below.

2 Thee in thy glorious realm they praise,
And bow before thy throne;
We in the kingdom of thy grace:
The kingdoms are but one.

3   The holy to the holiest leads,
        From hence our spirits rise,
    And he that in thy statutes treads
        Shall meet thee in the skies.

CHARLES WESLEY 1707–88

See also

219 Let our choirs new anthems raise
224–231 For any saint
381 Jerusalem the golden
432 O, what their joy and their glory must be
478 Ye watchers and ye holy ones

SAINTS OF ENGLAND

November 8th

199 *Office Hymn 223*

GOD, whose city's sure foundation
    Stands upon his holy hill,
By his mighty inspiration
    Chose of old and chooseth still
Men of every race and nation
    His good pleasure to fulfil.

2   Here in England through the ages,
        While the Christian years went by,
    Saints, confessors, martyrs, sages,
        Strong to live and strong to die,
    Wrote their names upon the pages
        Of God's blessèd company.

3 Some there were like lamps of learning
  Shining in a faithless night,
Some on fire with love, and burning
  With a flaming zeal for right,
Some by simple goodness turning
  Souls from darkness unto light.

4 As we now with high thanksgiving
  Their triumphant names record,
Grant that we, like them, believing
  In the promise of thy word,
May, like them, in all good living,
  Praise and magnify the Lord.

C. A. ALINGTON 1872-1955

See also

479 Faith of our fathers, taught of old

ST ANDREW

Patron of Scotland

November 30th

200 *Office Hymns 213, 214*

JESUS calls us! O'er the tumult
  Of our life's wild restless sea
Day by day his voice is sounding,
  Saying, 'Christian, follow me':

2 As of old Saint Andrew heard it
  By the Galilean lake,
Turned from home and toil and kindred,
  Leaving all for his dear sake.

3 Jesus calls us from the worship
    Of the vain world's golden store,
From each idol that would keep us,
    Saying, 'Christian, love me more'.

4 In our joys and in our sorrows,
    Days of toil and hours of ease,
Still he calls, in cares and pleasures,
    'Christian, love me more than these'.

5 Jesus calls us! By thy mercies,
    Saviour, may we hear thy call,
Give our hearts to thy obedience,
    Serve and love thee best of all.

MRS C. F. ALEXANDER 1818–95†

See also

353 Dear Lord and Father of mankind

ST STEPHEN

December 26th

201 *Office Hymns 19, 20*

STEPHEN, first of Christian martyrs,
    Let the Church in hymns proclaim;
Following close the Saviour's passion,
    Thus he won immortal fame:
For his foes he prayed forgiveness
    While they stoned him unto death,
To the Lord his soul commending
    As he yielded up his breath.

2 Holy Spirit, gift of Jesus,
      Shed thy light upon our eyes,
   That we may behold with Stephen
      That fair realm beyond the skies,
   Where the Son of Man in glory
      Waits for us at God's right hand,
   King of saints and hope of martyrs,
      Lord of all the pilgrim band.

3 See him who went on before us
      Heavenly mansions to prepare,
   Who for us is ever pleading
      By his wounds of glory there;
   In that blessèd home of splendour
      Christ our Saviour reigns above,
   Calling us to share his rapture
      In the Father's boundless love.

4 Glory be to God the Father,
      Glory to his only Son,
   Dying, risen, ascending for us,
      Who the heavenly realm has won;
   Glory to the Holy Spirit,
      To One God in Persons Three,
   From the saints in earth and heaven,
      Glory, endless glory, be.   Amen.

EDITORS, partly based on verses
by CHRISTOPHER WORDSWORTH 1807–85

ST JOHN THE EVANGELIST
December 27th

202   *Office Hymns 19, 20*

WORD supreme, before creation
   Born of God eternally
Who didst will for our salvation
   To be born on earth, and die;
Well thy saints have kept their station,
   Watching till thine hour drew nigh.

2 Now 'tis come, and faith espies thee:
   Like an eagle in the morn,
John in steadfast worship eyes thee,
   Thy belov'd, thy latest born:
In thy glory he descries thee
   Reigning from the tree of scorn.

3 He first hoping and believing
   Did beside the grave adore;
Latest he, the warfare leaving,
   Landed on the eternal shore;
And his witness we receiving
   Own thee Lord for evermore.

4 Much he asked in loving wonder,
   On thy bosom leaning, Lord!
In that secret place of thunder,
   Answer kind didst thou accord,
Wisdom for thy Church to ponder
   Till the day of dread award.

5 Thee, the Almighty King eternal,
    Father of the eternal Word;
Thee, the Father's Word supernal,
    Thee, of both, the Breath adored;
Heaven, and earth, and realms infernal
    Own, one glorious God and Lord.   Amen.

JOHN KEBLE 1792–1866

THE HOLY INNOCENTS
December 28th

203   *Office Hymns 19, 20*

WHEN Christ was born in Bethlehem,
    Fair peace on earth to bring,
In lowly state of love he came
    To be the children's King.

2 A mother's heart was there his throne,
    His orb a maiden's breast,
Whereby he made through love alone
    His kingdom manifest.

3 And round him, then, a holy band
    Of children blest was born,
Fair guardians of his throne to stand
    Attendant night and morn.

4 And unto them this grace was given
    A Saviour's name to own,
And die for him who out of heaven
    Had found on earth a throne.

5   O blessèd babes of Bethlehem,
     Who died to save our King,
  You share the Martyr's diadem,
     And in their anthem sing!

6* Your lips, on earth that never spake,
     Now sound the eternal word;
  And in the courts of love you make
     Your children's voices heard.

7* Lord Jesus Christ, eternal Child,
     Make thou our childhood thine;
  That we with these the meek and mild
     May share the love divine.

LAURENCE HOUSMAN 1865–1959

See also

39 Unto us a boy is born

DEDICATION FESTIVAL

If the date of the consecration of the church is unknown, or if it occurs at an inconvenient season, this festival is kept on the first Sunday in October.

204 OFFICE HYMN

Urbs beata Jerusalem

BLESSÈD City, heavenly Salem,
  Vision dear of peace and love,
Who, of living stones upbuilded,
  Art the joy of heaven above,
And, with angel cohorts circled,
  As a bride to earth dost move!

2 From celestial realms descending,
    Bridal glory round her shed,
To his presence, decked with jewels,
    By her Lord shall she be led:
All her streets, and all her bulwarks,
    Of pure gold are fashionèd.

3 Bright with pearls her portals glitter,
    They are open evermore;
And, by virtue of his merits,
    Thither faithful souls may soar,
Who for Christ's dear name in this world
    Pain and tribulation bore.

4 Many a blow and biting sculpture
    Fashioned well those stones elect,
In their places now compacted
    By the heavenly Architect,
Who therewith hath willed for ever
    That his palace should be decked.

5 Laud and honour to the Father;
    Laud and honour to the Son;
Laud and honour to the Spirit;
    Ever Three, and ever One:
One in love, and One in splendour,
    While unending ages run.   Amen.

Latin c 7th century
Tr J. M. NEALE 1818–66‡

For a procession at the Dedication Festival see

205 Christ is made the sure foundation
210 Only-begotten, Word of God eternal

205 *Suitable for use in Procession*

Angularis fundamentum

CHRIST is made the sure foundation,
    And the precious corner-stone,
Who, the two walls underlying,
    Bound in each, binds both in one,
Holy Sion's help for ever,
    And her confidence alone.

2 All that dedicated city,
    Dearly loved by God on high,
In exultant jubilation
    Pours perpetual melody,
God the One, in Threefold glory,
    Singing everlastingly.

3 To this temple, where we call thee,
    Come, O Lord of hosts, today;
With thy wonted loving-kindness,
    Hear thy people as they pray;
And thy fullest benediction
    Shed within its walls for ay.

4 Here vouchsafe to all thy servants
    Gifts of grace by prayer to gain;
Here to have and hold for ever,
    Those good things their prayers obtain,
And hereafter, in thy glory,
    With thy blessèd ones to reign.

5   Laud and honour to the Father,
      Laud and honour to the Son,
   Laud and honour to the Spirit,
      Ever Three and ever One,
   One in love, and One in splendour,
      While unending ages run.   Amen.

Latin c 7th century
Tr J. M. NEALE 1818–66†

206   CHRIST is our corner-stone,
         On him alone we build;
      With his true saints alone
         The courts of heaven are filled:
            On his great love
               Our hopes we place
               Of present grace
            And joys above.

2   Oh, then with hymns of praise
      These hallowed courts shall ring;
   Our voices we will raise
      The Three in One to sing;
         And thus proclaim
            In joyful song,
            Both loud and long,
         That glorious Name.

3   Here may we gain from heaven
        The grace which we implore;
    And may that grace, once given,
        Be with us evermore,
            Until that day
                When all the blest
                To endless rest
            Are called away.

Latin c 7th century
Tr JOHN CHANDLER 1806–76

207   ETERNAL Power, whose high abode
          Becomes the grandeur of a God,
          Infinite lengths beyond the bounds
          Where stars revolve their little rounds:

2   Thee while the first archangel sings,
     He hides his face behind his wings;
     And ranks of shining ones around
     Fall worshipping and spread the ground.

3   Lord, what shall earth and ashes do?
     We would adore our Maker too!
     From sin and dust to thee we cry,
     The great, the holy, and the high!

ISAAC WATTS 1674–1748

208 *In remembrance of past worshippers*

IN our day of thanksgiving one psalm let us offer
    For the saints who before us have found their
        reward;
When the shadow of death fell upon them, we
    sorrowed,
    But now we rejoice that they rest in the Lord.

2 In the morning of life, and at noon, and at even
    He called them away from our worship below;
But not till his love, at the font and the altar,
    Had girt them with grace for the way they
        should go.

3 These stones that have echoed their praises are
        holy,
    And dear is the ground where their feet have
        once trod;
Yet here they confessed they were strangers and
    pilgrims,
    And still they were seeking the city of God.

4 Sing praise then, for all who here sought and
        here found him,
    Whose journey is ended, whose perils are past:
They believed in the Light; and its glory is
    round them,
    Where the clouds of earth's sorrow are lifted
        at last.

WILLIAM DRAPER 1855–1933

This hymn is also suitable for a Patronal Festival

209 LO! God is here! let us adore
    And own how dreadful is this place!
Let all within us feel his power,
    And silent bow before his face,
Who know his power, his grace who prove,
Serve him with awe, with reverence love.

2 Lo! God is here! Him day and night
    The united choirs of angels sing;
To him, enthroned above all height,
    Heaven's hosts their noblest praises bring;
To thee may all our thoughts arise
Ceaseless, accepted Sacrifice.

German, G. TERSTEEGEN 1697–1769
Tr JOHN WESLEY 1703–91

210 *Suitable for use in Procession*

Christe cunctorum Dominator alme

ONLY-BEGOTTEN, Word of God eternal,
Lord of Creation, merciful and mighty,
Hear thou thy servants, when their tuneful voices
    Rise to thy presence.

2 Thus in our solemn Feast of Dedication,
Graced with returning rites of due devotion,
Ever thy children, year by year rejoicing,
    Chant in thy temple.

3 This is thy palace; here thy presence-chamber;
Here may thy servants, at the mystic banquet,
Daily adoring, take thy body broken,
    Drink of thy chalice.

4 Here for thy children stands the holy laver,
Fountain of pardon for the guilt of nature,
Cleansed by whose water springs a race
anointed,
Liegemen of Jesus.

5 Here in our sickness, healing grace aboundeth,
Light in our blindness, in our toil refreshment;
Sin is forgiven, hope o'er fear prevaileth,
Joy over sorrow.

6 Hallowed this dwelling where the Lord abideth,
This is none other than the gate of heaven;
Strangers and pilgrims, seeking homes eternal,
Pass through its portals.

7 Lord, we beseech thee, as we throng thy temple
By thy past blessings, by thy present bounty,
Smile on thy children, and with tender mercy
Hear our petitions.

8 God in Three Persons, Father everlasting,
Son co-eternal, ever-blessèd Spirit,
Thine be the glory, praise, and adoration,
Now and for ever. Amen.

Latin c 9th century
Tr M. J. BLACKER 1822–88

211 O WORD of God above,
Who fillest all in all,
Hallow this house with thy sure love,
And bless our festival.

2   Here at the font is given
       The new birth from above,
And here the Spirit's gift from heaven
       Confirms the soul in love.

3   Here Christ to faithful hearts
       His body gives for food,
And here the living Lord imparts
       The chalice of his blood.

4   Here guilty souls that pine
       May health and healing win,
Forgiveness free and grace divine
       Restore the dead in sin.

5   The God enthroned on high
       Comes in this house to dwell,
Here souls at prayer may find him nigh
       And know that all is well.

6   All glory evermore
       To God the Three in One,
The God whom heaven and earth adore
       While endless ages run.   Amen.

EDITORS, based upon the Latin
of CHARLES GUIET 1601–64

212 *Sequence*

Jerusalem et Sion filiae

SION'S daughters, sons of Jerusalem,
All ye hosts of heavenly chivalry,
Lift your voices, singing right merrily
      Alleluya!

2 Christ our Saviour weds on this festival
   Holy Church, the pattern of righteousness,
   Whom from depths of uttermost misery
         He hath rescued.

3 Now the Bride receiveth his benison,
   Tasteth now the joys of the Paraclete,
   Kings and queens with jubilant melody
         Call her blessèd.

4 Mother meet for sinful humanity,
   Life's sure haven, rest for the sorrowful,
   Strong protectress, born in a mystery
         Ever wondrous.

5 Not more bright the sun in his majesty,
   Not more fair the moon in her loveliness,
   Radiant as the stars in the firmament,
         Perfect as the dawn:

6 So the Church shines forth on her pilgrimage,
   Cleansed in Jordan's waters of penitence,
   Drawn to hear the wisdom of Solomon
         From the world's end.

7 So, foretold in figures and prophecies,
   Clothed in nuptial vesture of charity,
   Joined to Christ, o'er heaven's glad citizens
         Now she reigneth.

8 Welcome, feast of light and felicity,
   Bride to Bridegroom wedded in unity,
   In her mystic marriage is typified
         Our salvation.

9 Christ, whose joys we joyfully celebrate,
    Grant us all a place with thy chosen ones,
    True delights, ineffable happiness,
              Rest eternal.

Latin, 12th century
Tr GABRIEL GILLETT 1873–1948†

The ancient theme of the Feast of Dedication is the Church as the Bride of Christ. See Revelation 21

For the plainsong melody see 522

See also

362 Glorious things of thee are spoken
426 O praise the Lord, ye servants of the Lord
441 Pray that Jerusalem may have
479 Faith of our fathers, taught of old
484 The Church's one foundation
485 Thy hand, O God, has guided

FESTIVALS AND OTHER HOLY DAYS
(II) GENERAL

APOSTLES AND EVANGELISTS

213 OFFICE HYMN

Aeterna Christi munera

THE eternal gifts of Christ the King,
The Apostles' glorious deeds, we sing;
And while due hymns of praise we pay,
Our thankful hearts cast grief away.

2 The Church in these her princes boasts,
These victor chiefs of warrior hosts;
The soldiers of the heavenly hall,
The lights that rose on earth for all.

3 'Twas thus the yearning faith of saints,
The unconquered hope that never faints,
The love of Christ that knows not shame,
The prince of this world overcame.

4 In these the Father's glory shone;
In these the will of God the Son;
In these exults the Holy Ghost;
Through these rejoice the heavenly host.

5 Redeemer, hear us of thy love,
That, with this glorious band above,
Hereafter, of thine endless grace,
Thy servants also may have place.   Amen.

Attributed to St Ambrose c 340–97
Tr J. M. Neale 1818–66

214 Office Hymn

Exultet caelum laudibus

LET the round world with songs rejoice,
Let heaven return the joyful voice,
All mindful of the Apostles' fame,
Let heaven and earth their praise proclaim.

2 Ye servants who once bore the light
Of gospel truth o'er heathen night,
Still may your work that light impart,
To glad our eyes and cheer our heart.

3 O God, by whom to them was given
The key that shuts and opens heaven,
Our chains unbind, our loss repair,
And grant us grace to enter there.

4 For at thy will they preached the word
Which cured disease, which health conferred;
O may thy healing power once more
Our souls to grace and health restore.

5 That when as judge thy Son shall come
To bring his ransomed people home,
He may with them pronounce us blest,
And place us in thine endless rest.

6 To God the Father, God the Son,
And God the Spirit, Three in One,
Be honour, praise and majesty,
Now and throughout eternity.   Amen.

Latin c 10th century
Tr RICHARD MANT 1776–1848‡

215   CAPTAINS of the saintly band,
Lights who lighten every land,
Princes who with Jesus dwell,
Judges of his Israel:

2 On the nations sunk in night
   Ye have shed the Gospel light;
   Sin and error flee away;
   Truth reveals the promised day.

3 Not by warrior's spear and sword,
   Not by art of human word,
   Preaching but the Cross of shame,
   Rebel hearts for Christ ye tame.

4 Earth, that long in sin and pain
   Groaned in Satan's deadly chain,
   Now to serve its God is free
   In the law of liberty.

5 Distant lands with one acclaim
   Tell the honour of your name,
   Who, wherever man has trod,
   Teach the mysteries of God.

6 Glory to the Three in One
   While eternal ages run,
   Who from deepest shades of night
   Called us to his glorious light.

Latin, J. B. DE SANTEUIL 1630–97
Tr H. W. BAKER 1821–77

216   *Supreme, quales, Arbiter*

DISPOSER supreme, and judge of the earth,
   Who choosest for thine the weak and the poor,
To frail earthen vessels, and things of no worth,
   Entrusting thy riches which ay shall endure;

2 Throughout the wide world their message is
       heard,
     And swift as the wind it circles the earth;
   It echoes the voice of the heavenly Word,
     And brings unto mortals the hope of new
       birth.

3 Their cry thunders forth, 'Christ Jesus is Lord',
     Then Satan doth fear, his citadels fall:
   As when those shrill trumpets were raised at thy
       word,
     And one long blast shattered proud Jericho's
       wall.

4 O loud be the call, and stirring the sound,
     To rouse us, O Lord, from sin's deadly sleep;
   May lights which thou kindlest in darkness
       around,
     The dull soul awaken, her vigil to keep.

5 All honour and praise, dominion and might,
     To thee, Three in One, eternally be,
   Who pouring around us thy glorious light,
     Dost call us from darkness thy glory to see.

                    Latin, J. B. DE SANTEUIL 1630–97
                         Tr ISAAC WILLIAMS 1802–65
                                    and EDITORS

                    See also
179 Saints of God! Lo, Jesu's people

217 OFFICE HYMN

For one martyr

Martyr Dei qui unicum

MARTYR of God, whose strength was steeled
    To follow close God's only Son,
Well didst thou brave thy battlefield,
    And well thy heavenly bliss was won!

2 Now join thy prayers with ours, who pray
    That God may pardon us and bless;
For prayer keeps evil's plague away,
    And draws from life its weariness.

3 Long, long ago, were loosed the chains
    That held thy body once in thrall;
For us how many a bond remains!
    O Love of God release us all.

4 All praise to God the Father be,
    All praise to thee, eternal Son;
All praise, O Holy Ghost, to thee,
    While never-ending ages run.   Amen.

Latin c 10th century
Tr PERCY DEARMER 1867–1936

218 OFFICE HYMN

For one or many martyrs

Deus tuorum militum

O GOD, thy soldiers' crown and guard,
And their exceeding great reward,
From bonds of evil set us free,
Who sing thy martyrs' victory.

2 Right valiantly they kept the faith,
And glorified thee unto death;
For thee their blood they dared to pour,
And thence have joy for evermore.

3 Look down upon us from above,
Uplift our hearts, O God of love,
And as our hymns to thee we raise,
Accept thy people's prayer and praise.

4 On this the martyrs' triumph-day,
Let every voice its tribute pay
To those who counted all things loss
For love of him who bore the cross.

5 O Christ, most loving King, to thee
With God the Father, glory be,
And glory to the Holy Ghost,
From men and from the angel-host.   Amen.

Latin c 6th century
Tr J. M. NEALE 1818–66
and EDITORS

219 LET our choirs new anthems raise,
　　Bright the morn with gladness,
When God turned to joy and praise
　　All his servants' sadness:
This the day that won their crown,
　　Opened heaven's wide portal;
They, mortality laid down,
　　Entered life immortal.

2 Now they stand before the throne
　　Clothed in robes of splendour,
Death and torment overthrown,
　　Praise to God they render;
Praise alike to Christ their King
　　From their lips is sounding,
As they adoration bring
　　For his grace abounding.

3 Let us then due honour pay,
　　As we raise our voices,
For the saints in whom today
　　All the Church rejoices;
Let God's people here below
　　Still recount their story,
How they fought against the foe
　　For the Saviour's glory.

EDITORS, verse 1 based
on J. M. NEALE 1818–66

220 OFFICE HYMN

Iste Confessor

HE who bore witness by a good confession,
He whom thy people join this day to honour,
Now in the heavenly mansions of the blessèd
    Liveth for ever.

2   Many the gifts with which thou didst endow
      him,
   Many the virtues which adorned his spirit,
   Through all the years while in this mortal body
      Daily he served thee.

3   Wherefore together, giving thee the glory,
   Sing we his praises on this holy feast-day,
   Praying for grace to follow in his footsteps
      Now and hereafter.

4   Glory and honour, love and adoration,
   Be in the highest unto thee who reignest
   Threefold in splendour, source of life eternal,
      Blessed for ever.   Amen.

EDITORS, freely based on
the Latin c 9th century

221 OFFICE HYMN

O GOD, thy loving care for man
Devised for us salvation's plan,
And sent thy Son to be the way
To bring us to eternal day.

2 The Shepherd bled to save the sheep,
And gave his own strict watch to keep,
That souls bought at so great a cost
Might never from the fold be lost.

3 All praise be thine, O Lord of heaven,
For those to whom the charge is given
To tend and feed the souls of men,
Until thy Son shall come again.

4 So, for that pastor of the sheep
Whose entrance into bliss we keep,
Thanksgiving unto thee be made,
While honour due to him is paid.

5 O God the Father, God the Son,
And God the Spirit, Three in One,
Blest Trinity, our strength and stay,
Guard thou thy flock by night and day.   Amen.

EDITORS

222 OFFICE HYMN

For a woman saint

AS we remember, Lord, thy faithful handmaid,
Who on this day attained the heavenly mansions,
Grant to thy servants, met in due devotion,
      Mercy and blessing.

2 Lo, unto thee, her Lord and mystic Bridegroom,
Gladly she yielded all her heart's devotion,
While in her soul the flame of love burned
    brightly
      Unto thy glory.

3 Fountain of mercy, Saviour and Redeemer,
Deepen our love and pardon our transgressions,
So that hereafter, we with her may ever
      Joyful behold thee.

4 There, where the angels throng thy presence-
    chamber,
Spirits attendant in celestial splendour,
May we thy servants, in the courts of glory
      Offer our praises.

5 Thine be the worship, Father, Son and Spirit,
God everlasting, Trinity eternal,
From all thy creatures, here and in the heavens,
      Now and for ever.   Amen.

EDITORS

223 OFFICE HYMN

For one or several saints

Jesu, redemptor omnium

O JESU, Saviour of mankind,
In whom the saints their glory find,
On this commemoration day
Hear thou thy people as they pray.

2 Contending for thy holy name,
Thy servants won their saintly fame,
Which Christian hearts with praise recall,
And bless the Lord and God of all.

3 Earth's fleeting pleasures counting nought,
For higher, truer joys they sought,
And now, with angels round thy throne,
Unfading glories are their own.

4 O grant that we, most gracious God,
May follow in the steps they trod,
And freed from every bond of sin,
As they have won, may also win.

5 To thee, O Christ, most loving King,
All glory, praise and thanks we bring,
Whom with the Father we adore,
And Holy Spirit, evermore.   Amen.

Latin c 8th century
Tr FATHER BENSON SSJE 1824–1915
and EDITORS

224   FOR all thy saints, O Lord,
         Who strove in thee to live,
    Who followed thee, obeyed, adored,
         Our grateful hymn receive.

2   For all thy saints, O Lord,
         Who strove in thee to die,
    Who counted thee their great reward,
         Accept our thankful cry.

3   O Lord, thy name we bless,
         And humbly pray that we
    May follow them in holiness
         Who lived and died in thee.

4   Thine earthly members fit
         To join thy saints above,
    In one communion ever knit,
         One fellowship of love.

5   All praise to thee, O Lord,
         The Father and the Son
    And Holy Spirit, God adored
         While endless ages run.   Amen.

                    RICHARD MANT 1776–1848‡

225   GIVE me the wings of faith to rise
         Within the veil, and see
    The saints above, how great their joys,
         How bright their glories be.

2 Once they were mourning here below,
   And wet their couch with tears;
They wrestled hard, as we do now,
   With sins and doubts and fears.

3 I ask them whence their victory came;
   They, with united breath,
Ascribe their conquest to the Lamb,
   Their triumph to his death.

4 They marked the footsteps that he trod,
   His zeal inspired their breast,
And, following their incarnate God,
   Possess the promised rest.

5 Our glorious Leader claims our praise
   For his own pattern given;
While the long cloud of witnesses
   Show the same path to heaven.

ISAAC WATTS 1674-1748

226   HARK! the sound of holy voices,
          Chanting at the crystal sea,
       Alleluya, Alleluya,
          Alleluya, Lord, to thee:
       Multitude, which none can number,
          Like the stars in glory stands,
       Clothed in white apparel, holding
          Palms of victory in their hands.

2 Patriarch and holy prophet,
     Who prepared the way of Christ,
   King, apostle, saint, confessor,
     Martyr and evangelist,
   Saintly maiden, godly matron,
     Widows who have watched to prayer,
   Joined in holy concert, singing
     To the Lord of all, are there.

3 They have come from tribulation,
     And have washed their robes in blood,
   Washed them in the blood of Jesus;
     Tried they were, and firm they stood;
   Gladly, Lord, with thee they suffered;
     Gladly, Lord, with thee they died,
   And by death to life immortal
     They were born, and glorified.

4 Now they reign in heavenly glory,
     Now they walk in golden light,
   Now they drink, as from a river,
     Holy bliss and infinite;
   Love and peace they taste for ever,
     And all truth and knowledge see
   In the beatific vision
     Of the blessèd Trinity.

5 God of God, the One-begotten,
     Light of light, Emmanuel,
   In whose Body joined together
     All the saints for ever dwell;
   Pour upon us of thy fullness,
     That we may for evermore
   God the Father, God the Son, and
     God the Holy Ghost adore.   Amen.

CHRISTOPHER WORDSWORTH 1807–85†

247

227   HOW bright these glorious spirits shine!
      Whence all their white array?
   How came they to the blissful seats
      Of everlasting day?

2   Lo! these are they from sufferings great
      Who came to realms of light,
   And in the blood of Christ have washed
      Those robes that shine so bright.

3   Now with triumphal palms they stand
      Before the throne on high,
   And serve the God they love amidst
      The glories of the sky.

4   Hunger and thirst are felt no more,
      Nor sun with scorching ray:
   God is their sun, whose cheering beams
      Diffuse eternal day.

5   The Lamb, who dwells amid the throne,
      Shall o'er them still preside,
   Feed them with nourishment divine,
      And all their footsteps guide.

6   In pastures green he'll lead his flock
      Where living streams appear;
   And God the Lord from every eye
      Shall wipe off every tear.

ISAAC WATTS 1674–1748 and others

228   *With verse 6 suitable for any saint's day*

JERUSALEM, thou City blest,
  Fair home of God's elect!
No sun, in all his radiance bright,
  Thy glory could reflect.

2 In thee no sickness may be seen,
     No hurt, no ache, no sore;
   In thee there is no dread of death,
     But life for evermore.

3 The blessèd saints, who've run their race,
     With glory there are crowned;
   Nor tongue can tell, nor heart conceive
     What joys in thee they've found.

4 God is their sun, and Christ their light,
     They see him face to face;
   The Spirit's perfect bond of love
     Doth every heart embrace.

5 O happy ones, in heaven who dwell,
     Pour forth for us your prayer,
   That God our Father, through his Son,
     May bring us with you there.

6* And praise and honour be to him
      Whom earth and heaven obey,
    For that blest saint whose festival
      Doth glorify this day.

EDITORS

229 *Supernae matris gaudia*

JOY and triumph everlasting
  Hath the heavenly Church on high;
For that pure immortal gladness
  All our feast-days mourn and sigh:
Yet in death's dark desert wild
Doth the mother aid her child,
Guards celestial thence attend us,
Stand in combat to defend us.

2 Here the world's perpetual warfare
    Holds from heaven the soul apart;
  Legioned foes in shadowy terror
    Vex the Sabbath of the heart.
  O how happy that estate
  Where delight doth not abate;
  For that home the spirit yearneth,
  Where none languisheth nor mourneth.

3 There the body hath no torment,
    There the mind is free from care,
  There is every voice rejoicing,
    Every heart is loving there.
  Angels in that city dwell;
  Them their King delighteth well:
  Still they joy and weary never,
  More and more desiring ever.

4 There the seers and fathers holy,
    There the prophets glorified,
  All their doubts and darkness ended,
    In the Light of light abide.
  There the Saints, whose memories old
  We in faithful hymns uphold,
  Have forgot their bitter story
  In the joy of Jesu's glory.

5 There from lowliness exalted
    Dwelleth Mary, Queen of grace,
Ever with her presence pleading
    'Gainst the sin of Adam's race.
To that glory of the blest,
By their prayers and faith confest,
Us, us too, when death hath freed us,
Christ of his good mercy lead us.

A Latin Sequence by
ADAM OF ST VICTOR c 1150
Tr ROBERT BRIDGES 1844–1930

230 PALMS of glory, raiment bright,
    Crowns that never fade away,
Gird and deck the saints in light,
    Priests, and kings, and conquerors they.

2 Yet the conquerors bring their palms
    To the Lamb amidst the throne,
And proclaim in joyful psalms
    Victory through his cross alone.

3 Kings for harps their crowns resign,
    Crying, as they strike the chords,
'Take the kingdom, it is thine,
    King of kings, and Lord of lords.'

4 Round the altar priests confess,
    If their robes are white as snow,
'Twas the Saviour's righteousness,
    And his blood, that made them so.

5 They were mortal too like us;
   Ah! when we like them must die,
May our souls translated thus
   Triumph, reign, and shine on high.

JAMES MONTGOMERY 1771–1854

231 WHO are these, like stars appearing,
   These before God's throne who stand?
Each a golden crown is wearing;
   Who are all this glorious band?
      Alleluya, hark! they sing,
      Praising loud their heavenly King.

2 Who are these of dazzling brightness,
   These in God's own truth arrayed,
Clad in robes of purest whiteness,
   Robes whose lustre ne'er shall fade,
      Ne'er be touched by time's rude hand—
      Whence comes all this glorious band?

3 These are they who have contended
   For their Saviour's honour long,
Wrestling on till life was ended,
   Following not the sinful throng;
      These, who well the fight sustained,
      Triumph through the Lamb have gained.

4 These are they whose hearts were riven,
   Sore with woe and anguish tried,
Who in prayer full oft have striven
   With the God they glorified;
      Now, their painful conflict o'er,
      God has bid them weep no more.

5 These like priests have watched and waited,
　　Offering up to Christ their will,
Soul and body consecrated,
　　Day and night to serve him still:
　　　Now, in God's most holy place
　　　Blest they stand before his face.

German, H. T. SCHENCK 1656–1727
Tr FRANCES COX 1812–97

See also

197 For all the saints who from their labours rest
198 The Church triumphant in thy love
381 Jerusalem the golden
432 O what their joy and their glory must be
478 Ye watchers and ye holy ones

and for English saints

199 God, whose city's sure foundation
479 Faith of our fathers, taught of old

PART II

TIMES AND SEASONS

232   AWAKE, my soul, and with the sun
Thy daily stage of duty run;
Shake off dull sloth, and joyful rise
To pay thy morning sacrifice.

2   Redeem thy mis-spent time that's past,
Live this day as if 'twere thy last:
Improve thy talent with due care;
For the great day thyself prepare.

3   Let all thy converse be sincere,
Thy conscience as the noon-day clear;
Think how all-seeing God thy ways
And all thy secret thoughts surveys.

4   Awake, awake, ye heavenly choir,
May your devotion me inspire,
That I like you my age may spend,
Like you may on my God attend.

5   Praise God, from whom all blessings flow,
Praise him, all creatures here below,
Praise him above, ye heavenly host,
Praise Father, Son, and Holy Ghost.   Amen.

THOMAS KEN 1637–1711

233 GLORY to thee, who safe hast kept
And hast refreshed me whilst I slept;
Grant, Lord, when I from death shall wake
I may of endless light partake.

2 Wake, and lift up thyself, my heart,
And with the angels bear thy part,
Who all night long unwearied sing
High praise to the eternal King.

3 Lord, I my vows to thee renew;
Scatter my sins as morning dew;
Guard my first springs of thought and will,
And with thyself my spirit fill.

4 Direct, control, suggest, this day
All I design, or do, or say;
That all my powers, with all their might,
In thy sole glory may unite.

5 Praise God, from whom all blessings flow,
Praise him all creatures here below,
Praise him above, ye heavenly host,
Praise Father, Son, and Holy Ghost.   Amen.

THOMAS KEN 1637–1711

234 CHRIST, whose glory fills the skies,
   Christ, the true, the only light,
Sun of Righteousness, arise,
   Triumph o'er the shades of night;
Dayspring from on high, be near;
Daystar, in my heart appear.

2 Dark and cheerless is the morn
    Unaccompanied by thee;
Joyless is the day's return,
    Till thy mercy's beams I see;
Till they inward light impart,
Glad my eyes, and warm my heart.

3 Visit then this soul of mine,
    Pierce the gloom of sin and grief;
Fill me, radiancy divine,
    Scatter all my unbelief;
More and more thyself display,
Shining to the perfect day.

CHARLES WESLEY 1707–88

235 FORTH in thy name, O Lord, I go,
    My daily labour to pursue;
Thee, only thee, resolved to know,
    In all I think or speak or do.

2 The task thy wisdom hath assigned
    O let me cheerfully fulfil;
In all my works thy presence find,
    And prove thy good and perfect will.

3 Preserve me from my calling's snare,
    And hide my simple heart above,
Above the thorns of choking care,
    The gilded baits of worldly love.

4 Thee may I set at my right hand,
   Whose eyes my inmost substance see,
And labour on at thy command,
   And offer all my works to thee.

5 Give me to bear thy easy yoke,
   And every moment watch and pray,
And still to things eternal look,
   And hasten to thy glorious day;

6 For thee delightfully employ
   Whate'er thy bounteous grace hath given,
And run my course with even joy,
   And closely walk with thee to heaven.

CHARLES WESLEY 1707–88†

236   *Psalm 5*

LORD, as I wake I turn to you,
   Yourself the first thought of my day:
My King, my God, whose help is sure,
   Yourself the help for which I pray.

2 There is no blessing, Lord, from you
   For those who make their will their way,
No praise for those who will not praise,
   No peace for those who will not pray.

3 Your loving gifts of grace to me,
   Those favours I could never earn,
Call for my thanks in praise and prayer,
   Call me to love you in return.

4   Lord, make my life a life of love,
     Keep me from sin in all I do;
  Lord, make your law my only law,
     Your will my will, for love of you.

BRIAN FOLEY b 1919

237   MORNING has broken
     Like the first morning,
     Blackbird has spoken
       Like the first bird.
       Praise for the singing,
       Praise for the morning,
       Praise for them springing
        Fresh from the Word.

2   Sweet the rain's new fall
     Sunlit from heaven,
     Like the first dewfall
       On the first grass.
       Praise for the sweetness
       Of the wet garden,
       Sprung in completeness
        Where his feet pass.

3   Mine is the sunlight,
     Mine is the morning
     Born of the one light
       Eden saw play.
       Praise with elation,
       Praise every morning,
       God's re-creation
        Of the new day.

ELEANOR FARJEON 1881–1965

238 NEW every morning is the love
Our wakening and uprising prove;
Through sleep and darkness safely brought,
Restored to life, and power, and thought.

2 New mercies, each returning day,
Hover around us while we pray;
New perils past, new sins forgiven,
New thoughts of God, new hopes of heaven.

3 If on our daily course our mind
Be set to hallow all we find,
New treasures still, of countless price,
God will provide for sacrifice.

4 The trivial round, the common task,
Would furnish all we ought to ask,
Room to deny ourselves, a road
To bring us daily nearer God.

5 Only, O Lord, in thy dear love
Fit us for perfect rest above;
And help us this and every day
To live more nearly as we pray.

JOHN KEBLE 1792–1866

See also

239 Lord of all hopefulness, Lord of all joy
240 When all the world to life is waking
473 When morning gilds the skies

239 LORD of all hopefulness, Lord of all joy,
Whose trust, ever child-like, no cares could
destroy,
Be there at our waking, and give us, we pray,
Your bliss in our hearts, Lord, at the break of
the day.

2 Lord of all eagerness, Lord of all faith,
Whose strong hands were skilled at the plane
and the lathe,
Be there at our labours, and give us, we pray,
Your strength in our hearts, Lord, at the noon of
the day.

3 Lord of all kindliness, Lord of all grace,
Your hands swift to welcome, your arms to
embrace,
Be there at our homing, and give us, we pray,
Your love in our hearts, Lord, at the eve of the
day.

4 Lord of all gentleness, Lord of all calm,
Whose voice is contentment, whose presence is
balm,
Be there at our sleeping, and give us, we pray,
Your peace in our hearts, Lord, at the end of the
day.

JAN STRUTHER 1901–53

240 WHEN all the world to life is waking,
　　And night withdraws from earth and sky,
Creation's song to thee is making
　　Its praises heard, O Lord most high.
Thine is the splendour of the morning,
　　Thine is the evening's tranquil light;
Thine, too, the veil which till the dawning
　　Shrouds all the earth in peaceful night.

2 Maker of worlds beyond our knowing,
　　Realms which no human eye can scan,
Yet by a wondrous love bestowing
　　Through Christ thy saving aid to man;
Lord, while the hymns of all creation
　　Rise ever to thy throne above,
We too would join in adoration,
　　Owning thee God of changeless love.

JACK WINSLOW 1882–1974
and EDITORS

EVENING

241 OFFICE HYMN Compline

Te lucis ante terminum

BEFORE the ending of the day,
Creator of the world, we pray
That with thy wonted favour thou
Wouldst be our guard and keeper now.

2 From all ill dreams defend our eyes,
  From nightly fears and fantasies;
Tread under foot our ghostly foe,
  That no pollution we may know.

3 O Father, that we ask be done,
  Through Jesus Christ, thine only Son;
Who, with the Holy Ghost and thee,
  Doth live and reign eternally.   Amen.

Latin, *Tr* J. M. NEALE 1818–66

242   *Labente jam solis rota*

AS now the sun's declining rays
  At eventide descend,
E'en so our years are sinking down
  To their appointed end.

2 Lord, on the cross thine arms were stretched
  To draw the nations nigh;
O grant us then that cross to love,
  And in those arms to die.

3 To God the Father, God the Son,
  And God the Holy Ghost,
All glory be from saints on earth,
  And from the angel host.   Amen.

Latin, CHARLES COFFIN 1676–1749
Tr JOHN CHANDLER 1806–76

243 AT even when the sun was set
    The sick, O Lord, around thee lay;
O, in what divers pains they met!
    O with what joy they went away!

2 Once more 'tis eventide, and we
    Oppressed with various ills draw near;
What if thy form we cannot see?
    We know and feel that thou art here.

3 O Saviour Christ, our woes dispel;
    For some are sick, and some are sad,
And some have never loved thee well,
    And some have lost the love they had;

4 And some have found the world is vain,
    Yet from the world they break not free;
And some have friends who give them pain,
    Yet have not sought a friend in thee;

5 And none, O Lord, have perfect rest,
    For none are wholly free from sin;
And they who fain would serve thee best
    Are conscious most of wrong within.

6 O Saviour Christ, thou too art Man;
    Thou hast been troubled, tempted, tried;
Thy kind but searching glance can scan
    The very wounds that shame would hide;

7 Thy touch has still its ancient power,
    No word from thee can fruitless fall;
Hear in this solemn evening hour,
    And in thy mercy heal us all.

HENRY TWELLS 1823–1900

263

244 GLORY to thee, my God, this night
For all the blessings of the light;
Keep me, O keep me, King of kings,
Beneath thy own almighty wings.

2 Forgive me, Lord, for thy dear Son,
The ill that I this day have done,
That with the world, myself and thee,
I, ere I sleep, at peace may be.

3 Teach me to live, that I may dread
The grave as little as my bed;
Teach me to die, that so I may
Rise glorious at the aweful day.

4 O may my soul on thee repose,
And with sweet sleep my eyelids close,
Sleep that may me more vigorous make
To serve my God when I awake.

5 Praise God from whom all blessings flow,
Praise him all creatures here below,
Praise him above, ye heavenly host,
Praise Father, Son, and Holy Ghost.

THOMAS KEN 1637–1711

245 GOD, that madest earth and heaven,
    Darkness and light;
Who the day for toil hast given,
    For rest the night;
May thine angel-guards defend us,
Slumber sweet thy mercy send us,
Holy dreams and hopes attend us,
    This livelong night.

2 Guard us waking, guard us sleeping;
    And, when we die,
May we in thy mighty keeping
    All peaceful lie:
When the last dread call shall wake us,
Do not thou our God forsake us,
But to reign in glory take us
    With thee on high.

Verse 1, REGINALD HEBER 1783–1826
Verse 2, RICHARD WHATELY 1787–1863

246 HOLY Father, cheer our way
With thy love's perpetual ray;
Grant us every closing day
    Light at evening time.

2 Holy Saviour, calm our fears
When earth's brightness disappears;
Grant us in our latter years
    Light at evening time.

3 Holy Spirit, be thou nigh
When in mortal pains we lie;
Grant us, as we come to die,
    Light at evening time.

4 Holy, blessèd Trinity,
Darkness is not dark with thee;
Those thou keepest always see
    Light at evening time.

RICHARD ROBINSON 1842–1892

247   O GLADSOME light, O grace
       Of God the Father's face,
The eternal splendour wearing;
    Celestial, holy, blest,
    Our Saviour Jesus Christ,
Joyful in thine appearing.

2   Now, ere day fadeth quite,
      We see the evening light,
Our wonted hymn outpouring;
    Father of might unknown,
    Thee, his incarnate Son,
And Holy Spirit adoring.

3   To thee of right belongs
      All praise of holy songs,
O Son of God, Lifegiver;
    Thee, therefore, O Most High,
    The world doth glorify,
And shall exalt for ever.

Greek, before 4th century
Tr ROBERT BRIDGES 1844–1930

248   *Rerum Deus tenax vigor*

O STRENGTH and Stay upholding all
    creation,
  Who ever dost thyself unmoved abide,
Yet day by day the light in due gradation
  From hour to hour through all its changes
    guide;

2 Grant to life's day a calm unclouded ending,
    An eve untouched by shadows of decay,
The brightness of a holy death-bed blending
    With dawning glories of the eternal day.

3 Hear us, O Father, gracious and forgiving,
    Through Jesus Christ thy co-eternal Word,
Who, with the Holy Ghost, by all things living
    Now and to endless ages art adored.   Amen.

Latin, St Ambrose 340–397
Tr John Ellerton 1826–93
and F. J. A. Hort 1828–92

249   ROUND me falls the night;
      Saviour, be my light:
Through the hours in darkness shrouded
Let me see thy face unclouded:
    Let thy glory shine
    In this heart of mine.

2   Earthly work is done,
      Earthly sounds are none;
Rest in sleep and silence seeking,
Let me hear thee softly speaking;
    In my spirit's ear
    Whisper, 'I am near.'

3   Blessèd, heavenly light,
      Shining through earth's night;
Voice, that oft of love hast told me;
Arms, so strong to clasp and hold me;
    Thou thy watch wilt keep,
    Saviour, o'er my sleep.

William Romanis 1824–99

250 SAVIOUR, again to thy dear name we raise
With one accord our parting hymn of praise.
Guard thou the lips from sin, the hearts from
    shame,
That in this house have called upon thy name.

2 Grant us thy peace, Lord, through the coming
    night;
Turn thou for us its darkness into light;
From harm and danger keep thy children free,
For dark and light are both alike to thee.

3 Grant us thy peace throughout our earthly life;
Peace to thy Church from error and from strife
Peace to our land, the fruit of truth and love;
Peace in each heart, thy Spirit from above:

4 Thy peace in life, the balm of every pain;
Thy peace in death, the hope to rise again;
Then, when thy voice shall bid our conflict
    cease,
Call us, O Lord, to thine eternal peace.

JOHN ELLERTON 1826–93

251 SUN of my soul, thou Saviour dear,
It is not night if thou be near:
O may no earth-born cloud arise
To hide thee from thy servant's eyes.

2 When the soft dews of kindly sleep
My wearied eyelids gently steep,
Be my last thought, how sweet to rest
For ever on my Saviour's breast.

3 Abide with me from morn till eve,
  For without thee I cannot live;
  Abide with me when night is nigh,
  For without thee I dare not die.

4 If some poor wand'ring child of thine
  Have spurned to-day the voice divine,
  Now, Lord, the gracious work begin;
  Let him no more lie down in sin.

5 Watch by the sick; enrich the poor
  With blessings from thy boundless store;
  Be every mourner's sleep to-night
  Like infant's slumbers, pure and light.

6 Come near and bless us when we wake,
  Ere through the world our way we take;
  Till in the ocean of thy love
  We lose ourselves in heaven above.

JOHN KEBLE 1792–1866

252 THE day thou gavest, Lord, is ended,
      The darkness falls at thy behest;
    To thee our morning hymns ascended,
      Thy praise shall sanctify our rest.

  2 We thank thee that thy Church unsleeping,
      While earth rolls onward into light,
    Through all the world her watch is keeping,
      And rests not now by day or night.

3   As o'er each continent and island
      The dawn leads on another day,
  The voice of prayer is never silent,
      Nor dies the strain of praise away.

4   The sun that bids us rest is waking
      Our brethren 'neath the western sky,
  And hour by hour fresh lips are making
      Thy wondrous doings heard on high.

5   So be it, Lord; thy throne shall never,
      Like earth's proud empires, pass away;
  Thy kingdom stands, and grows for ever,
      Till all thy creatures own thy sway.

JOHN ELLERTON 1826–93

253   THE duteous day now closeth,
      Each flower and tree reposeth,
        Shade creeps o'er wild and wood:
      Let us, as night is falling,
      On God our Maker calling,
        Give thanks to him, the Giver good.

2   Now all the heavenly splendour
      Breaks forth in starlight tender
        From myriad worlds unknown;
      And man, the marvel seeing,
      Forgets his selfish being,
        For joy of beauty not his own.

3 His care he drowneth yonder,
   Lost in the abyss of wonder;
      To heaven his soul doth steal:
   This life he disesteemeth,
   The day it is that dreameth,
      That doth from truth his vision seal.

4 Awhile his mortal blindness
   May miss God's loving kindness,
      And grope in faithless strife:
   But when life's day is over
   Shall death's fair night discover
      The fields of everlasting life.

German, PAUL GERHARDT 1607–76
Tr ROBERT BRIDGES 1844–1930

See also

239 Lord of all hopefulness, Lord of all joy
240 When all the world to life is waking
331 Abide with me, fast falls the eventide

SUNDAY

254 COME, let us with our Lord arise,
     Our Lord who made both earth and skies;
     Who died to save the world he made,
     And rose triumphant from the dead;
     He rose, the prince of life and peace,
     And stamped the day for ever his.

2   This is the day the Lord has made,
     That all may see his love displayed,
     May feel his resurrection's power,
     And rise again to fall no more,
     In perfect righteousness renewed,
     And filled with all the life of God.

3   Then let us render him his own,
     With solemn prayer approach the throne,
     With meekness hear the gospel word,
     With thanks his dying love record;
     Our joyful hearts and voices raise
     To fill his courts with songs of praise.

CHARLES WESLEY 1707–88

255   MOST glorious Lord of life, that on this day
     Didst make thy triumph over death and sin,
  And having harrowed hell, didst bring away
     Captivity thence captive, us to win:

2   This joyous day, dear Lord, with joy begin,
     And grant that we for whom thou diddest die,
  Being with thy dear blood clean washed from
     sin,
     May live for ever in felicity:

3   And that thy love we weighing worthily,
     May likewise love thee for the same again;
  And for thy sake, that all like dear didst buy,
     With love may one another entertain;

4   So let us love, dear Love, like as we ought;
     Love is the lesson which the Lord us taught.

EDMUND SPENSER 1552–99

256   ON this day, the first of days,
God the Father's name we praise,
Who, creation's Lord and spring,
Did the world from darkness bring.

2   On this day his only Son
Over death the triumph won;
On this day the Spirit came
With his gifts of living flame.

3   On this day his people raise
One pure sacrifice of praise,
And, with all the saints above,
Tell of Christ's redeeming love.

4   Praise, O God, to thee be given,
Praise on earth and praise in heaven,
Praise to thy eternal Son,
Who this day our victory won.

H. W. BAKER 1821–77
and EDITORS

257   THIS is the day the Lord has made,
He calls the hours his own;
Let heaven rejoice, let earth be glad,
And praise surround his throne.

2   Blest be the Lord who came to men
With heavenly truth and grace,
Who came in God his Father's name,
To save a sinful race.

3   Today he rose and left the dead,
        And Satan's empire fell;
     Today the saints his triumphs spread,
        And all his wonders tell.

                              ISAAC WATTS 1674–1748
                                    and EDITORS

258   *Suitable also for general use*

     O CHRIST the same through all our story's
        pages,
     Our loves and hopes, our failures and our
        fears;
     Eternal Lord, the King of all the ages,
     Unchanging still, amid the passing years:
     O living Word, the source of all creation,
     Who spread the skies, and set the stars ablaze,
     O Christ the same, who wrought man's whole
        salvation,
     We bring our thanks for all our yesterdays.

2   O Christ the same, the friend of sinners, sharing
     Our inmost thoughts, the secrets none can hide,
     Still as of old upon your body bearing
     The marks of love, in triumph glorified:
     O Son of Man, who stooped for us from heaven,
     O Prince of life, in all your saving power,
     O Christ the same, to whom our hearts are given,
     We bring our thanks for this the present hour.

3 O Christ the same, secure within whose keeping
   Our lives and loves, our days and years remain,
   Our work and rest, our waking and our sleeping,
   Our calm and storm, our pleasure and our pain:
   O Lord of love, for all our joys and sorrows,
   For all our hopes, when earth shall fade and flee,
   O Christ the same, for all our brief tomorrows,
   We bring our thanks for all that is to be.

TIMOTHY DUDLEY-SMITH b 1926

See also

393 Lead us, heavenly Father, lead us
417 O God, our help in ages past
467 Through all the changing scenes of life
472 When all thy mercies, O my God

HARVEST

259 COME, ye thankful people, come,
   Raise the song of harvest-home!
   All be safely gathered in,
   Ere the winter storms begin;
   God, our Maker, doth provide
   For our wants to be supplied;
   Come to God's own temple, come;
   Raise the song of harvest-home!

2 All the world is God's own field,
   Fruit unto his praise to yield;
   Wheat and tares together sown,
   Unto joy or sorrow grown;
   First the blade and then the ear,
   Then the full corn shall appear:
   Grant, O harvest Lord, that we
   Wholesome grain and pure may be.

3 For the Lord our God shall come,
And shall take his harvest home;
From his field shall purge away
All that doth offend, that day;
Give his angels charge at last
In the fire the tares to cast,
But the fruitful ears to store
In his garner evermore.

4 Then, thou Church triumphant, come,
Raise the song of harvest-home;
All be safely gathered in,
Free from sorrow, free from sin,
There for ever purified
In God's garner to abide:
Come, ten thousand angels, come,
Raise the glorious harvest-home!

HENRY ALFORD 1810–71

260 FAIR waved the golden corn
In Canaan's pleasant land,
When full of joy, some shining morn,
Went forth the reaper-band.

2 To God so good and great
Their cheerful thanks they pour;
Then carry to his temple-gate
The choicest of their store.

3 Like Israel, Lord, we give
Our earliest fruits to thee,
And pray that, long as we shall live,
We may thy children be.

4   Thine is our youthful prime,
       And life and all its powers;
Be with us in our morning time,
       And bless our evening hours.

5   In wisdom let us grow,
       As years and strength are given,
That we may serve thy Church below,
       And join thy saints in heaven.

JOHN HAMPDEN GURNEY 1802–62

261   TO thee, O Lord, our hearts we raise
       In hymns of adoration;
To thee bring sacrifice of praise
       With shouts of exultation.
Bright robes of gold the fields adorn,
       The hills with joy are ringing,
The valleys stand so thick with corn
       That even they are singing.

2   And now, on this our festal day,
       Thy bounteous hand confessing,
Upon thine altar, Lord, we lay
       The first-fruits of thy blessing;
By thee the souls of men are fed
       With gifts of grace supernal;
Thou who dost give us daily bread,
       Give us the bread eternal.

3 We bear the burden of the day,
   And often toil seems dreary;
But labour ends with sunset ray,
   And rest is for the weary;
May we, the angel-reaping o'er,
   Stand at the last accepted,
Christ's golden sheaves for evermore
   To garners bright elected.

4 O blessèd is that land of God,
   Where saints abide for ever;
Where golden fields spread fair and broad,
   Where flows the crystal river:
The strains of all its holy throng
   With ours to-day are blending;
Thrice blessèd is that harvest-song
   Which never hath an ending.

W. CHATTERTON DIX 1837–98

262 WE plough the fields, and scatter
   The good seed on the land,
But it is fed and watered
   By God's almighty hand;
He sends the snow in winter,
   The warmth to swell the grain,
The breezes and the sunshine,
   And soft refreshing rain:
   All good gifts around us
   Are sent from heaven above,
   Then thank the Lord, O thank the Lord,
   For all his love.

2   He only is the Maker
      Of all things near and far,
  He paints the wayside flower,
      He lights the evening star.
  The winds and waves obey him,
      By him the birds are fed;
  Much more to us, his children,
      He gives our daily bread:

3   We thank thee then, O Father,
      For all things bright and good;
  The seed-time and the harvest,
      Our life, our health, our food.
  No gifts have we to offer
      For all thy love imparts,
  But that which thou desirest,
      Our humble, thankful hearts:

German, MATTHIAS CLAUDIUS 1740–1815
Tr JANE CAMPBELL 1817–78

See also

264 All things bright and beautiful
285 For the beauty of the earth
397 Let us with a gladsome mind
493 Rejoice, O land, in God thy might

GOD IN NATURE

263 ALL creatures of our God and King,
    Lift up your voice and with us sing
        Alleluya, alleluya!
    Thou burning sun with golden beam,
    Thou silver moon with softer gleam:
                O praise him, O praise him,
                Alleluya, Alleluya, Alleluya!

 2 Thou rushing wind that art so strong,
    Ye clouds that sail in heaven along,
        O praise him, Alleluya!
    Thou rising morn, in praise rejoice,
    Ye lights of evening, find a voice:

 3 Thou flowing water, pure and clear,
    Make music for thy Lord to hear,
        Alleluya, Alleluya!
    Thou fire so masterful and bright,
    That givest man both warmth and light:

 4 Dear mother earth, who day by day
    Unfoldest blessings on our way,
        O praise him, Alleluya!
    The flowers and fruits that in thee grow,
        Let them his glory also show:

 5* And all ye men of tender heart,
    Forgiving others, take your part,
        O sing ye, Alleluya!
    Ye who long pain and sorrow bear,
    Praise God and on him cast your care:

6* And thou, most kind and gentle death,
    Waiting to hush our latest breath,
      O praise him, Alleluya!
    Thou leadest home the child of God,
    And Christ our Lord the way hath trod:

7 Let all things their Creator bless,
    And worship him in humbleness,
      O praise him, Alleluya!
    Praise, praise the Father, praise the Son,
      And praise the Spirit, three in One:

ST FRANCIS OF ASSISI 1182–1226
Tr WILLIAM DRAPER 1855–1933

264 *ALL things bright and beautiful,*
    All creatures great and small,
    All things wise and wonderful,
      The Lord God made them all.

2 Each little flower that opens,
    Each little bird that sings,
    He made their glowing colours,
    He made their tiny wings.

3 The purple-headed mountain,
    The river running by,
    The sunset and the morning,
    That brightens up the sky;

4   The cold wind in the winter,
     The pleasant summer sun,
  The ripe fruits in the garden,—
     He made them every one;

5*   The tall trees in the greenwood,
     The meadows for our play,
  The rushes by the water,
     To gather every day;—

6   He gave us eyes to see them,
     And lips that we might tell
  How great is God Almighty,
     Who has made all things well.

MRS C. F. ALEXANDER 1818–95

265   LORD of beauty, thine the splendour
     Shown in earth and sky and sea,
  Burning sun and moonlight tender,
     Hill and river, flower and tree:
  Lest we fail our praise to render
     Touch our eyes that they may see.

2   Lord of wisdom, whom obeying
     Mighty waters ebb and flow,
  While unhasting, undelaying,
     Planets on their courses go:
  In thy laws thyself displaying,
     Teach our minds thyself to know.

3 Lord of life, alone sustaining
  All below and all above,
Lord of love, by whose ordaining
  Sun and stars sublimely move:
In our earthly spirits reigning,
  Lift our hearts that we may love.

4 Lord of beauty, bid us own thee,
  Lord of truth, our footsteps guide,
Till as Love our hearts enthrone thee,
  And, with vision purified,
Lord of all, when all have known thee,
  Thou in all art glorified.

C. A. ALINGTON 1872–1955

266   *Psalm 93*

THE Lord reigns clothed in strength and power,
  And beauty is his royal robe:
For his eternal throne he poised
  The pillars of the solid globe.

2 The thunder of the brooks in spate,
  The restless motion of the tides,
Those voices of the springs proclaim
  The Lord whose majesty abides.

3 Then in the splendour of his house
  Now and for ever glorify
The Lord whose covenant stands firm,
  Who built the earth and sea and sky.

MICHAEL HODGETTS b 1936

267 THE spacious firmament on high,
With all the blue ethereal sky,
And spangled heavens, a shining frame,
Their great Original proclaim.
The unwearied sun from day to day
Does his Creator's power display,
And publishes to every land
The works of an almighty hand.

2 Soon as the evening shades prevail
The moon takes up the wondrous tale,
And nightly to the listening earth
Repeats the story of her birth;
Whilst all the stars that round her burn,
And all the planets in their turn,
Confirm the tidings, as they roll,
And spread the truth from pole to pole.

3 What though in solemn silence all
Move round the dark terrestrial ball;
What though nor real voice nor sound
Amid their radiant orbs be found;
In reason's ear they all rejoice,
And utter forth a glorious voice;
For ever singing as they shine,
'The hand that made us is divine.'

JOSEPH ADDISON 1672–1719

See also

285 For the beauty of the earth
397 Let us with a gladsome mind
405 Lord of the boundless curves of space
433 O worship the King
458 The Lord my pasture shall prepare

PART III

SACRAMENTS AND OTHER RITES

HOLY COMMUNION

268 OFFICE HYMN   Corpus Christi

Pangue lingua gloriosi corporis mysterium

OF the glorious body telling,
    O my tongue, its mysteries sing,
And the blood, all price excelling,
    Which the world's eternal King,
In a spotless womb once dwelling,
    Shed for this world's ransoming.

2 Given for us, for us descending,
    Of a virgin to proceed,
Man with man in converse blending,
    Scattered he the gospel seed,
Till his sojourn drew to ending,
    Which he closed in wondrous deed.

3 At the last great supper lying
    Circled by his chosen band,
Duly with the law complying,
    First he finished its command,
Then, immortal food supplying,
    Gave himself by his own hand.

4 Word-made-flesh, by word he maketh
    Bread his very flesh to be;
Man in wine Christ's blood partaketh:
    And if senses fail to see,
Faith alone the true heart waketh
    To behold the mystery.

PART 2   *Tantum ergo*

5 Therefore we, before him bending,
      This great sacrament revere:
   Types and shadows have their ending,
      For the newer rite is here;
   Faith, our outward sense befriending,
      Makes the inward vision clear.

6 Glory let us give and blessing
      To the Father and the Son,
   Honour, might and praise addressing,
      While eternal ages run;
   Ever too his love confessing,
      Who, from both, with both is one.   Amen.

ST THOMAS AQUINAS 1227–74
Tr J. M. NEALE 1818–66
and others

269   OFFICE HYMN   Corpus Christi

Verbum supernum prodiens, nec Patris

THE heavenly Word proceeding forth
   Yet leaving not his Father's side,
And going to his work on earth,
   Had reached at length life's eventide.

2 By false disciple to be given
      To foemen for his blood athirst,
   Himself, the living bread from heaven,
      He gave to his disciples first.

3 In twofold form of sacrament,
    He gave his flesh, he gave his blood,
That man, of soul and body blent,
    Might wholly feed on mystic food.

4 In birth man's fellow-man was he,
    His meat while sitting at the board;
He died, our ransomer to be,
    He reigns to be our great reward.

PART 2   *O salutaris hostia*

5 O saving Victim, opening wide
    The gate of heaven to man below;
Our foes press hard on every side,
    Thine aid supply, thy strength bestow.

6 All praise and thanks to thee ascend
    For evermore, blest One in Three;
O grant us life that shall not end,
    In our true native land with thee.   Amen.

St Thomas Aquinas 1227–74
Tr J. M. Neale 1818–66
and others

270   *Suitable for Maundy Thursday*

ACCORDING to thy gracious word,
  In meek humility,
This will I do, my dying Lord,
  I will remember thee.

2 Thy body, broken for my sake,
    My bread from heaven shall be;
  Thy testamental cup I take,
    And thus remember thee.

3 Gethsemane can I forget?
    Or there thy conflict see,
  Thine agony and bloody sweat,
    And not remember thee?

4 When to the cross I turn mine eyes
    And rest on Calvary
  O Lamb of God, my sacrifice,
    I must remember thee:

5 Remember thee, and all thy pains,
    And all thy love to me;
  Yea, while a breath, a pulse remains,
    Will I remember thee.

6 And when these failing lips grow dumb,
    And mind and memory flee,
  When thou shalt in thy kingdom come,
    Jesu, remember me.

JAMES MONTGOMERY 1771–1854

271 ALLELUYA, sing to Jesus,
    His the sceptre, his the throne;
  Alleluya, his the triumph,
    His the victory alone:
  Hark the songs of peaceful Sion
    Thunder like a mighty flood;
  Jesus, out of every nation,
    Hath redeemed us by his blood.

2   Alleluya, not as orphans
      Are we left in sorrow now;
    Alleluya, he is near us,
      Faith believes, nor questions how;
    Though the cloud from sight received him
      When the forty days were o'er,
    Shall our hearts forget his promise,
      'I am with you evermore'?

3   Alleluya, Bread of Angels,
      Thou on earth our food, our stay;
    Alleluya, here the sinful
      Flee to thee from day to day;
    Intercessor, Friend of sinners,
      Earth's Redeemer, plead for me,
    Where the songs of all the sinless
      Sweep across the crystal sea.

4   Alleluya, King eternal,
      Thee the Lord of lords we own;
    Alleluya, born of Mary,
      Earth thy footstool, heaven thy throne:
    Thou within the veil hast entered,
      Robed in flesh, our great High Priest;
    Thou on earth both Priest and Victim
      In the Eucharistic Feast.

W. CHATTERTON DIX 1837–98

272   ALL for Jesus! all for Jesus!
      This our song shall ever be;
    For we have no hope nor Saviour
      If we have not hope in thee.

2   All for Jesus! thou wilt give us
       Strength to serve thee hour by hour:
    None can move us from thy presence
       While we trust thy love and power.

3   All for Jesus! at thine altar
       Thou dost give us sweet content;
    There, dear Saviour, we receive thee
       In thy holy sacrament.

4   All for Jesus! thou hast loved us,
       All for Jesus! thou hast died,
    All for Jesus! thou art with us,
       All for Jesus, glorified!

5   All for Jesus! All for Jesus!
       This the Church's song shall be,
    Till at last the flock is gathered
       One in love, and one in thee.

W. J. SPARROW-SIMPSON 1859–1952†

273 AND now, O Father, mindful of the love
      That bought us, once for all, on Calvary's tree,
  And having with us him that pleads above,
      We here present, we here spread forth to thee
  That only offering perfect in thine eyes,
  The one true, pure, immortal sacrifice.

2 Look, Father, look on his anointed face,
      And only look on us as found in him;
  Look not on our misusings of thy grace,
      Our prayer so languid, and our faith so dim;
  For lo, between our sins and their reward
  We set the passion of thy Son our Lord.

3 And then for those, our dearest and our best,
   By this prevailing presence we appeal;
O fold them closer to thy mercy's breast,
   O do thine utmost for their souls' true weal;
From tainting mischief keep them white and clear
And crown thy gifts with grace to persevere.

4 And so we come: O draw us to thy feet
   Most patient Saviour, who canst love us still;
And by this food, so aweful and so sweet,
   Deliver us from every touch of ill:
In thine own service make us glad and free,
And grant us nevermore to part from thee.

WILLIAM BRIGHT 1824–1901

274   AUTHOR of life divine,
          Who hast a table spread,
       Furnished with mystic wine
          And everlasting bread,
       Preserve the life thyself hast given,
       And feed and train us up for heaven.

2   Our needy souls sustain
          With fresh supplies of love,
       Till all thy life we gain,
          And all thy fullness prove,
       And, strengthened by thy perfect grace,
       Behold without a veil thy face.

CHARLES WESLEY 1707–88

275 BLESSED Jesu, Mary's son,
    For mankind to earth thou camest,
But the saving battle won,
    Now at God's right hand thou reignest:
On thy people pour thy blessing,
Gathered here, thy name confessing.

2 By this sacramental sign,
    Token of thy bitter passion,
Through these gifts of bread and wine
    Thine own image in us fashion:
By this food thy grace doth send us
From all ills of soul defend us.

3 In this mystery of grace
    Which we celebrate before thee,
Come, O Saviour, show thy face
    To the faithful who adore thee:
All our sins by thee forgiven,
Grant us here the joys of heaven.

G. B. TIMMS b 1910

276 BREAD of heaven, on thee we feed,
    For thy flesh is meat indeed;
Ever may our souls be fed
With this true and living bread,
Day by day with strength supplied
Through the life of him who died.

2   Vine of heaven, thy blood supplies
      This blest cup of sacrifice;
   'Tis thy wounds our healing give;
      To thy cross we look and live:
   Thou our life! O let us be
   Rooted, grafted, built on thee.

JOSIAH CONDER 1789–1855

277   BREAD of the world in mercy broken,
      Wine of the soul in mercy shed,
   By whom the words of life were spoken,
      And in whose death our sins are dead:
   Look on the heart by sorrow broken,
      Look on the tears by sinners shed,
   And be thy feast to us the token
      That by thy grace our souls are fed.

REGINALD HEBER 1783–1826

278   CHRIST be with me, Christ within me,
      Christ behind me, Christ before me,
   Christ beside me, Christ to win me,
      Christ to comfort and restore me.

2   Christ beneath me, Christ above me,
      Christ in quiet, Christ in danger,
   Christ in hearts of all who love me,
      Christ in mouth of friend and stranger.

From *St Patrick's Breastplate* see 159)
Tr MRS C. F. ALEXANDER 1818–95

279   COME, risen Lord, and deign to be our guest;
     Nay, let us be thy guests; the feast is thine;
Thyself at thine own board make manifest,
     In thine own sacrament of bread and wine.

2   We meet, as in that upper room they met;
     Thou, at thy table, blessing, yet dost stand:
'This is my body'—so thou givest yet;
     Faith still receives the cup as from thy hand.

3   One body we, one body who partake,
     One Church united in communion blest;
One name we bear, one bread of life we break,
     With all thy saints on earth and saints at rest.

4   One with each other, Lord, for one in thee,
     Who art one Saviour and one living Head;
Then open thou our eyes, that we may see:
     Be known to us in breaking of the bread.

G. W. BRIGGS 1875–1959

280   DECK thyself, my soul, with gladness,
Leave the gloomy haunts of sadness,
Come into the daylight's splendour,
There with joy thy praises render
Unto him whose grace unbounded
Hath this wondrous banquet founded;
High o'er all the heavens he reigneth,
Yet to dwell with thee he deigneth.

2* Now I sink before thee lowly,
    Filled with joy most deep and holy,
As with trembling awe and wonder
    On thy mighty works I ponder;
How, by mystery surrounded,
Depths no man hath ever sounded,
None may dare to pierce unbidden
Secrets that with thee are hidden.

3 Sun, who all my life dost brighten;
Light, who dost my soul enlighten;
Joy, the sweetest man e'er knoweth;
Fount, whence all my being floweth;
At thy feet I cry, my Maker,
Let me be a fit partaker
Of this blessèd food from heaven,
For our good, thy glory, given.

4 Jesus, Bread of Life, I pray thee,
Let me gladly here obey thee;
Never to my hurt invited,
Be thy love with love requited:
From this banquet let me measure,
Lord, how vast and deep its treasure;
Through the gifts thou here dost give me,
As thy guest in heaven receive me.

           German, JOHANN FRANCK 1618–77
           Tr CATHERINE WINKWORTH 1827–78

281   *Sancti, venite, Christi Corpus sumite*

    DRAW nigh, and take the body of the Lord,
    And drink the holy blood for you outpoured,
    Saved by that body, hallowed by that blood,
    Whereby refreshed we render thanks to God.

2　Salvation's giver, Christ the only Son,
　　By that his cross and blood the victory won.
　　Offered was he for greatest and for least:
　　Himself the Victim, and himself the Priest.

3　Victims were offered by the law of old,
　　That, in a type, celestial mysteries told.
　　He, Ransomer from death and Light from shade,
　　Giveth his holy grace his saints to aid.

4　Approach ye then with faithful hearts sincere,
　　And take the safeguard of salvation here.
　　He that in this world rules his saints and shields,
　　To all believers life eternal yields:

5　With heavenly bread makes them that hunger
　　　　whole,
　　Gives living waters to the thirsty soul.
　　Alpha and Omega, to whom shall bow
　　All nations at the doom, is with us now.

Latin, 7th century
Tr J. M. NEALE 1818–66

282　FAITHFUL Shepherd, feed me
　　　　In the pastures green;
　　　　Faithful Shepherd, lead me
　　　　Where thy steps are seen.

2　Hold me fast, and guide me
　　　In the narrow way;
　　So, with thee beside me,
　　　I shall never stray.

3   Daily bring me nearer
     To the heavenly shore;
  May my faith grow clearer,
     May I love thee more.

4   Hallow every pleasure,
     Every gift and pain;
  Be thyself my treasure,
     Though none else I gain.

5   Day by day prepare me
     As thou seest best,
  Then let angels bear me
     To thy promised rest.

T. B. POLLOCK 1836–96

283   FATHER, see thy children bending at thy
      throne,
Pleading here the Passion of thine only Son,
Pleading here before thee all his dying love,
As he pleads it ever in the courts above.

2   Not for our wants only we this offering plead,
But for all thy children who thy mercy need:
Bless thy faithful people, win thy wandering
    sheep,
Keep the souls departed who in Jesus sleep.

WILLIAM JERVOIS 1852–1905
and W. B. TREVELYAN 1853–1929

284 FATHER, we thank thee who hast planted
Thy holy name within our hearts.
Knowledge and faith and life immortal
Jesus thy Son to us imparts.

2 Thou, Lord, didst make all for thy pleasure,
Didst give us food for all our days,
Giving in Christ the bread eternal;
Thine is the power, be thine the praise.

3 Watch o'er thy Church, O Lord, in mercy,
Save it from evil, guard it still,
Perfect it in thy love, unite it,
Cleansed and conformed unto thy will.

4 As grain, once scattered on the hillsides,
Was in this broken bread made one,
So from all lands thy Church be gathered
Into thy kingdom by thy Son.

From the *Didache* (1st century)
Tr F. BLAND TUCKER (1895–1984)

285 FOR the beauty of the earth,
For the beauty of the skies,
For the love which from our birth
Over and around us lies:
Lord of all, to thee we raise
This our sacrifice of praise.

2 For the beauty of each hour,
Of the day and of the night,
Hill and vale, and tree and flower,
Sun and moon and stars of light:

3 For the joy of ear and eye,
 For the heart and brain's delight,
 For the mystic harmony
 Linking sense to sound and sight:

4 For the joy of human love,
 Brother, sister, parent, child,
 Friends on earth and friends above,
 For all gentle thoughts and mild:

5 For each perfect gift of thine,
 To our race so freely given,
 Graces human and divine,
 Flowers of earth and buds of heaven:

6* For thy Church that evermore
 Lifteth holy hands above,
 Offering up on every shore
 This pure sacrifice of love:

F. S. PIERPOINT 1835–1917

286 *After Communion*

FROM glory to glory advancing, we praise thee,
 O Lord;
Thy name with the Father and Spirit be ever
 adored.
From strength unto strength we go forward on
 Sion's highway,
To appear before God in the city of infinite day.

2 Thanksgiving and glory and worship and
   blessing and love,
One heart and one song have the saints upon
   earth and above.
O Lord, evermore to thy servants thy presence
   be nigh;
Ever fit us by service on earth for thy service on
   high.

Liturgy of ST JAMES
Tr CHARLES HUMPHREYS 1840–1921

287 GLORY, love and praise and honour
       For our food, now bestowed,
         Render we the Donor.
     Bounteous God, we now confess thee;
       God who thus, blessest us,
         Meet it is to bless thee.

2   Thankful for our every blessing,
      Let us sing Christ the Spring,
        Never, never ceasing.
    Source of all our gifts and graces,
      Christ we own; Christ alone
        Calls for all our praises.

3   He dispels our sin and sadness,
      Life imparts, cheers our hearts,
        Fills with food and gladness.
    Who himself for all has given,
      Us he feeds, us he leads
        To a feast in heaven.

CHARLES WESLEY 1707–88

288 GOD everlasting, wonderful and holy,
    Father most gracious, we who stand before
       thee
    Here at thine altar, as thy Son has taught us,
      Come to adore thee.

2 Countless the mercies thou has lavished on us,
    Source of all blessing to all creatures living,
    To thee we render, for thy love o'erflowing,
      Humble thanksgiving.

3 Now in remembrance of our great Redeemer,
    Dying on Calvary, rising and ascending,
    Through him we offer what he ever offers,
      Sinners befriending.

4 Strength to the living, rest to the departed,
    Grant, Holy Father, through this pure oblation;
    May the life-giving Bread for ever bring us
      Health and salvation.

HAROLD RILEY b 1903

289   *Ave, verum corpus natum*

    HAIL, true Body, born of Mary,
      Spotless Virgin's virgin birth;
    Thou who truly hangedst weary
      On the cross for sons of earth;
    Thou whose sacred side was riven,
      Whence the water flowed and blood,
    O may'st thou, dear Lord, be given
      At death's hour to be our food:
    O most kind, O gracious one,
    O sweetest Jesu, holy Mary's Son.

Latin, 14th century
Tr H. N. OXENHAM 1829–88

290 HOLY God, we show forth here
Jesus' death our sins to clear,
Jesus' life our life to be,
Jesus' love the world to free.
Stay the faithful, win the strayed,
Bless the living and the dead.
Father lead us,
Saviour feed us,
Spirit be our store,
Now and evermore.

2 Lord, unite us every one
Each to other, through thy Son;
Join us truly heart to heart,
Let us ne'er be drawn apart:
All one bread, one body we,
Bound by love to all and thee.
Blessèd Master,
Bind us faster;
In thy love divine,
Love we thee and thine!

PERCY DEARMER 1867–1936

291 *The Rosy Sequence*

Jesu, dulcis memoria

JESU!—the very thought is sweet!
In that dear name all heart-joys meet;
But sweeter than the honey far
The glimpses of his presence are.

2   No word is sung more sweet than this:
No name is heard more full of bliss:
No thought brings sweeter comfort nigh,
Than Jesus, Son of God most high.

3   Jesu! the hope of souls forlorn!
How good to them for sin that mourn!
To them that seek thee, O how kind!
But what art thou to them that find?

4   Jesu, thou sweetness, pure and blest,
Truth's fountain, Light of souls distrest,
Surpassing all that heart requires,
Exceeding all that soul desires!

5   No tongue of mortal can express,
No letters write its blessedness:
Alone who hath thee in his heart
Knows, love of Jesus, what thou art.

6* I seek for Jesus in repose,
When round my heart its chambers close;
Abroad, and when I shut the door,
I long for Jesus evermore.

7* With Mary in the morning gloom
I seek for Jesus at the tomb;
For him, with love's most earnest cry,
I seek with heart and not with eye.

8* Jesus, to God the Father gone,
Is seated on the heavenly throne;
My heart hath also passed from me,
That where he is there it may be.

9   We follow Jesus now, and raise
     The voice of prayer, the hymn of praise,
    That he at last may make us meet
     With him to gain the heavenly seat.

Latin, 12th century
Tr J. M. NEALE 1818–66

292   *Jesu, dulcedo cordium*

JESU, thou joy of loving hearts,
   Thou fount of life, thou light of men,
From the best bliss that earth imparts
   We turn unfilled to thee again.

2   Thy truth unchanged hath ever stood,
     Thou savest those that on thee call,
   To them that seek thee thou art good,
     To them that find thee, all in all.

3   We taste thee, O thou living bread,
     And long to feast upon thee still;
   We drink of thee, the fountain-head,
     And thirst our souls from thee to fill.

4   Our restless spirits yearn for thee,
     Where'er our changeful lot is cast,
   Glad when thy gracious smile we see,
     Blest when our faith can hold thee fast.

5   O Jesu, ever with us stay,
     Make all our moments calm and bright;
   Chase the dark night of sin away,
     Shed o'er the world thy holy light.

Latin, 12th century
Tr RAY PALMER 1808–87

293   JESUS, our Master, on the night that they
             came
       To take you to prison, to death and to shame,
       You called to your table the friends that you
             knew,
       And asked them to do this in remembrance of
             you.

2   Still through the ages your new friends draw
             near,
       And know when they do so, that you will be
             here;
       We know you are present, though just out of
             view,
       To meet those who gather in remembrance of
             you.

3   When it is over, and all gone away,
       Come back to our thoughts for the rest of the
             day,
       And stay with us always, who met here to do
       The thing you commanded, in remembrance of
             you.

                                 MICHAEL HEWLETT b 1916

294   JUST as I am, without one plea
       But that thy blood was shed for me,
       And that thou bidd'st me come to thee,
        O Lamb of God, I come.

2   Just as I am, though tossed about
       With many a conflict, many a doubt,
       Fightings within, and fears without,

3 Just as I am, poor, wretched, blind;
  Sight, riches, healing of the mind,
  Yea all I need, in thee to find,

4 Just as I am, thou wilt receive,
  Wilt welcome, pardon, cleanse, relieve:
  Because thy promise I believe,

5 Just as I am (thy love unknown
  Has broken every barrier down),
  Now to be thine, yea thine alone,

6 Just as I am, of that free love
  The breadth, length, depth and height to prove,
  Here for a season then above,
    O Lamb of God, I come.

CHARLOTTE ELLIOTT 1789–1871

295 LET all mortal flesh keep silence
    And with fear and trembling stand;
  Ponder nothing earthly-minded,
    For with blessing in his hand
  Christ our God to earth descendeth,
    Our full homage to demand.

2 King of kings, yet born of Mary,
    As of old on earth he stood,
  Lord of lords, in human vesture,
    In the body and the blood:
  He will give to all the faithful
    His own self for heavenly food.

3 Rank on rank the host of heaven
   Spreads its vanguard on the way,
As the Light of light descendeth
   From the realms of endless day,
That the powers of hell may vanish
   As the darkness clears away.

4 At his feet the six-winged seraph;
   Cherubim with sleepless eye,
Veil their faces to the Presence,
   As with ceaseless voice they cry,
Alleluya, Alleluya,
   Alleluya, Lord most high!

Liturgy of ST JAMES
Tr GERARD MOULTRIE 1829–85

296 LORD, enthroned in heavenly splendour,
   First-begotten from the dead,
Thou alone, our strong defender,
   Liftest up thy people's head.
      Alleluya,
   Jesu, true and living Bread!

2 Here our humblest homage pay we;
   Here in loving reverence bow;
Here for Faith's discernment pray we,
   Lest we fail to know thee now.
      Alleluya,
   Thou art here, we ask not how.

3 Though the lowliest form doth veil thee
    As of old in Bethlehem,
Here as there thine angels hail thee,
    Branch and Flower of Jesse's stem.
        Alleluya,
    We in worship join with them.

4 Paschal Lamb, thine Offering, finished
    Once for all when thou wast slain,
In its fullness undiminished
    Shall for evermore remain,
        Alleluya,
    Cleansing souls from every stain.

5 Life-imparting heavenly Manna,
    Stricken Rock with streaming side,
Heaven and earth with loud hosanna
    Worship thee, the Lamb who died,
        Alleluya,
    Risen, ascended, glorified!

                    G. H. BOURNE 1840–1925

297   LORD Jesus Christ,
        You have come to us,
        You are one with us,
            Mary's Son;
        Cleansing our souls from all their sin,
        Pouring your love and goodness in;
        Jesus, our love for you we sing,
            Living Lord.

2   Lord Jesus Christ,
Now and every day
Teach us how to pray,
   Son of God.
You have commanded us to do
This in remembrance, Lord, of you:
Into our lives your power breaks through,
   Living Lord.

3   Lord Jesus Christ,
You have come to us,
Born as one of us,
   Mary's Son;
Led out to die on Calvary,
Risen from death to set us free,
Living Lord Jesus, help us see
   You are Lord.

4   Lord Jesus Christ,
I would come to you,
Live my life for you,
   Son of God.
All your commands I know are true,
Your many gifts will make me new,
Into my life your power breaks through,
   Living Lord.

PATRICK APPLEFORD b 1924

298   MAY the grace of Christ our Saviour,
    And the Father's boundless love,
With the Holy Spirit's favour,
    Rest upon us from above.

2 Thus may we abide in union
  With each other and the Lord,
And possess in sweet communion,
  Joys which earth cannot afford.

3 To the God whose wisdom made us,
  To the Son who set us free,
To the sanctifying Spirit,
  Glory, endless glory, be!   Amen.

JOHN NEWTON 1725–1807
and EDITORS

299 MY spirit longs for thee
  Within my troubled breast,
Though I unworthy be
  Of so divine a guest.

2 Of so divine a guest
  Unworthy though I be,
Yet has my heart no rest
  Unless it come from thee.

3 Unless it come from thee,
  In vain I look around;
In all that I can see
  No rest is to be found.

4 No rest is to be found
  But in thy blessèd love:
O, let my wish be crowned,
  And send it from above!

JOHN BYROM 1692–1763

300   *O esca viatorum*

O FOOD of men wayfaring,
The Bread of Angels sharing,
   O Manna from on high!
We hunger; Lord, supply us,
Nor thy delights deny us,
   Whose hearts to thee draw nigh.

2   O Stream of love past telling,
O purest Fountain, welling
   From out the Saviour's side!
We faint with thirst; revive us,
Of thine abundance give us,
   And all we need provide.

3   O Jesu, by thee bidden,
We here adore thee, hidden
   'Neath forms of bread and wine.
Grant when the veil is riven,
We may behold, in heaven,
   Thy countenance divine.

Latin, 17th century
Tr ATHELSTAN RILEY 1858–1945

301   O, MOST merciful!
O, most bountiful!
God the Father Almighty!
By the Redeemer's
Sweet intercession
Hear us, help us when we cry.

REGINALD HEBER 1783–1826

311

302 O THOU, who at thy Eucharist didst pray
      That all thy Church might be for ever one,
Grant us at every Eucharist to say
      With longing heart and soul, 'Thy will be
          done.'
Oh, may we all one Bread, one Body be,
One through this Sacrament of unity.

2 For all thy Church, O Lord, we intercede;
      Make thou our sad divisions soon to cease;
Draw us the nearer each to each, we plead,
      By drawing all to thee, O Prince of Peace:
Thus may we all one Bread, one Body be,
One through this Sacrament of unity.

3 We pray thee too for wanderers from thy fold;
      O bring them back, good Shepherd of the
          sheep,
Back to the faith which saints believed of old,
      Back to the Church which still that faith doth
          keep:
Soon may we all one Bread, one Body be,
One through this Sacrament of unity.

4 So, Lord, at length when sacraments shall cease,
      May we be one with all thy Church above,
One with thy saints in one unbroken peace,
      One with thy saints in one unbounded love:
More blessèd still, in peace and love to be
One with the Trinity in Unity.

WILLIAM TURTON 1856–1938

303   O WORD immortal of eternal God,
      Only-begotten of the only Source,
      For our salvation stooping to the course
Of human life, and born of Mary's blood;
Sprung from the ever-virgin womanhood
      Of her who bare thee, God immutable,
      Incarnate, made as man with man to dwell,
And condescending to the bitter Rood;

2   Save us, O Christ our God, for thou hast died
      To save thy people to the uttermost,
      And dying tramplest death in victory;
      One of the ever-blessèd Trinity,
      In equal honour with the Holy Ghost,
And with the eternal Father glorified.

Greek, 6th century
Tr T. A. LACEY 1853–1931

304   ONCE, only once, and once for all,
      His precious life he gave;
Before the Cross in faith we fall,
      And own it strong to save.

2   'One offering, single and complete,'
      With lips and hearts we say;
But what he never can repeat
      He shows forth day by day.

3   For as the priest of Aaron's line
      Within the holiest stood,
And sprinkled all the mercy-shrine
      With sacrificial blood;

4 So he, who once atonement wrought,
    Our Priest of endless power,
Presents himself for those he bought
    In that dark noontide hour.

5 His Manhood pleads where now it lives
    On heaven's eternal throne,
And where in mystic rite he gives
    Its presence to his own.

6 And so we show thy death, O Lord,
    Till thou again appear,
And feel, when we approach thy board,
    We have an altar here.

WILLIAM BRIGHT 1824–1901

305 *Anima Christi*

SOUL of my Saviour, sanctify my breast,
Body of Christ, be thou my saving guest,
Blood of my Saviour, bathe me in thy tide,
Wash me with water flowing from thy side.

2 Strength and protection may thy passion be,
O blessèd Jesu, hear and answer me;
Deep in thy wounds, Lord, hide and shelter me,
So shall I never, never part from thee.

3 Guard and defend me from the foe malign,
In death's dread moments make me only thine;
Call me and bid me come to thee on high
Where I may praise thee with thy saints for ay.

Latin, 14th century
Tr Anonymous

314

306 *After communion*

STRENGTHEN for service, Lord, the hands
  That holy things have taken;
Let ears that now have heard thy songs
  To clamour never waken.

2 Lord, may the tongues which 'Holy' sang
  Keep free from all deceiving;
The eyes which saw thy love be bright,
  Thy blessèd hope perceiving.

3 The feet that tread thy holy courts
  From light do thou not banish;
The bodies by thy Body fed
  With thy new life replenish.

> Syrian, 4th century
> *Tr* C. W. HUMPHREYS 1840–1921
> and PERCY DEARMER 1867–1936

307 *A hymn to Christ in his sacramental presence.*

SWEET Sacrament divine,
  Hid in thine earthly home,
Lo, round thy lowly shrine,
  With suppliant hearts we come;
Jesu, to thee our voice we raise
In songs of love and heartfelt praise:
  Sweet Sacrament divine.

2 Sweet Sacrament of peace,
    Dear home for every heart,
Where restless yearnings cease
    And sorrows all depart;
There in thine ear all trustfully
We tell our tale of misery:
    Sweet Sacrament of peace.

3 Sweet Sacrament of rest,
    Ark from the ocean's roar,
Within thy shelter blest
    Soon may we reach the shore;
Save us, for still the tempest raves,
Save, lest we sink beneath the waves:
    Sweet Sacrament of rest.

4 Sweet Sacrament divine,
    Earth's light and jubilee,
In thy far depths doth shine
    The Godhead's majesty;
Sweet light, so shine on us, we pray
That earthly joys may fade away:
    Sweet Sacrament divine.

FRANCIS STANFIELD 1835-1914

308   *Adoro te devote*

THEE we adore, O hidden Saviour, thee,
Who in thy Sacrament art pleased to be;
Both flesh and spirit in thy presence fail,
Yet here thy presence we devoutly hail.

2 O blest memorial of our dying Lord,
   Who living bread to men doth here afford!
   O may our souls for ever feed on thee,
   And thou, O Christ, for ever precious be.

3 Fountain of goodness, Jesu, Lord and God,
   Cleanse us, unclean, with thy most cleansing
      blood;
   Increase our faith and love, that we may know
   The hope and peace which from thy presence
      flow.

4 O Christ, whom now beneath a veil we see,
   May what we thirst for soon our portion be,
   To gaze on thee unveiled, and see thy face,
   The vision of thy glory and thy grace.

St Thomas Aquinas 1227–74
Tr James Woodford 1820–85

309 VICTIM Divine, thy grace we claim
      While thus thy precious death we show;
      Once offered up, a spotless Lamb,
      In thy great temple here below,
      Thou didst for all mankind atone,
      And standest now before the throne.

2 Thou standest in the holiest place,
   As now for guilty sinners slain;
   Thy blood of sprinkling speaks and prays
   All-prevalent for helpless man;
   Thy blood is still our ransom found,
   And spreads salvation all around.

3 We need not now go up to heaven
To bring the long-sought Saviour down;
Thou art to all already given,
Thou dost e'en now thy banquet crown:
To every faithful soul appear,
And show thy real presence here.

CHARLES WESLEY 1707–88

310 WE hail thy presence glorious,
O Christ our great high priest,
O'er sin and death victorious,
At thy thanksgiving feast:
As thou art interceding
For us in heaven above,
Thy Church on earth is pleading
Thy perfect work of love.

2 Through thee in every nation
Thine own their hearts upraise,
Offering one pure oblation,
One sacrifice of praise:
With thee in blest communion
The living and the dead
Are joined in closest union,
One body with one head.

3 O living Bread from heaven,
Jesu, our Saviour good,
Who thine own self hast given
To be our souls' true food;
For us thy body broken
Hung on the cross of shame:
This bread, its hallowed token,
We break in thy dear name.

4 O stream of love unending,
   Poured from the one true vine,
With our weak nature blending
   The strength of life divine;
Our thankful faith confessing
   In thy life-blood outpoured,
We drink this cup of blessing
   And praise thy name, O Lord.

RICHARD PARSONS 1882–1948

311 WE pray thee, heavenly Father,
   To hear us in thy love,
And pour upon thy children
   The unction from above;
That so in love abiding,
   From all defilement free,
We may in pureness offer
   Our Eucharist to thee.

2 All that we have we offer,
   For it is all thine own,
All gifts, by thine appointment,
   In bread and cup are shown;
One thing alone we bring not,
   The wilfulness of sin,
And all we bring is nothing
   Save that which is within.

319

3   Within the pure oblation,
     Beneath the outward sign,
By that his operation,—
     The Holy Ghost divine,—
Lies hid the sacred body,
     Lies hid the precious blood,
Once slain, now ever glorious,
     Of Christ our Lord and God.

4   Wherefore, though all unworthy
     To offer sacrifice,
We pray that this our duty
     Be pleasing in thine eyes;
For praise, and thanks and worship,
     For mercy and for aid,
The catholic oblation
     Of Jesus Christ is made.

V. S. STUCKEY COLES 1845–1929

312   WHERE the appointed sacrifice
     Of worship, praise and fervent prayer,
Ascends from earth unto the skies,
     The very gate of heaven is there.

2   He whom the worlds cannot contain,
     Our great, our universal Lord,
Among his people here doth deign
     His living presence to afford.

3   Open our eyes, O Christ, to see
     The heavenly glory with us here;
These sacramental gifts shall be
     Effectual signs that thou art near.

4   Father, through him we offer up
        Ourselves for ever thine to be,
    Who by this bread and by this cup
        Are one with Christ our Lord in thee.

G. B. TIMMS b 1910
verses 1 and 2 based on lines by
W. DRENNAN 1754–1820

313   WHEREFORE, O Father, we thy humble
            servants
        Here bring before thee Christ thy well-belovèd,
        All-perfect Offering, Sacrifice immortal,
                Spotless Oblation.

2   See now thy children, making intercession
    Through him our Saviour, Son of God
        incarnate,
    For all thy people, living and departed,
            Pleading before thee.

WILLIAM JERVOIS 1852–1905

314   WITH solemn faith we offer up,
            And spread before thy glorious eyes
        That only ground of all our hope,
            That all-sufficient sacrifice,
        Which brings thy grace on sinners down,
        And perfects all our souls in one.

2 Father, behold thy dying Son,
  And hear the blood that speaks above;
On us let all thy grace be shown,
  Peace, righteousness and joy and love:
Thy kingdom come to every heart,
And all thou hast, and all thou art.

CHARLES WESLEY 1707–88†

315 *For a gradual*

WORD of the Father, source of all things living,
Word once made flesh, our true and only
  Saviour,
Grow in our hearts, O seed of heaven's harvest,
  Jesus, Redeemer.

2 Gospel from heaven, living Word incarnate,
Open our minds, Lord, teach us your true
  wisdom;
Lamp to our footsteps, scatter all our darkness,
  Day-star of glory.

3 Lord of the faithful, guide us on our journey;
Pilgrims, we hunger for the life of heaven;
Jesus, our manna, feed us with your goodness,
  Here and hereafter.

G. B. TIMMS b 1910

See also
Hymns for Sunday 254–257

316   *Of Infants*

SING to the Lord glad hymns of praise,
    His works of grace proclaim,
Who guides his children all their days,
    From age to age the same.

2   Forth from his home in heaven above
        He came mankind to save;
    In life revealed the Father's love,
        In death subdued the grave.

3   He at a maiden's breast was fed,
        Though Son of God was he;
    He learned the first small words he said
        At a virgin mother's knee.

4   Close to his heart of love he holds
        The children of his grace,
    With everlasting arms enfolds
        The babes of human race.

5   Here in baptismal water blest
        He claims them for his own,
    While in their souls, with faith confessed,
        The seed of life is sown.

6 Keep them, O Lord, in thy strong love,
  That, guarded by thy grace,
They may at length in heaven above
  Behold our Father's face.

EDITORS, partly based on
verses by R. S. HAWKER 1804–75

See also

344 Children of the heavenly King
387 Jesus, good above all other

317 *Of Adults*

WITH Christ we share a mystic grave,
  With Christ we buried lie:
But not within the darksome cave
  By mournful Calvary.

2 The pure and bright baptismal flood
    Entombs our nature's stain:
New creatures from the cleansing wave
    In Christ we rise again.

3 Thrice blest, if through this world of sin,
    Of lust and selfish care,
Our resurrection robe of white
    All undefiled we wear.

4 Thrice blest, if through the gate of death,
    Glorious at last and free,
We to our joyful rising pass,
    O risen Lord with thee.

5   And now to thy thrice holy Name,
        The God whom we adore,
    To Father, Son, and Spirit blest,
        Be glory evermore.   Amen.

Attributed to J. M. NEALE 1818–66†

See also

58 The sinless one to Jordan came
114 Now is eternal life
369 Happy are they, they that love God

CONFIRMATION

318   MY God, accept my heart this day
             And make it always thine,
         That I from thee no more may stray,
             No more from thee decline.

2   Before the cross of him who died,
        Behold, I prostrate fall;
    Let every sin be crucified,
        And Christ be all in all.

3   Anoint me with thy heavenly grace,
        And seal me for thine own,
    That I may run this earthly race
        In thy strong might alone.

4   Let every thought and work and word
        To thee be ever given,
    Then life shall be thy service, Lord,
        And death the gate of heaven.

5   The vision of thy glory there
      Shall be my hope and song,
  That where thou dost a place prepare,
      I may at length belong.

MATTHEW BRIDGES 1800–94
and EDITORS

See also

MARRIAGE

319 O GOD, whose loving hand has led
    Thy children to this joyful day,
    We pray that thou wilt bless them now
    As, one in thee, they face life's way.

2 Grant them the will to follow Christ
    Who graced the feast in Galilee,
    And through his perfect life of love
    Fulfilment of their love to see.

3 Give them the power to make a home
  Where peace and honour shall abide,
  Where Christ shall be the gracious head,
  The trusted friend, the constant guide.

JOHN BOYD MOORE

320 O PERFECT Love, all human thought
    transcending,
  Lowly we kneel in prayer before thy throne,
That theirs may be the love that knows no
    ending
  Whom thou for evermore dost join in one.

2 O perfect Life, be thou their full assurance
  Of tender charity and steadfast faith,
Of patient hope, and quiet brave endurance,
  With childlike trust that fears nor pain nor
    death.

3 Grant them the joy that brightens earthly
    sorrow,
  Grant them the peace which calms all earthly
    strife;
And to life's day the glorious unknown morrow
  That dawns upon eternal love and life.

DOROTHY F. GURNEY 1858–1932

See also

357 Father, hear the prayer we offer
369 Happy are they, they that love God
393 Lead us, heavenly Father, lead us
408 Love divine, all loves excelling
419 O Holy Spirit, Lord of grace
459 The Lord's my shepherd, I'll not want

321   *Suitable also for general use*

GO forth for God; go forth to the world in
     peace;
Be of good courage, armed with heavenly grace,
In God's good Spirit daily to increase,
Till in his kingdom we behold his face.

2   Go forth for God; go forth to the world in
       strength;
Hold fast the good, be urgent for the right,
Render to no man evil; Christ at length
Shall overcome all darkness with his light.

3   Go forth for God; go forth to the world in love;
Strengthen the faint, give courage to the weak,
Help the afflicted; richly from above
His love supplies the grace and power we seek.

4   Go forth for God; go forth to the world in joy,
To serve Christ's brethren every day and hour,
And serving Christ, his every gift employ,
Rejoicing in the Holy Spirit's power.

5   Sing praise to him who brought us on our way,
Sing praise to him who bought us with his blood,
Sing praise to him who sanctifies each day,
Sing praise to him who reigns one Lord and
     God.

J. R. PEACEY 1896–1971
and EDITORS

322 POUR out thy Spirit from on high;
    Lord, thine assembled servants bless;
Graces and gifts to each supply,
    And clothe thy priests with righteousness.

2 Within the temple when they stand,
    To teach the truth, as taught by thee,
Saviour, like stars in thy right hand
    May all thy Church's pastors be.

3 Wisdom, and zeal, and faith impart,
    Firmness with meekness, from above,
To bear thy people in their heart,
    And love the souls whom thou dost love:

4 To watch, and pray, and never faint,
    By day and night, strict guard to keep,
To warn the sinner, cheer the saint,
    Nourish thy lambs, and feed thy sheep.

5 Then, when their work is finished here,
    May they in hope their charge resign;
When the Chief Shepherd shall appear,
    O God, may they and we be thine.

JAMES MONTGOMERY 1771–1854‡

See also

141 Holy Spirit, ever dwelling
361 Forth in the peace of Christ we go
431 O thou who camest from above
482 Spread, O spread, thou mighty word
483 The Church of God a kingdom is
486 We have a gospel to proclaim

323   FATHER of mercy, God of consolation,
    Look on your people, gathered here to praise
        you,
    Pity our weakness, come in power to aid us,
        Source of all blessing.

  2   Son of the Father, Lord of all creation,
    Come as our Saviour, Jesus, friend of sinners,
    Grant us forgiveness, lift our downcast spirit,
        Heal us and save us.

  3   Life-giving Spirit, be our light in darkness,
    Come to befriend us, help us bear our burdens,
    Give us true courage, breathe your peace around
        us,
        Stay with us always.

  4   God in Three Persons, Father, Son and Spirit,
    Come to renew us, fill your Church with glory,
    Grant us your healing, pledge of resurrection,
        Foretaste of heaven.

JAMES QUINN, S. J. b 1919

While of general use also, this hymn is specially suitable at the laying-on-of-hands or anointing of the sick.

324   THINE arm, O Lord, in days of old
    Was strong to heal and save;
  It triumphed o'er disease and death,
    O'er darkness and the grave;
  To thee they went, the blind, the dumb,
    The palsied and the lame,
  The leper with his tainted life,
    The sick with fevered frame.

2 And lo! thy touch brought life and health,
     Gave speech, and strength, and sight;
   And youth renewed and frenzy calmed
     Owned thee the Lord of light;
   And now, O Lord, be near to bless,
     Almighty as of yore,
   In crowded street, by restless couch,
     As by Gennesareth's shore.

3 Be thou our great deliverer still,
     Thou Lord of life and death;
   Restore and quicken, soothe and bless
     With thine almighty breath;
   To hands that work, and eyes that see,
     Give wisdom's heavenly lore,
   That whole and sick, and weak and strong,
     May praise thee evermore.

EDWARD PLUMPTRE 1821–91

325 *Intercession for the sick*

THOU to whom the sick and dying
  Ever came, nor came in vain,
With thy healing hands replying
  To their wearied cry of pain,
    Hear us, Jesu, as we meet
    Suppliant at thy mercy seat.

2　Still the weary, sick and dying
　　　Call for hands of loving care;
On thy help and grace relying,
　　　Grant we may their burden share,
　　　　And thy heart of love intreat,
　　　　Suppliant at thy mercy seat.

3　May thy people all be willing,
　　　Ready both in mind and heart,
Thus the heavenly law fulfilling,
　　　Strength and solace to impart,
　　　　And thy heart of love intreat,
　　　　Suppliant at thy mercy seat.

4　So may sickness, sin and sadness
　　　To thy powerful presence yield,
And the sick and sad, in gladness,
　　　Rescued, ransomed, cleansed and healed,
　　　　Joyful, praise thy heart of love
　　　　With the heavenly Church above.

EDITORS, altered from verses by
GODFREY THRING 1823–1903

See also

102　A brighter dawn is breaking
139　Come, thou Holy Spirit, come
243　At even, when the sun was set
378　Immortal love, for ever full
415　O for a thousand tongues to sing

326   *Hic breve vivitur*

BRIEF life is here our portion,
   Brief sorrow, short-lived care;
The life that knows no ending,
   The tearless life is there.

2 O happy retribution,
      Short toil, eternal rest;
   For mortals and for sinners
      A mansion with the blest.

3 There grief is turned to pleasure,
      Such pleasure as below
   No human voice can utter,
      No human heart can know.

4 For he whom now we trust in
      Shall then be seen and known,
   And they that know and see him,
      Shall have him for their own.

5 The morning shall awaken,
      The shadows shall decay,
   And each true-hearted servant
      Shall shine as doth the day.

6 Then all the halls of Sion
      For ay shall be complete,
   And in the Land of Beauty,
      All things of beauty meet.

BERNARD OF CLUNY 12th century
Tr J. M. NEALE 1818–66

327   *De profundis Ps 130*

CHRIST, enthroned in highest heaven,
    Hear us, crying from the deep
For the faithful ones departed,
    For the souls of all that sleep;
As thy kneeling Church entreateth,
    Hearken, Shepherd of the sheep.

2★ King of glory, hear our voices,
    Grant the faithful rest, we pray;
We have sinned and may not bide it,
    If thou mark our steps astray,
Yet we plead that saving victim,
    Which for them we bring today.

3★ That which thou thyself hast offered
    To thy Father, offer we:
By thy sacrifice, O Jesu,
    From sin's burden set them free;
Hear us, loving friend of sinners,
    Merciful and gracious be.

4 They are thine, O take them to thee;
    Thou their hope, O raise them high;
In thy mercy ever trusting,
    Confident we make our cry
That the souls whom thou hast purchased
    May unto thy heart be nigh.

5 Let thy plenteous loving-kindness
    On them evermore be poured;
Let them through thy boundless mercy
    Be to boundless life restored,
And within thy Father's mansions
    Give to each a place, O Lord.

6 Where the saints, thy throne surrounding,
   Join in the angelic song,
Where thy Mother, raised in glory,
   Leads the great redeemèd throng,
Grant that we, with souls departed,
   May through grace at length belong.

Latin, 13th century Sequence
Tr R. F. LITTLEDALE 1833–90
and revised by EDITORS

328 GOD be in my head,
      And in my understanding;

2 God be in mine eyes,
   And in my looking;

3 God be in my mouth,
   And in my speaking;

4 God be in my heart,
   And in my thinking;

5 God be at mine end,
   And at my departing.

Horae B. V. M. (Sarum) 1514

329 *At Holy Communion*

JESU, Son of Mary,
   Fount of life alone,
Here we hail thee present
   On thine altar-throne.
Humbly we adore thee,
   Lord of endless might,
In the mystic symbols
   Veiled from earthly sight.

2 Think, O Lord, in mercy
   On the souls of those
Who, in faith gone from us,
   Now in death repose.
Here 'mid stress and conflict
   Toils can never cease;
There, the warfare ended,
   Bid them rest in peace.

3 Often were they wounded
   In the deadly strife;
Heal them, Good Physician,
   With the balm of life.
Every taint of evil,
   Frailty and decay,
Good and gracious Saviour,
   Cleanse and purge away.

4 Rest eternal grant them,
   After weary fight;
Shed on them the radiance
   Of thy heavenly light.
Lead them onward, upward,
   To the holy place,
Where thy saints made perfect
   Gaze upon thy face.

Swahili, *Tr* EDMUND PALMER 1856–1931

330   WHAT sweet of life endureth
      Unmixed with bitter pain?
   'Midst earthly change and chances
      What glory doth remain?

2 All is a feeble shadow,
      A dream that will not stay;
Death cometh in a moment,
      And taketh all away.

3 O Christ, a light transcendent
      Shines in thy countenance,
And none can tell the sweetness,
      The beauty of thy glance.

4 In this may thy poor servants
      Their joy eternal find;
Thou calledst them, O rest them,
      Thou lover of mankind!

Greek, ST JOHN OF DAMASCUS c 750
Tr ATHELSTAN RILEY 1858–1945

See also

PART IV

GENERAL HYMNS

331   ABIDE with me; fast falls the eventide;
The darkness deepens; Lord, with me abide!
When other helpers fail, and comforts flee,
Help of the helpless, O abide with me.

2   Swift to its close ebbs out life's little day;
Earth's joys grow dim, its glories pass away;
Change and decay in all around I see;
O thou who changest not, abide with me.

3   I need thy presence every passing hour;
What but thy grace can foil the tempter's power?
Who like thyself my guide and stay can be?
Through cloud and sunshine, O abide with me.

4   I fear no foe with thee at hand to bless;
Ills have no weight, and tears no bitterness.
Where is death's sting? where, grave, thy
        victory?
I triumph still, if thou abide with me.

5   Hold thou thy cross before my closing eyes;
Shine through the gloom, and point me to the
        skies:
Heaven's morning breaks, and earth's vain
        shadows flee;
In life, in death, O Lord, abide with me!

H. F. LYTE 1793–1847

332 ALL hail the power of Jesu's name;
    Let angels prostrate fall;
Bring forth the royal diadem
    To crown him Lord of all.

2* Crown him, ye morning stars of light,
    Who fixed this floating ball;
Now hail the Strength of Israel's might,
    And crown him Lord of all.

3* Crown him, ye martyrs of your God,
    Who from his altar call;
Praise him whose way of pain ye trod,
    And crown him Lord of all.

4 Ye seed of Israel's chosen race,
    Ye ransomed of the fall,
Hail him who saves you by his grace,
    And crown him Lord of all.

5 Hail him, ye heirs of David's line,
    Whom David Lord did call;
The God incarnate, Man divine,
    And crown him Lord of all.

6 Sinners, whose love can ne'er forget
    The wormwood and the gall,
Go spread your trophies at his feet,
    And crown him Lord of all.

7 Let every tribe and every tongue
    To him their hearts enthral,
Lift high the universal song,
    And crown him Lord of all.

EDWARD PERRONET 1726–92
and others

333 ALL my hope on God is founded;
  He doth still my trust renew.
Me through change and chance he guideth,
  Only good and only true.
   God unknown,
   He alone
  Calls my heart to be his own.

2 Pride of man and earthly glory,
  Sword and crown betray his trust;
What with care and toil he buildeth,
  Tower and temple, fall to dust
   But God's power,
   Hour by hour,
  Is my temple and my tower.

3 God's great goodness aye endureth,
  Deep his wisdom, passing thought:
Splendour, light and life attend him,
  Beauty springeth out of naught.
   Evermore
   From his store
  New-born worlds rise and adore.

4 Daily doth th'Almighty giver
  Bounteous gifts on us bestow;
His desire our soul delighteth,
  Pleasure leads us where we go.
   Love doth stand
   At his hand;
  Joy doth wait on his command.

5 Still from man to God eternal
   Sacrifice of praise be done,
High above all praises praising
   For the gift of Christ his Son.
     Christ doth call
     One and all:
   Ye who follow shall not fall.

ROBERT BRIDGES 1844–1930
based on the German of
J. NEANDER 1650–80

334   *Psalm 100*

ALL people that on earth do dwell,
   Sing to the Lord with cheerful voice;
Him serve with fear, his praise forth tell,
   Come ye before him, and rejoice.

2 The Lord, ye know, is God indeed,
   Without our aid he did us make;
We are his folk, he doth us feed,
   And for his sheep he doth us take.

3 O enter then his gates with praise,
   Approach with joy his courts unto;
Praise, laud, and bless his name always,
   For it is seemly so to do.

4 For why? the Lord our God is good:
   His mercy is for ever sure;
His truth at all times firmly stood,
   And shall from age to age endure.

5   To Father, Son, and Holy Ghost,
      The God whom heaven and earth adore,
  From men and from the Angel-host
      Be praise and glory evermore.   Amen.

WILLIAM KETHE d 1594

335   ALL praise to thee, for thou, O King divine,
      Didst yield the glory that of right was thine,
      That in our darkened hearts thy grace might
          shine:
                           Alleluya!

2   Thou cam'st to us in lowliness of thought;
    By thee the outcast and the poor were sought,
    And by thy death was God's salvation wrought:
                          Alleluya!

3   Let this mind be in us which was in thee,
    Who wast a servant that we might be free,
    Humbling thyself to death on Calvary:
                          Alleluya!

4   Wherefore, by God's eternal purpose, thou
    Art high exalted o'er all creatures now,
    And giv'n the name to which all knees shall bow:
                          Alleluya!

5 Let ev'ry tongue confess with one accord
  In heav'n and earth that Jesus Christ is Lord;
  And God the Father be by all adored:

  Alleluya!

F. BLAND TUCKER 1895–1984
based on Philippians 2. 5–11

336 ANGEL-VOICES ever singing
      Round thy throne of light,
    Angel-harps for ever ringing,
      Rest not day nor night;
    Thousands only live to bless thee
      And confess thee
        Lord of might.

2 Thou who art beyond the farthest
      Mortal eye can scan,
    Can it be that thou regardest
      Songs of sinful man?
    Can we know that thou art near us,
      And wilt hear us?
        Yes, we can.

3 For we know that thou rejoicest
      O'er each work of thine;
    Thou didst ears and hands and voices
      For thy praise design;
    Craftsman's art and music's measure
      For thy pleasure
        All combine.

4 In thy house, great God, we offer
    Of thine own to thee;
And for thine acceptance proffer
    All unworthily
Hearts and minds and hands and voices
    In our choicest
        Psalmody.

5 Honour, glory, might and merit
    Thine shall ever be,
Father, Son and Holy Spirit,
    Blessed Trinity.
Of the best which thou hast given
    Earth and heaven
        Render thee.

FRANCIS POTT 1832–190

337   *Psalm 42*

AS pants the hart for cooling streams
    When heated in the chase,
So longs my soul, O God, for thee,
    And thy refreshing grace.

2 For thee, my God, the living God,
    My thirsty soul doth pine:
O when shall I behold thy face,
    Thou Majesty Divine!

3 Why restless, why cast down, my soul?
    Hope still, and thou shalt sing
The praise of him who is thy God,
    Thy health's eternal spring.

4 To Father, Son, and Holy Ghost,
   The God whom we adore,
Be glory, as it was, is now,
   And shall be evermore. Amen.

      TATE and BRADY New Version 1696

338   AT the name of Jesus
      Every knee shall bow,
   Every tongue confess him
      King of glory now;
   'Tis the Father's pleasure
      We should call him Lord,
   Who from the beginning
      Was the mighty Word.

2 At his voice creation
      Sprang at once to sight,
   All the angel faces,
      All the hosts of light,
   Thrones and dominations,
      Stars upon their way,
   All the heavenly orders,
      In their great array.

3 Humbled for a season,
      To receive a name
   From the lips of sinners
      Unto whom he came,
   Faithfully he bore it
      Spotless to the last,
   Brought it back victorious
      When from death he passed:

4 Bore it up triumphant
    With its human light,
Through all ranks of creatures,
    To the central height,
To the throne of Godhead,
    To the Father's breast;
Filled it with the glory
    Of that perfect rest.

5 In your hearts enthrone him;
    There let him subdue
All that is not holy,
    All that is not true:
He is God the Saviour,
    He is Christ the Lord,
Ever to be worshipped,
    Trusted, and adored.

6* Brothers, this Lord Jesus
    Shall return again,
With the Father's glory,
    With his angel train;
For all wreaths of empire
    Meet upon his brow,
And our hearts confess him
    King of glory now.

CAROLINE NOEL 1817–77

339 BE thou my vision, O Lord of my heart,
Be all else but naught to me, save that thou art,
Be thou my best thought in the day and the
     night,
Both waking and sleeping, thy presence my
     light.

2 Be thou my wisdom, be thou my true word
Be thou ever with me, and I with thee, Lord,
Be thou my great Father, and I thy true son,
Be thou in me dwelling, and I with thee one.

3 Be thou my breastplate, my sword for the fight,
Be thou my whole armour, be thou my true
     might,
Be thou my soul's shelter, be thou my strong
     tower,
O raise thou me heavenward, great Power of my
     power.

4 Riches I heed not, nor man's empty praise,
Be thou my inheritance now and always,
Be thou and thou only the first in my heart,
O Sovereign of heaven, my treasure thou art.

5 High King of heaven, thou heaven's bright
     Sun,
O grant me its joys after vict'ry is won,
Great Heart of my own heart, whatever befall,
Still be thou my vision, O Ruler of all.

Irish c 8th century
Tr MARY BYRNE 1880–1931
Versified ELEANOR HULL 1860–1935

340 BEYOND all mortal praise
        God's name be ever blest,
Unsearchable his ways,
        His glory manifest;
                From his high throne
                        In power and might
                        By wisdom's light
                He rules alone.

2 Our times are in his hand
        To whom all flesh is grass,
While as their Maker planned
        The changing seasons pass.
                He orders all:
                        Before his eyes
                        Earth's empires rise
                Her kingdoms fall.

3 He gives to humankind,
        Dividing as he will,
All powers of heart and mind,
        Of spirit, strength and skill:
                Nor dark nor night
                        But must lay bare
                        Its secrets, where
                He dwells in light.

4 To God the only Lord,
        Our fathers' God, be praise;
His holy name adored
        Through everlasting days.
                His mercies trace
                        In answered prayer,
                        In love and care,
                And gifts of grace.

TIMOTHY DUDLEY-SMITH b 1926

341   BLEST are the pure in heart,
For they shall see our God,
The secret of the Lord is theirs,
    Their soul is Christ's abode.

2   The Lord, who left the heavens
Our life and peace to bring,
To dwell in lowliness with men,
    Their pattern and their King;

3   Still to the lowly soul
He doth himself impart,
And for his dwelling and his throne
    Chooseth the pure in heart.

4   Lord, we thy presence seek;
May ours this blessing be;
Give us a pure and lowly heart,
    A temple meet for thee.

JOHN KEBLE 1792–1866
and others

342   BREATHE on me, Breath of God,
Fill me with life anew,
That I may love what thou dost love,
    And do what thou wouldst do.

2   Breathe on me, Breath of God,
Until my heart is pure,
Until with thee I will one will,
    To do and to endure.

3   Breathe on me, Breath of God,
       Till I am wholly thine,
Until this earthly part of me
       Glows with the fire divine.

4   Breathe on me, Breath of God,
       So shall I never die,
But live with thee the perfect life
       Of thine eternity.

EDWIN HATCH 1835–89

343   BRIGHT the vision that delighted
       Once the sight of Judah's seer;
Sweet the countless tongues united
       To entrance the prophet's ear.

2   Round the Lord in glory seated
       Cherubim and seraphim
Filled his temple, and repeated
       Each to each the alternate hymn:

3   'Lord, thy glory fills the heaven;
       Earth is with its fullness stored;
Unto thee be glory given,
       Holy, Holy, Holy, Lord.'

4   Heaven is still with glory ringing,
       Earth takes up the angels' cry,
'Holy, Holy, Holy,' singing,
       'Lord of hosts, the Lord most high.'

5 With his seraph train before him,
   With his holy Church below,
Thus unite we to adore him,
   Bid we thus our anthem flow:

6 'Lord thy glory fills the heaven;
   Earth is with its fullness stored;
Unto thee be glory given,
   Holy, Holy, Holy, Lord.'

RICHARD MANT 1776–1848

344 CHILDREN of the heavenly King,
   As ye journey sweetly sing;
Sing your Saviour's worthy praise,
Glorious in his works and ways.

2 We are travelling home to God,
   In the way the fathers trod;
They are happy now, and we
Soon their happiness shall see.

3 Fear not, brethren; joyful stand
   On the borders of your land:
Jesus Christ your Father's Son,
Bids you undismayed go on.

4 Lift your eyes ye sons of light,
   Sion's city is in sight;
There our endless home shall be,
There our Lord in glory see.

JOHN CENNICK 1718–55†

345 CHRIST is the King, O friends rejoice!
Brothers and sisters, with one voice
Make all men know he is your choice:
> Alleluya.

2 The first Apostles round them drew
Thousands of faithful men and true,
Sharing a faith for ever new:
> Alleluya.

3 Then magnify the Lord and raise
Anthems of joy and holy praise
For Christ's brave saints of ancient days:
> Alleluya.

4 O Christian women, Christian men,
All the world over, seek again
The Way disciples followed then:
> Alleluya.

5 Christ through all ages is the same;
Place the same hope in his great name,
With the same faith his word proclaim:
> Alleluya.

6 Let Love's unconquerable might
God's people everywhere unite
In service to the Lord of light:
> Alleluya.

GEORGE BELL 1883–1958†

346 CITY of God, how broad and far
        Outspread thy walls sublime!
    The true thy chartered freemen are
        Of every age and clime.

2 One holy Church, one army strong,
        One steadfast, high intent;
    One working band, one harvest-song,
        One King omnipotent.

3 How purely hath thy speech come down
        From man's primaeval youth!
    How grandly hath thine empire grown
        Of freedom, love and truth!

4 How gleam thy watch-fires through the night
        With never-fainting ray!
    How rise thy towers, serene and bright,
        To meet the dawning day!

5 In vain the surge's angry shock,
        In vain the drifting sands:
    Unharmed upon the eternal Rock
        The eternal City stands.

SAMUEL JOHNSON 1822–82

347 COME, gracious Spirit, heavenly Dove,
    With light and comfort from above;
    Be thou our guardian, thou our guide,
    O'er every thought and step preside.

2 The light of truth to us display,
　And make us know and choose thy way;
Plant faith and love in every heart,
　That we from God may ne'er depart.

3 Lead us to Christ, the living Way,
　Nor let us from our shepherd stray;
Lead us to holiness, the road
　That brings us to our home in God.

4 Lead us to heaven, that we may share
　Fulness of joy for ever there;
Lead us to God, the heart's true rest,
　To dwell with him, for ever blest.

SIMON BROWNE 1680–1732
and others

348 *Suitable for the Gradual*

COME, Holy Ghost, our hearts inspire,
　Let us thine influence prove;
Source of the old prophetic fire,
　Fountain of life and love.

2 Come, Holy Ghost—for, moved by thee,
　Thy prophets wrote and spoke—
Unlock the truth, thyself the key,
　Unseal the sacred book.

3 Expand thy wings, celestial Dove,
　Brood o'er our nature's night;
On our disordered spirits move,
　And let there now be light.

4 God, through himself, we then shall know,
   If thou within us shine;
And sound, with all thy saints below,
   The depths of love divine.

CHARLES WESLEY 1707–88

349 COME, let us join our cheerful songs
   With angels round the throne;
Ten thousand thousand are their tongues,
   But all their joys are one.

2 'Worthy the Lamb that died,' they cry,
   'To be exalted thus;'
'Worthy the Lamb,' our lips reply,
   'For he was slain for us.'

3 Jesus is worthy to receive
   Honour and power divine;
And blessings more than we can give
   Be, Lord, for ever thine.

4 Let all creation join in one
   To bless the sacred name
Of him that sits upon the throne,
   And to adore the Lamb.

ISAAC WATTS 1674–1748†

350 COME, O thou Traveller unknown,
   Whom still I hold, but cannot see;
My company before is gone,
   And I am left alone with thee;
With thee all night I mean to stay
And wrestle till the break of day.

2   I need not tell thee who I am,
      My misery and sin declare;
  Thyself hast called me by my name,
      Look on thy hands and read it there:
  But who, I ask thee, who art thou?
  Tell me thy name, and tell me now.

3   In vain thou strugglest to get free;
      I never will unloose my hold:
  Art thou the Man that died for me?
      The secret of thy love unfold:
  Wrestling, I will not let thee go
  Till I thy name, thy nature know.

4   Yield to me now, for I am weak,
      But confident, in self-despair;
  Speak to my heart, in blessings speak,
      Be conquered by my instant prayer:
  Speak, or thou never hence shalt move,
  And tell me if thy name is Love.

5   'Tis Love, 'tis Love! Thou diedst for me!
      I hear thy whisper in my heart;
  The morning breaks, the shadows flee,
      Pure, universal Love thou art:
  To me, to all, thy mercies move;
  Thy nature and thy name is Love.

Cento from verses by
CHARLES WESLEY 1707–88

The hymn is based on Jacob's wrestling with the angel in Genesis 32. 24–30.

351 COME, ye faithful, raise the anthem,
  Cleave the skies with shouts of praise;
Sing to him who found the ransom,
  Ancient of eternal days,
God eternal, Word incarnate,
  Whom the heaven of heaven obeys.

2 Ere he raised the lofty mountains,
  Formed the sea, or built the sky,
Love eternal, free, and boundless,
  Forced the Lord of life to die,
Lifted up the Prince of princes
  On the throne of Calvary.

3 Now on those eternal mountains
  Stands the sapphire throne, all bright,
With the ceaseless alleluyas
  Which they raise, the sons of light;
Sion's people tell his praises,
  Victor after hard-won fight.

4 Bring your harps, and bring your incense,
  Sweep the string and pour the lay;
Let the earth proclaim his wonders,
  King of that celestial day;
He the Lamb once slain is worthy,
  Who was dead, and lives for ay.

5 Laud and honour to the Father,
  Laud and honour to the Son,
Laud and honour to the Spirit,
  Ever Three and ever One,
One in love, and One in splendour,
  While unending ages run.   Amen.

JOB HUPTON 1762–1849
and J. M. NEALE 1818–66

352   CROWN him with many crowns,
        The Lamb upon his throne;
Hark! how the heavenly anthem drowns
        All music but its own:
        Awake, my soul, and sing
        Of him who died for thee,
And hail him as thy matchless King
        Through all eternity.

2   Crown him the Virgin's Son,
        The God incarnate born,
Whose arm those crimson trophies won
        Which now his brow adorn:
        Fruit of the mystic Rose,
        As of that Rose the Stem;
The Root whence mercy ever flows,
        The Babe of Bethlehem.

3   Crown him the Lord of love!
        Behold his hands and side,
Rich wounds yet visible above
        In beauty glorified:
        No angel in the sky
        Can fully bear that sight,
But downward bends his burning eye
        At mysteries so bright.

4   Crown him the Lord of peace,
        Whose power a sceptre sways
From pole to pole, that wars may cease,
        Absorbed in prayer and praise:
        His reign shall know no end,
        And round his piercèd feet
Fair flowers of Paradise extend
        Their fragrance ever sweet.

5   Crown him the Lord of years,
      The Potentate of time,
Creator of the rolling spheres,
    Ineffably sublime.
    Glassed in a sea of light,
    Where everlasting waves
Reflect his throne—the Infinite!
    Who lives—and loves—and saves.

MATTHEW BRIDGES 1800–94

The 'mystic Rose' in verse 2 is a mediaeval title for the Blessed Virgin

353   DEAR Lord and Father of mankind,
      Forgive our foolish ways!
Re-clothe us in our rightful mind,
In purer lives thy service find,
    In deeper reverence praise.

2   In simple trust like theirs who heard,
      Beside the Syrian sea,
The gracious calling of the Lord,
Let us, like them, without a word
    Rise up and follow thee.

3*   O Sabbath rest by Galilee!
      O calm of hills above,
Where Jesus knelt to share with thee
The silence of eternity,
    Interpreted by love!

4   Drop thy still dews of quietness,
        Till all our strivings cease;
    Take from our souls the strain and stress,
    And let our ordered lives confess
        The beauty of thy peace.

5   Breathe through the heats of our desire
        Thy coolness and thy balm;
    Let sense be dumb, let flesh retire;
    Speak through the earthquake, wind, and fire,
        O still small voice of calm!

JOHN WHITTIER 1807–92

354   ETERNAL Father, strong to save,
        Whose arm doth bind the restless wave,
        Who bidd'st the mighty ocean deep
        Its own appointed limits keep;
            O hear us when we cry to thee
            For those in peril on the sea.

2   O Saviour, whose almighty word
    The winds and waves submissive heard,
    Who walkedst on the foaming deep,
    And calm amid its rage didst sleep:
        O hear us when we cry to thee
        For those in peril on the sea.

3   O sacred Spirit, who didst brood
    Upon the chaos dark and rude,
    Who bad'st its angry tumult cease,
    And gavest light and life and peace:
        O hear us when we cry to thee
        For those in peril on the sea.

4 O Trinity of love and power,
Our brethren shield in danger's hour;
From rock and tempest, fire and foe,
Protect them whereso'er they go:
And ever let there rise to thee
Glad hymns of praise from land and sea.

WILLIAM WHITING 1825–78

355 ETERNAL Ruler of the ceaseless round
Of circling planets singing on their way;
Guide to the nations from the night profound
Into the glory of the perfect day;
Rule in our hearts, that we may ever be
Guided and strengthened and upheld by thee.

2 We are of thee, the children of thy love,
The brothers of thy well-belovèd Son;
Descend, O Holy Spirit, like a dove,
Into our hearts, that we may be as one:
As one with thee, to whom we ever tend;
As one with him, our Brother and our Friend.

3 We would be one in hatred of all wrong,
One in our love of all things sweet and fair,
One with the joy that breaketh into song,
One with the grief that trembleth into prayer,
One in the power that makes the children free
To follow truth, and thus to follow thee.

4   O clothe us with thy heavenly armour, Lord,
     Thy trusty shield, thy sword of love divine;
  Our inspiration be thy constant word;
     We ask no victories that are not thine:
  Give or withhold, let pain or pleasure be;
  Enough to know that we are serving thee.

JOHN CHADWICK 1840–1904

356   FATHER eternal, Lord of the ages,
     You who have made us, you who have called us:
     Look on your children gathered before you;
     Worship they bring you, Father of all.

2   Jesus our Saviour, born of a virgin,
     Truth from high heaven you came to teach us:
     You are the way that leads to the Father;
     Be now our life, both here and above.

3   Spirit all-holy, Spirit of mercy,
     Bind us in one with Christ and the Father:
     Give us all joy and peace in believing,
     Firm on the rock of faith in our God.

4   Father eternal; Jesus redeemer;
     Spirit all-holy; Trinity perfect:
     Unity endless, Love everlasting:
     Praise evermore we offer to you.

G. B. TIMMS b 1910

357 FATHER, hear the prayer we offer:
    Not for ease that prayer shall be,
But for strength that we may ever
    Live our lives courageously.

2 Not for ever in green pastures
    Do we ask our way to be;
But the steep and rugged pathway
    May we tread rejoicingly.

3 Not for ever by still waters
    Would we idly rest and stay;
But would smite the living fountains
    From the rocks along our way.

4 Be our strength in hours of weakness,
    In our wanderings be our guide;
Through endeavour, failure, danger,
    Father, be thou at our side.

MARIA WILLIS 1824–1908

358 FATHER of heaven, whose love profound
A ransom for our souls hath found,
Before thy throne we sinners bend:
To us thy pardoning love extend.

2 Almighty Son, incarnate Word,
Our Prophet, Priest, Redeemer, Lord,
Before thy throne we sinners bend:
To us thy saving grace extend.

3 Eternal Spirit, by whose breath
The soul is raised from sin and death,
Before thy throne we sinners bend:
To us thy quickening power extend.

4 Thrice Holy! Father, Spirit, Son,
Mysterious Godhead, Three in One,
Before thy throne we sinners bend:
Grace, pardon, life to us extend.   Amen.

EDWARD COOPER 1770–1833

359   FIGHT the good fight with all thy might,
Christ is thy strength, and Christ thy right;
Lay hold on life, and it shall be
Thy joy and crown eternally.

2 Run the straight race through God's good grace,
Lift up thine eyes, and seek his face;
Life with its way before us lies,
Christ is the path, and Christ the prize.

3 Cast care aside, upon thy Guide
Lean, and his mercy will provide;
Lean, and the trusting soul shall prove
Christ is its life, and Christ its love.

4 Faint not nor fear, his arms are near,
   He changeth not, and thou art dear;
   Only believe, and thou shalt see
   That Christ is all in all to thee.

J. S. B. MONSELL 1811–75

360 FIRMLY I believe and truly
           God is Three, and God is One;
        And I next acknowledge duly
           Manhood taken by the Son.

2 And I trust and hope most fully
      In that Manhood crucified;
   And each thought and deed unruly
      Do to death, as he has died.

3 Simply to his grace and wholly
      Light and life and strength belong,
   And I love supremely, solely,
      Him the holy, him the strong.

4 And I hold in veneration,
      For the love of him alone,
   Holy Church as his creation,
      And her teachings as his own.

5 Adoration ay be given,
      With and through the angelic host,
   To the God of earth and heaven,
      Father, Son, and Holy Ghost.   Amen.

JOHN HENRY NEWMAN 1801–90

361   *Prophets, priests, and kings*

FORTH in the peace of Christ we go;
  Christ to the world with joy we bring;
Christ in our minds, Christ on our lips,
  Christ in our hearts, the world's true King.

2 King of our hearts, Christ makes us kings;
    Kingship with him his servants gain;
  With Christ, the Servant-Lord of all,
    Christ's world we serve to share Christ's
      reign.

3 Priests of the world, Christ sends us forth
    This world of time to consecrate,
  This world of sin by grace to heal,
    Christ's world in Christ to re-create.

4 Christ's are our lips, his word we speak;
    Prophets are we whose deeds proclaim
  Christ's truth in love, that we may be
    Christ in the world, to spread Christ's name.

5 We are the Church; Christ bids us show
    That in his Church all nations find
  Their hearth and home, where Christ restores
    True peace, true love, to all mankind.

JAMES QUINN, S. J. b 1919

362 GLORIOUS things of thee are spoken,
    Sion, city of our God;
He whose word cannot be broken
    Formed thee for his own abode:
On the Rock of Ages founded,
    What can shake thy sure repose?
With salvation's walls surrounded,
    Thou may'st smile at all thy foes.

2 See, the streams of living waters,
    Springing from eternal love,
Well supply thy sons and daughters,
    And all fear of want remove:
Who can faint, while such a river
    Ever flows their thirst to assuage?
Grace, which like the Lord the giver,
    Never fails from age to age.

3 Saviour, if of Sion's city
    I through grace a member am,
Let the world deride or pity,
    I will glory in thy name:
Fading is the worldling's pleasure,
    All his boasted pomp and show;
Solid joys and lasting treasure
    None but Sion's children know.

JOHN NEWTON 1725–1807

363   *Gloria in excelsis*

GLORY in the highest to the God of heaven!
Peace to all your people through the earth be
    given:
Mighty God and Father, thanks and praise we
    bring,
Singing alleluyas to our heavenly King.

2 Jesus Christ is risen, God the Father's Son:
With the Holy Spirit, you are Lord alone!
Lamb once killed for sinners, all our guilt to
    bear,
Show us now your mercy, now receive our
    prayer.

3 Christ the world's true Saviour, high and holy
    one,
Seated now and reigning from your Father's
    throne:
Lord and God, we praise you; highest heaven
    adores:
In the Father's glory, all the praise be yours!

CHRISTOPHER IDLE b 1938

364   GOD is Love: let heav'n adore him;
      God is Love: let earth rejoice;
    Let creation sing before him,
      And exalt him with one voice.
    He who laid the earth's foundation,
      He who spread the heav'ns above,
    He who breathes through all creation,
      He is Love, eternal Love.

2 God is Love: and he enfoldeth
      All the world in one embrace;
   With unfailing grasp he holdeth
      Every child of every race.
   And when human hearts are breaking
      Under sorrow's iron rod,
   Then they find that selfsame aching
      Deep within the heart of God.

3 God is Love: and though with blindness
      Sin afflicts the souls of men,
   God's eternal loving-kindness
      Holds and guides them even then.
   Sin and death and hell shall never
      O'er us final triumph gain;
   God is Love, so Love for ever
      O'er the universe must reign.

TIMOTHY REES 1874–1939

365 GOD moves in a mysterious way
            His wonders to perform;
         He plants his footsteps in the sea,
            And rides upon the storm.

2 Deep in unfathomable mines
      Of never-failing skill
   He treasures up his bright designs,
      And works his sovereign will.

3 Ye fearful saints, fresh courage take,
      The clouds ye so much dread
   Are big with mercy, and shall break
      In blessings on your head.

4 Judge not the Lord by feeble sense,
    But trust him for his grace;
Behind a frowning providence
    He hides a smiling face.

5 His purposes will ripen fast,
    Unfolding every hour;
The bud may have a bitter taste,
    But sweet will be the flower.

6 Blind unbelief is sure to err,
    And scan his work in vain;
God is his own interpreter,
    And he will make it plain.

WILLIAM COWPER 1731–1800

366   *Psalm 67*

GOD of mercy, God of grace,
Show the brightness of thy face:
Shine upon us, Saviour, shine,
Fill thy Church with light divine;
And thy saving health extend
Unto earth's remotest end.

2 Let the people praise thee, Lord;
Be by all that live adored:
Let the nations shout and sing,
Glory to their Saviour King;
At thy feet their tributes pay,
And thy holy will obey.

3 Let the people praise thee, Lord;
   Earth shall then her fruits afford;
   God to man his blessing give,
   Man to God devoted live;
   All below, and all above,
   One in joy, and light, and love.

H. F. LYTE 1793–1847

367 GRACIOUS Spirit, Holy Ghost,
   Taught by thee, we covet most
   Of thy gifts at Pentecost,
      Holy, heavenly love.

2 Love is kind, and suffers long,
   Love is meek, and thinks no wrong,
   Love than death itself more strong;
      Therefore give us love.

3 Prophecy will fade away,
   Melting in the light of day;
   Love will ever with us stay;
      Therefore give us love.

4 Faith will vanish into sight;
   Hope be emptied in delight;
   Love in heaven will shine more bright;
      Therefore give us love.

5 Faith and hope and love we see
   Joining hand in hand agree;
   But the greatest of the three,
      And the best, is love.

6   From the overshadowing
     Of thy gold and silver wing
     Shed on us, who to thee sing,
       Holy, heavenly love.

CHRISTOPHER WORDSWORTH 1807–85

368   GUIDE me, O thou great Redeemer,
      Pilgrim through this barren land;
    I am weak, but thou art mighty,
      Hold me with thy powerful hand:
       Bread of heaven,
    Feed me till I want no more.

2   Open now the crystal fountain
      Whence the healing stream doth flow;
    Let the fire and cloudy pillar
      Lead me all my journey through:
       Strong deliverer,
    Be thou still my strength and shield.

3   When I tread the verge of Jordan,
      Bid my anxious fears subside;
    Death of death, and hell's Destruction
      Land me safe on Canaan's side:
       Songs of praises
    I will ever give to thee.

Welsh, WILLIAM WILLIAMS 1717–91
Tr PETER WILLIAMS 1727–96
and others

369   *O quam juvat fratres*

HAPPY are they, they that love God,
  Whose hearts have Christ confest,
Who by his Cross have found their life,
  And 'neath his yoke their rest.

2 Glad is the praise, sweet are the songs,
    When they together sing;
  And strong the prayers that bow the ear
    Of heaven's eternal King.

3 Christ to their homes giveth his peace,
    And makes their loves his own:
  But ah, what tares the evil one
    Hath in his garden sown!

4 Sad were our lot, evil this earth,
    Did not its sorrows prove
  The path whereby the sheep may find
    The fold of Jesu's love.

5 Then shall they know, they that love him,
    How all their pain is good;
  And death itself cannot unbind
    Their happy brotherhood.

ROBERT BRIDGES 1844–1930
based on the Latin of
CHARLES COFFIN 1676–1749

370   *Suitable for the Gradual*

HELP us, O Lord, to learn
  The truths thy word imparts:
To study that thy laws may be
  Inscribed upon our hearts.

2 Help us, O Lord, to live
    The faith which we proclaim,
That all our thoughts and words and deeds
    May glorify thy name.

3 Help us, O Lord, to teach
    The beauty of thy ways,
That all who seek may find the Christ,
    And sing aloud his praise.

WILLIAM WATKINS REID JR. b 1923

371   HE wants not friends that hath thy love,
    And may converse and walk with thee
And with thy saints, here and above,
    With whom for ever I must be.

2 Within the fellowship of saints
    Is wisdom, safety and delight;
And when my heart declines and faints,
    It's raisèd by their heat and light.

3 As for my friends, they are not lost:
    The several vessels of thy fleet
Though parted now, by tempests tossed,
    Shall safely in the haven meet.

4 We still are centred all in thee,
    Though distant, members of one Head;
Within one family we be,
    And by one faith and spirit led.

5 Before thy throne we daily meet
    As joint-petitioners to thee;
In spirit each the other greet,
    And shall again each other see.

6 The heavenly hosts, world without end,
    Shall be my company above;
And thou, my best and surest Friend,
    Who shall divide me from thy love?

RICHARD BAXTER 1615–91‡

372 HE who would valiant be
    'Gainst all disaster,
    Let him in constancy
      Follow the Master.
    There's no discouragement
    Shall make him once relent
    His first avowed intent
      To be a pilgrim.

2 Who so beset him round
    With dismal stories,
    Do but themselves confound—
      His strength the more is.
    No foes shall stay his might,
    Though he with giants fight:
    He will make good his right
      To be a pilgrim.

3 Since, Lord, thou dost defend
   Us with thy Spirit,
We know we at the end
   Shall life inherit.
Then fancies flee away!
I'll fear not what men say,
I'll labour night and day
   To be a pilgrim.

JOHN BUNYAN 1628–88
and PERCY DEARMER 1867–1936

373 HOW shall I sing that majesty
   Which angels do admire?
Let dust in dust and silence lie;
   Sing, sing, ye heavenly choir.
Thousands of thousands stand around
   Thy throne, O God most high;
Ten thousand times ten thousand sound
   Thy praise; but who am I?

2 Thy brightness unto them appears,
   Whilst I thy footsteps trace;
A sound of God comes to my ears,
   But they behold thy face.
They sing because thou art their Sun;
   Lord, send a beam on me;
For where heaven is but once begun
   There alleluyas be.

3 Enlighten with faith's light my heart,
  Inflame it with love's fire;
Then shall I sing and bear a part
  With that celestial choir.
I shall, I fear, be dark and cold,
  With all my fire and light;
Yet when thou dost accept their gold,
  Lord, treasure up my mite.

4 How great a being, Lord, is thine,
  Which doth all beings keep!
Thy knowledge is the only line
  To sound so vast a deep.
Thou art a sea without a shore,
  A sun without a sphere;
Thy time is now and evermore,
  Thy place is everywhere.

JOHN MASON c 1645–1694

374 HOW sweet the name of Jesus sounds
  In a believer's ear!
It soothes his sorrows, heals his wounds,
  And drives away his fear.

2 It makes the wounded spirit whole,
  And calms the troubled breast;
'Tis manna to the hungry soul,
  And to the weary rest.

3 Dear name! the rock on which I build,
  My shield and hiding-place,
My never-failing treasury filled
  With boundless stores of grace.

4 Jesus! my Shepherd, Brother, Friend,
    My Prophet, Priest, and King,
My Lord, my Life, my Way, my End,
    Accept the praise I bring.

5 Weak is the effort of my heart,
    And cold my warmest thought;
But when I see thee as thou art,
    I'll praise thee as I ought.

6 Till then I would thy love proclaim
    With every fleeting breath;
And may the music of thy name
    Refresh my soul in death.

JOHN NEWTON 1725–1807

375 I DANCED in the morning when the world
      was begun,
    And I danced in the moon and the stars and
      the sun,
I came down from heaven and I danced on the
    earth;
    At Bethlehem I had my birth.

Dance, then, wherever you may be;
I am the Lord of the Dance, said he,
And I'll lead you all, wherever you may be,
And I'll lead you all in the dance, said he.

2 I danced for the scribe and the pharisee,
    But they would not dance and they would not
      follow me.
I danced for the fishermen, for James and
    John—
    They came with me and the dance went on.

3 I danced on the Sabbath and I cured the lame;
  The holy people said it was a shame.
They whipped and they stripped and they hung
    me on high;
  They left me there on a cross to die.

4 I danced on a Friday when the sky turned
    black—
  It's hard to dance with the devil on your
    back.
They buried my body and they thought I'd
    gone;
  But I'm the dance and I still go on.

5 They cut me down and I leapt up high;
  I am the life that will never, never die;
I'll live in you if you'll live in me—
  I am the Lord of the Dance said he.

SYDNEY CARTER b 1915

376 I HEARD the voice of Jesus say,
  'Come unto me and rest;
Lay down, thou weary one, lay down
  Thy head upon my breast:'
I came to Jesus as I was,
  Weary, and worn, and sad;
I found in him a resting-place,
  And he has made me glad.

2 I heard the voice of Jesus say,
    'Behold, I freely give
The living water, thirsty one;
    Stoop down, and drink, and live:'
I came to Jesus, and I drank
    Of that life-giving stream;
My thirst was quenched, my soul revived,
    And now I live in him.

3 I heard the voice of Jesus say,
    'I am this dark world's Light;
Look unto me, thy morn shall rise,
    And all thy day be bright:'
I looked to Jesus, and I found
    In him my Star, my Sun;
And in that light of life I'll walk
    Till travelling days are done.

HORATIUS BONAR 1808–89

377 IMMORTAL, invisible, God only wise,
In light inaccessible hid from our eyes,
Most blessèd, most glorious, the Ancient of
    Days,
Almighty, victorious, thy great name we praise.

2 Unresting, unhasting, and silent as light,
Nor wanting, nor wasting, thou rulest in might;
Thy justice like mountains high soaring above
Thy clouds which are fountains of goodness and
    love.

3 To all life thou givest—to both great and small;
In all life thou livest, the true life of all;
We blossom and flourish as leaves on the tree,
And wither and perish—but nought changeth
thee.

4 Great Father of glory, pure Father of light,
Thine angels adore thee, all veiling their sight;
All laud we would render: O help us to see
'Tis only the splendour of light hideth thee.

W. CHALMERS SMITH 1824–1908

378 IMMORTAL love for ever full,
For ever flowing free,
For ever shared, for ever whole,
A never-ebbing sea!

2 Our outward lips confess the name,
All other names above;
Love only knoweth whence it came
And comprehendeth love.

3 We may not climb the heavenly steeps
To bring the Lord Christ down;
In vain we search the lowest deeps,
For him no depths can drown;

4 But warm, sweet, tender, even yet
A present help is he;
And faith has still its Olivet,
And love its Galilee.

5 The healing of his seamless dress
    Is by our beds of pain;
  We touch him in life's throng and press,
    And we are whole again.

6 Through him the first fond prayers are said
    Our lips of childhood frame;
  The last low whispers of our dead
    Are burdened with his name.

7 Alone, O Love ineffable,
    Thy saving name is given;
  To turn aside from thee is hell,
    To walk with thee is heaven.

JOHN WHITTIER 1807–92

379 IN the Cross of Christ I glory,
    Towering o'er the wrecks of time;
  All the light of sacred story
    Gathers round its head sublime.

2 When the woes of life o'ertake me,
    Hopes deceive and fears annoy,
  Never shall the Cross forsake me:
    Lo! it glows with peace and joy.

3 When the sun of bliss is beaming
    Light and love upon my way,
  From the Cross the radiance streaming,
    Adds more lustre to the day.

4 Bane and blessing, pain and pleasure,
    By the Cross are sanctified;
  Peace is there that knows no measure,
    Joys that through all time abide.

JOHN BOWRING 1792–1872

380   *Christ's perfect work*

IT is finished! Christ hath known
All the life of men wayfaring,
Human joys and sorrows sharing,
  Making human needs his own.
Lord, in us thy life renewing,
  Lead us where thy feet have trod,
Till, the way of truth pursuing,
  Human souls find rest in God.

2   It is finished! Christ is slain,
On the altar of creation,
Offering for a world's salvation
  Sacrifice of love and pain.
Lord, thy love through pain revealing,
  Purge our passions, scourge our vice,
Till, upon the tree of healing,
  Self is slain in sacrifice.

3   It is finished! Christ our King
Wins the victor's crown of glory;
Sun and stars recite his story,
  Floods and fields his triumph sing.
Lord, whose praise the world is telling,
  Lord, to whom all power is given,
By thy death, hell's armies quelling,
  Bring thy saints to reign in heaven.

GABRIEL GILLETT 1873–1948

381   *Urbs Sion aurea*

JERUSALEM the golden,
  With milk and honey blest,
Beneath thy contemplation
  Sink heart and voice opprest.
I know not, O I know not,
  What social joys are there,
What radiancy of glory,
  What light beyond compare.

2 They stand, those halls of Sion,
     Conjubilant with song,
   And bright with many an angel,
     And all the martyr throng;
   The Prince is ever in them,
     The daylight is serene,
   The pastures of the blessèd
     Are decked in glorious sheen.

3 There is the throne of David,
     And there, from care released,
   The song of them that triumph,
     The shout of them that feast;
   And they who, with their Leader,
     Have conquered in the fight,
   For ever and for ever
     Are clad in robes of white.

4   O sweet and blessèd country,
     Shall I ever see thy face?
  O sweet and blessèd country,
     Shall I ever win thy grace?
  Exult, O dust and ashes!
     The Lord shall be thy part:
  His only, his for ever,
     Thou shalt be, and thou art!

BERNARD OF CLUNY 12th century
Tr J. M. NEALE 1818–66

382   *Dignare me, O Jesu, rogo te*

JESU, grant me this, I pray,
Ever in thy heart to stay;
Let me evermore abide
Hidden in thy wounded side.

2 If the evil one prepare,
Or the world, a tempting snare,
I am safe when I abide
In thy heart and wounded side.

3 If the flesh, more dangerous still,
Tempt my soul to deeds of ill,
Naught I fear when I abide
In thy heart and wounded side.

4 Death will come one day to me;
Jesu, cast me not from thee:
Dying let me still abide
In thy heart and wounded side.

Latin 17th century
Tr H. W. BAKER 1821–77

383 JESU, Lover of my soul,
Let me to thy bosom fly,
While the nearer waters roll,
While the tempest still is high:
Hide me, O my Saviour, hide
Till the storm of life is past;
Safe into the haven guide,
O receive my soul at last.

2 Other refuge have I none,
Hangs my helpless soul on thee;
Leave, ah, leave me not alone,
Still support and comfort me.
All my trust on thee is stayed,
All my help from thee I bring;
Cover my defenceless head
With the shadow of thy wing.

3★ Thou, O Christ, art all I want,
More than all in thee I find:
Raise the fallen, cheer the faint,
Heal the sick, and lead the blind.
Just and holy is thy name,
I am all unrighteousness;
False and full of sin I am,
Thou art full of truth and grace.

4 Plenteous grace with thee is found,
    Grace to cover all my sin;
Let the healing streams abound,
    Make and keep me pure within.
Thou of life the fountain art,
    Freely let me take of thee,
Spring thou up within my heart,
    Rise to all eternity.

CHARLES WESLEY 1707–88

384   JESU, my Lord, my God, my All,
Hear me, blest Saviour, when I call;
Hear me, and from thy dwelling-place
Pour down the riches of thy grace:
    Jesu, my Lord, I thee adore,
    O make me love thee more and more.

2 Jesu, too late I thee have sought,
How can I love thee as I ought?
And how extol thy matchless fame,
The glorious beauty of thy name?

3 Jesu, what didst thou find in me,
That thou hast dealt so lovingly?
How great the joy that thou hast brought,
So far exceeding hope or thought!

4 Jesu, of thee shall be my song,
To thee my heart and soul belong;
All that I am or have is thine,
And thou, sweet Saviour, thou art mine.

HENRY COLLINS 1827–1919

385   *Jesu, dulcis memoria*

JESU, the very thought of thee
  With sweetness fills my breast;
But sweeter far thy face to see,
  And in thy presence rest.

2 Nor voice can sing, nor heart can frame,
    Nor can the memory find,
  A sweeter sound than thy blest name,
    O Saviour of mankind!

3 O hope of every contrite heart,
    O joy of all the meek,
  To those who fall, how kind thou art!
    How good to those who seek!

4 But what to those who find? Ah, this
    Nor tongue nor pen can show;
  The love of Jesus, what it is
    None but his loved ones know.

5 Jesu, our only joy be thou,
    As thou our prize wilt be;
  Jesu, be thou our glory now,
    And through eternity.

Latin c 12th century
Tr EDWARD CASWALL 1814–78

386   *Jesu, Rex admirabilis*

O JESU, King most wonderful,
  Thou Conqueror renowned,
Thou sweetness most ineffable,
  In whom all joys are found!

2 When once thou visitest the heart,
    Then truth begins to shine;
Then earthly vanities depart;
    Then kindles love divine.

3 O Jesu, Light of all below,
    Thou Fount of life and fire,
Surpassing all the joys we know,
    And all we can desire:

4 May every heart confess thy name,
    And ever thee adore;
And, seeking thee, itself inflame
    To seek thee more and more.

5 Thee may our tongues for ever bless,
    Thee may we love alone;
And ever in our lives express
    The image of thine own.

Latin c 12th century
Tr EDWARD CASWALL 1814–78

387 JESUS, good above all other,
    Gentle Child of gentle Mother,
    In a stable born our Brother,
        Give us grace to persevere.

2 Jesus, cradled in a manger,
For us facing every danger,
Living as a homeless stranger,
  Make we thee our King most dear.

3 Jesus, for thy people dying,
Risen Master, death defying,
Lord in heaven, thy grace supplying,
  Keep us to thy presence near.

4 Jesus, who our sorrows bearest,
All our thoughts and hopes thou sharest,
Thou to man the truth declarest;
  Help us all thy truth to hear.

5 Lord, in all our doings guide us;
Pride and hate shall ne'er divide us;
We'll go on with thee beside us,
  And with joy we'll persevere!

PERCY DEARMER 1867–1936

388 JESUS shall reign where'er the sun
Does his successive journeys run;
His kingdom stretch from shore to shore,
Till moons shall wax and wane no more.

2 People and realms of every tongue
Dwell on his love with sweetest song,
And infant voices shall proclaim
Their early blessings on his name.

3   Blessings abound where'er he reigns;
     The prisoner leaps to lose his chains;
     The weary find eternal rest,
     And all the sons of want are blest.

4   Let every creature rise and bring
     Peculiar honours to our King;
     Angels descend with songs again,
     And earth repeat the long Amen.

ISAAC WATTS 1674–1748

389   JESUS, these eyes have never seen
       That radiant form of thine;
     The veil of sense hangs dark between
       Thy blessèd face and mine.

2   I see thee not, I hear thee not,
      Yet art thou oft with me;
     And earth hath ne'er so dear a spot
      As where I met with thee.

3   Yet, though I have not seen, and still
      Must rest in faith alone,
     I love thee, dearest Lord, and will,
      Unseen, but not unknown.

4   When death these mortal eyes shall seal,
      And still this throbbing heart,
     The rending veil shall thee reveal
      All glorious as thou art.

RAY PALMER 1808–87

390   JESUS, where'er thy people meet,
There they behold thy mercy-seat;
Where'er they seek thee, thou art found,
And every place is hallowed ground.

2   For thou, within no walls confined,
Inhabitest the humble mind;
Such ever bring thee where they come,
And going, take thee to their home.

3   Dear Shepherd of thy chosen few,
Thy former mercies here renew;
Here to our waiting hearts proclaim
The sweetness of thy saving name.

4   Here may we prove the power of prayer,
To strengthen faith and sweeten care;
To teach our faint desires to rise,
And bring all heaven before our eyes.

5   Lord, we are few, but thou art near;
Nor short thine arm, nor deaf thine ear;
O rend the heavens, come quickly down,
And make a thousand hearts thine own!

WILLIAM COWPER 1731–1800

391   KING of glory, King of peace,
   I will love thee;
And that love may never cease,
   I will move thee.
Thou hast granted my request,
   Thou hast heard me;
Thou didst note my working breast,
   Thou hast spared me.

2 Wherefore with my utmost art
      I will sing thee,
And the cream of all my heart
      I will bring thee.
Though my sins against me cried,
      Thou didst clear me;
And alone, when they replied,
      Thou didst hear me.

3 Seven whole days, not one in seven,
      I will praise thee;
In my heart, though not in heaven,
      I can raise thee.
Small it is, in this poor sort
      To enrol thee:
E'en eternity's too short
      To extol thee.

GEORGE HERBERT 1593–1632

392 LEAD, kindly Light, amid the encircling
      gloom,
      Lead thou me on;
The night is dark, and I am far from home,
      Lead thou me on.
Keep thou my feet; I do not ask to see
The distant scene; one step enough for me.

2 I was not ever thus, nor prayed that thou
      Shouldst lead me on;
I loved to choose and see my path; but now
      Lead thou me on.
I loved the garish day, and, spite of fears,
Pride ruled my will: remember not past years.

3 So long thy power hath blest me, sure it still
    Will lead me on
O'er moor and fen, o'er crag and torrent, till
    The night is gone,
And with the morn those angel faces smile,
Which I have loved long since, and lost awhile.

JOHN HENRY NEWMAN 1801–90

393   LEAD us, heavenly Father, lead us
        O'er the world's tempestuous sea;
    Guard us, guide us, keep us, feed us,
        For we have no help but thee;
    Yet possessing every blessing
        If our God our Father be.

2 Saviour, breathe forgiveness o'er us,
    All our weakness thou dost know;
Thou didst tread this earth before us,
    Thou didst feel its keenest woe;
Self denying, death defying,
    Thou to Calvary didst go.

3 Spirit of our God, descending,
    Fill our hearts with heavenly joy;
Love with every passion blending,
    Pleasure that can never cloy;
Thus provided, pardoned, guided,
    Nothing can our peace destroy.

JAMES EDMESTON 1791–1867†

394   LET all the world in every corner sing,
          My God and King!
          The heavens are not too high,
          His praise may thither fly;
          The earth is not too low,
          His praises there may grow.
      Let all the world in every corner sing,
          My God and King!

2   Let all the world in every corner sing,
          My God and King!
          The Church with psalms must shout,
          No door can keep them out;
          But above all, the heart
          Must bear the longest part.
      Let all the world in every corner sing,
          My God and King!

GEORGE HERBERT 1593–1632

395   *The call of the bells*

      LET bells peal forth the universal fame,
      Creator Lord, of thy mysterious name;
      Conscience within, the boundless heavens
            above,
      Disclose to faith the hidden name of Love.

2   Loudly proclaim with each insistent chime
      How thine eternity redeems our time;
      Past sins forgiven, and future hopes restored,
      Reveal thy presence with us, gracious Lord.

3   Spirit divine, re-cast our faulty ways,
     Make them ring true and echo to thy praise;
     Through every change of circumstance and
        choice
     May we confess thee with a single voice.

4   Call us to worship, call us to obey,
     Call us to pilgrimage along life's way;
     Rouse us from sleep; renewed in mind and
        heart,
     Call us to love thee, Lord, since Love thou art.

PETER BAELZ b 1923

396   LET saints on earth in concert sing
       With those whose work is done;
     For all the servants of our King
       In earth and heaven are one.

2   One family, we dwell in him,
       One Church, above, beneath;
     Though now divided by the stream,
       The narrow stream of death.

3   One army of the living God,
       To his command we bow;
     Part of his host has crossed the flood,
       And part is crossing now.

4   E'en now to their eternal home
       There pass some spirits blest,
     While others to the margin come,
       Waiting their call to rest.

5 Jesu, be thou our constant Guide;
   Then, when the word is given,
   Bid Jordan's narrow stream divide,
   And bring us safe to heaven.

CHARLES WESLEY 1707–88
and others

397   *Psalm 136*

LET us, with a gladsome mind,
Praise the Lord, for he is kind:
For his mercies ay endure,
Ever faithful, ever sure.

2 Let us blaze his name abroad,
   For of gods he is the God:

3 He with all-commanding might
   Filled the new-made world with light:

4 He the golden-tressèd sun
   Caused all day his course to run:

5 And the hornèd moon by night,
   Mid her spangled sisters bright:

6 All things living he doth feed,
   His full hand supplies their need:

7 Let us, with a gladsome mind,
   Praise the Lord for he is kind:

JOHN MILTON 1608–74†

398 'LIFT up your hearts!' We lift them, Lord,
    to thee;
Here at thy feet none other may we see:
'Lift up your hearts!' E'en so, with one accord,
We lift them up, we lift them to the Lord.

2   Above the level of the former years,
The mire of sin, the slough of guilty fears,
The mist of doubt, the blight of love's decay,
O Lord of Light, lift all our hearts to-day!

3   Above the swamps of subterfuge and shame,
The deeds, the thoughts, that honour may not
    name,
The halting tongue that dares not tell the whole,
O Lord of Truth, lift every Christian soul!

4   Lift every gift that thou thyself hast given;
Low lies the best till lifted up to heaven:
Low lie the bounding heart, the teeming brain,
Till, sent from God, they mount to God again.

5   Then, as the trumpet-call, in after years,
'Lift up your hearts!' rings pealing in our ears,
Still shall those hearts respond, with full accord,
'We lift them up, we lift them to the Lord!'

HENRY MONTAGU BUTLER 1833–1918

399 LIGHT of the lonely pilgrim's heart,
    The star of coming day,
Arise, and with thy morning beams
    Chase all our griefs away.

2 Bid the whole earth, responsive now
    To that bright world above,
  Break forth in rapturous strains of joy
    To celebrate thy love.

3 Thine was the cross, with all its fruits
    Of grace and peace divine;
  And thine the crown of glory now,
    The palm of victory thine.

4 See how thy fair creation groans,
    The sky, the earth, the sea,
  In unison with all our hearts,
    And calls aloud for thee.

5 Come, blessèd Lord, let every shore
    And answering island sing
  The praises of thy royal name,
    And own thee as their king.

EDWARD DENNY 1796–1889‡

400 Light of the minds that know him:
    May Christ be light to mine;
  My sun in risen splendour,
    My light of truth divine;
  My guide in doubt and darkness,
    My true and living way,
  My clear light ever shining
    My dawn of heaven's day.

2   Life of the souls that love him:
      May Christ be ours indeed;
  The living bread from heaven
      On whom our spirits feed;
  Who died for love of sinners
      To bear our guilty load,
  And make of life's brief journey
      A new Emmaus road.

3   Strength of the wills that serve him:
      May Christ be strength to me,
  Who stilled the storm and tempest,
      Who calmed the tossing sea;
  His Spirit's power to move me,
      His will to master mine,
  His cross to carry daily
      And conquer in his sign.

4   May it be ours to know him
      That we may truly love,
  And loving, fully serve him
      As serve the saints above;
  Till in that home of glory
      With fadeless splendour bright,
  We serve in perfect freedom
      Our Strength, our Life, our Light.

TIMOTHY DUDLEY-SMITH b 1926
based on a prayer of
ST AUGUSTINE OF HIPPO 354–430

401   *Jerusalem luminosa*

LIGHT'S abode, celestial Salem,
  Vision dear whence peace doth spring,
Brighter than the heart can fancy,
  Mansion of the highest King;
O, how glorious are the praises
  Which of thee the prophets sing!

2 There for ever and for ever
    Alleluya is outpoured;
  For unending, for unbroken
    Is the feast-day of the Lord;
  All is pure and all is holy
    That within thy walls is stored.

3 There no cloud nor passing vapour
    Dims the brightness of the air;
  Endless noon-day, glorious noon-day,
    From the Sun of suns is there;
  There no night brings rest from labour,
    There unknown are toil and care.

4 O how glorious and resplendent,
    Fragile body, shalt thou be,
  When endued with so much beauty,
    Full of health, and strong, and free,
  Full of vigour, full of pleasure
    That shall last eternally!

5 Now with gladness, now with courage,
    Bear the burden on thee laid,
  That hereafter these thy labours
    May with endless gifts be paid,
  And in everlasting glory
    Thou with joy may'st be arrayed.

6 Laud and honour to the Father,
   Laud and honour to the Son,
Laud and honour to the Spirit,
   Ever Three and ever One,
One in love, and One in splendour,
   While unending ages run.   Amen.

Latin 15th century
Tr J. M. NEALE 1818–66

402   LORD, it belongs not to my care
      Whether I die or live;
   To love and serve thee is my share,
      And this thy grace must give.

2 If life be long, I will be glad
      That I may long obey;
   If short, yet why should I be sad
      To end my little day?

3 Christ leads me through no darker rooms
      Than he went through before;
   He that into God's kingdom comes
      Must enter by this door.

4 Come, Lord, when grace hath made me meet
      Thy blessèd face to see:
   For if thy work on earth be sweet,
      What will thy glory be!

5 My knowledge of that life is small,
   The eye of faith is dim;
But 'tis enough that Christ knows all,
   And I shall be with him.

RICHARD BAXTER 1615–91†

403 LORD of all being, throned afar,
   Thy glory flames from sun and star;
Centre and soul of every sphere,
   Yet to each loving heart how near!

2 Sun of our life, thy quickening ray
   Sheds on our path the glow of day;
Star of our hope, thy softened light
   Cheers the long watches of the night.

3 Our midnight is thy smile withdrawn,
   Our noontide is thy gracious dawn,
Our rainbow arch thy mercy's sign;
   All, save the clouds of sin, are thine.

4 Lord of all life, below, above,
   Whose light is truth, whose warmth is love,
Before thy ever-blazing throne
   We ask no lustre of our own.

5 Grant us thy truth to make us free
   And kindling hearts that burn for thee,
Till all thy living altars claim
   One holy light, one heavenly flame.

OLIVER WENDELL HOLMES 1809–94

404   LORD of our life, and God of our salvation,
Star of our night, and hope of every nation,
Hear and receive thy Church's supplication,
        Lord God Almighty.

2* See round thine ark the hungry billows curling;
See how thy foes their banners are unfurling;
Lord, while their darts envenomed they are
    hurling,
        Thou canst preserve us.

3 Lord, thou canst help when earthly armour
    faileth,
Lord, thou canst save when deadly sin assaileth;
Christ, o'er thy rock nor death nor hell
    prevaileth;
        Grant us thy peace, Lord.

4 Peace in our hearts, our evil thoughts
    assuaging;
Peace in thy Church, where brothers are
    engaging;
Peace, when the world its busy war is waging:
        Calm thy foes' raging.

5 Grant us thy help till backward they are driven,
Grant them thy truth, that they may be
    forgiven;
Grant peace on earth, and, after we have striven,
        Peace in thy heaven.

PHILIP PUSEY 1799–1855
based on the German of
M. VON LÖWENSTERN 1594–1648

405   LORD of the boundless curves of space,
        And time's deep mystery;
    To thy creative might we trace
        The fount of energy.

2   Thy mind conceived the galaxy,
        The atom's secret planned;
    And every age of history
        Thy purpose, Lord, has spanned.

3   Thy Spirit gave the living cell
        Its hidden vital force;
    The instincts which all life impel
        Derive from thee their source.

4   Thine is the image stamped on man,
        Though marred by man's own sin;
    And thine the liberating plan
        Devised his soul to win.

5   Science explores thy reason's ways,
        But faith draws near thy heart;
    And in the face of Christ we gaze
        Upon the Love thou art.

ALBERT F. BAYLY† 1901–84

406   LORD, teach us how to pray aright
        With reverence and with fear;
    Though dust and ashes in thy sight,
        We may, we must draw near.

2 We perish if we cease from prayer;
     O grant us power to pray;
  And when to meet thee we prepare,
     Lord, meet us by the way.

3 God of all grace, we come to thee
     With broken contrite hearts;
  Give, what thine eye delights to see,
     Truth in the inward parts;

4 Faith in the only sacrifice
     That can for sin atone;
  To cast our hopes, to fix our eyes,
     On Christ, on Christ alone;

5 Patience to watch, and wait, and weep,
     Though mercy long delay;
  Courage our fainting souls to keep,
     And trust thee though thou slay.

6 Give these, and then thy will be done;
     Thus, strengthened with all might,
  We, through thy Spirit and thy Son,
     Shall pray, and pray aright.

JAMES MONTGOMERY 1771–1854

407 LORD, thy word abideth,
     And our footsteps guideth;
     Who its truth believeth,
     Light and joy receiveth.

2 When our foes are near us,
   Then thy word doth cheer us,
   Word of consolation,
   Message of salvation.

3 When the storms are o'er us,
   And dark clouds before us,
   Then its light directeth,
   And our way protecteth.

4 Who can tell the pleasure,
   Who recount the treasure
   By thy word imparted
   To the simple-hearted?

5 Word of mercy, giving
   Succour to the living;
   Word of life, supplying
   Comfort to the dying.

6 O that we discerning
   Its most holy learning,
   Lord, may love and fear thee,
   Evermore be near thee!

H. W. Baker 1821–77

408 LOVE Divine, all loves excelling,
   Joy of heaven, to earth come down,
Fix in us thy humble dwelling,
   All thy faithful mercies crown.
Jesu, thou art all compassion,
   Pure unbounded love thou art;
Visit us with thy salvation,
   Enter every trembling heart.

2   Come, almighty to deliver,
     Let us all thy life receive;
  Suddenly return, and never,
     Never more thy temples leave.
  Thee we would be always blessing,
     Serve thee as thy hosts above,
  Pray, and praise thee, without ceasing,
     Glory in thy perfect love.

3   Finish then thy new creation,
     Pure and spotless let us be;
  Let us see thy great salvation,
     Perfectly restored in thee,
  Changed from glory into glory,
     Till in heaven we take our place,
  Till we cast our crowns before thee,
     Lost in wonder, love, and praise!

CHARLES WESLEY 1707–88

The Holy Spirit

409   LOVE of the Father, love of God the Son,
From whom all came, in whom was all begun;
Who formest heavenly beauty out of strife,
Creation's whole desire and breath of life.

2   Spirit all-holy, thou supreme in might,
Thou dost give peace, thy presence maketh
    right;
Thou with thy favour all things dost enfold,
With thine all-kindness free from harm wilt
    hold.

3 Hope of all comfort, splendour of all aid,
That dost not fail nor leave the heart afraid:
To all that cry thou dost all help accord,
The angels' armour, and the saints' reward.

4 Purest and highest, wisest and most just,
There is no truth save only in thy trust;
Thou dost the mind from earthly dreams recall,
And bring through Christ to him for whom are
all.

5 Eternal glory, all men thee adore,
Who art and shalt be worshipped evermore:
Us whom thou madest, comfort with thy might,
And lead us to enjoy thy heavenly light.

ROBERT BRIDGES 1844–1930
based on a 12th century
Latin hymn

410 MY God, how wonderful thou art,
Thy majesty how bright,
How beautiful thy mercy-seat,
In depths of burning light!

2 How dread are thine eternal years,
O everlasting Lord,
By prostrate spirits day and night
Incessantly adored!

3 How wonderful, how beautiful,
The sight of thee must be,
Thine endless wisdom, boundless power,
And aweful purity!

4 O, how I fear thee, living God,
   With deepest, tenderest fears,
And worship thee with trembling hope,
   And penitential tears!

5 Yet I may love thee too, O Lord,
   Almighty as thou art,
For thou hast stooped to ask of me
   The love of my poor heart.

6 No earthly father loves like thee,
   No mother, e'er so mild,
Bears and forbears as thou hast done
   With me thy sinful child.

7 Father of Jesus, love's reward,
   What rapture will it be
Prostrate before thy throne to lie,
   And gaze and gaze on thee.

F. W. FABER 1814–6

411   MY Lord, my Life, my Love,
          To thee, to thee I call;
       I cannot live if thou remove:
          Thou art my joy, my all.

2   My only sun to cheer
          The darkness where I dwell;
       The best and only true delight
          My song hath found to tell.

3   To thee in very heaven
      The angels owe their bliss;
  To thee the saints, whom thou hast called
      Where perfect pleasure is.

4   And how shall man, thy child,
      Without thee happy be,
  Who hath no comfort nor desire
      In all the world but thee?

5   Return my Love, my Life,
      Thy grace hath won my heart;
  If thou forgive, if thou return,
      I will no more depart.

ROBERT BRIDGES 1844–1930
based on verses by
ISAAC WATTS 1674–1748

412 MY soul, there is a country
      Far beyond the stars,
  Where stands a wingèd sentry
      All skilful in the wars.

2   There, above noise and danger,
      Sweet peace sits, crowned with smiles,
  And one born in a manger
      Commands the beauteous files.

3   He is thy gracious friend,
      And—O my soul, awake—
  Did in pure love descend,
      To die here for thy sake.

4   If thou canst get but thither,
  There grows the flower of peace,
 The rose that cannot wither,
  Thy fortress and thine ease.

5   Leave then thy foolish ranges,
  For none can thee secure
 But one who never changes,
  Thy God, thy life, thy cure.

HENRY VAUGHAN 1622–95

413 NOW thank we all our God,
  With heart and hands and voices,
   Who wondrous things hath done,
  In whom his world rejoices;
   Who from our mother's arms
    Hath blessed us on our way
   With countless gifts of love,
    And still is ours to-day.

2   O may this bounteous God
  Through all our life be near us,
   With ever joyful hearts
  And blessèd peace to cheer us;
   And keep us in his grace,
    And guide us when perplexed,
   And free us from all ills
    In this world and the next.

3   All praise and thanks to God
The Father now be given,
    The Son, and him who reigns
With them in highest heaven,
    The One eternal God,
     Whom earth and heaven adore;
For thus it was, is now,
     And shall be evermore.   Amen.

German, MARTIN RINKART 1586–1649
Tr CATHERINE WINKWORTH 1827–78

414   O FOR a closer walk with God,
    A calm and heavenly frame;
A light to shine upon the road
    That leads me to the Lamb!

2   Return, O holy Dove, return,
    Sweet messenger of rest;
I hate the sins that made thee mourn,
    And drove thee from my breast.

3   The dearest idol I have known,
    Whate'er that idol be,
Help me to tear it from thy throne,
    And worship only thee.

4   So shall my walk be close with God,
    Calm and serene my frame;
So purer light shall mark the road
    That leads me to the Lamb.

WILLIAM COWPER 1731–1800

415 O FOR a thousand tongues to sing
My dear Redeemer's praise,
The glories of my God and King,
The triumphs of his grace!

2 Jesus—the name that charms our fears,
That bids our sorrows cease;
'Tis music in the sinner's ears,
'Tis life, and health, and peace.

3* He breaks the power of cancelled sin,
He sets the prisoner free;
His blood can make the foulest clean;
His blood availed for me.

4 He speaks; and, listening to his voice,
New life the dead receive,
The mournful broken hearts rejoice,
The humble poor believe.

5 Hear him, ye deaf; his praise, ye dumb,
Your loosened tongues employ;
Ye blind, behold your Saviour come;
And leap, ye lame, for joy!

6 My gracious Master and my God,
Assist me to proclaim
And spread through all the earth abroad
The honours of thy name.

CHARLES WESLEY 1707–88

416 O GOD of Bethel, by whose hand
      Thy people still are fed,
Who through this weary pilgrimage
      Hast all our fathers led:

2 Our vows, our prayers, we now present
      Before thy throne of grace;
God of our fathers, be the God
      Of their succeeding race.

3 Through each perplexing path of life
      Our wandering footsteps guide;
Give us each day our daily bread,
      And raiment fit provide.

4 O spread thy covering wings around,
      Till all our wanderings cease,
And at our Father's loved abode
      Our souls arrive in peace.

PHILIP DODDRIDGE 1702–51

417   *Psalm 90*

O GOD, our help in ages past,
      Our hope for years to come,
Our shelter from the stormy blast,
      And our eternal home;

2 Under the shadow of thy throne
      Thy saints have dwelt secure;
Sufficient is thine arm alone,
      And our defence is sure.

3 Before the hills in order stood,
   Or earth received her frame,
From everlasting thou art God,
   To endless years the same.

4 A thousand ages in thy sight
   Are like an evening gone,
Short as the watch that ends the night
   Before the rising sun.

5 Time, like an ever-rolling stream,
   Bears all its sons away;
They fly forgotten, as a dream
   Dies at the opening day.

6 O God, our help in ages past,
   Our hope for years to come,
Be thou our guard while troubles last,
   And our eternal home.

ISAAC WATTS 1674–1748

418   O HAPPY band of pilgrims,
   If onward ye will tread
With Jesus as your fellow
   To Jesus as your Head!

2 O happy if ye labour
   As Jesus did for men;
O happy if ye hunger
   As Jesus hungered then!

3* The cross that Jesus carried
    He carried as your due;
The crown that Jesus weareth,
    He weareth it for you.

4* The faith by which ye see him,
    The hope in which ye yearn,
The love that through all troubles
    To him alone will turn,

5* What are they but forerunners
    To lead you to his sight?
What are they save the effluence
    Of uncreated light?

6 The trials that beset you,
    The sorrows ye endure,
The manifold temptations
    That death alone can cure,

7 What are they but his jewels
    Of right celestial worth?
What are they but the ladder
    Set up to heaven on earth?

8 O happy band of pilgrims,
    Look upward to the skies,
Where such a light affliction
    Shall win you such a prize!

J. M. NEALE 1818–66

419   *O fons amoris, Spiritus*

O HOLY Spirit, Lord of grace,
　　Eternal fount of love,
Inflame, we pray, our inmost hearts
　　With fire from heaven above.

2　As thou in bond of love dost join
　　　The Father and the Son,
　So fill us all with mutual love,
　　　And knit our hearts in one.

3　All glory to the Father be,
　　　All glory to the Son,
　All glory, Holy Ghost, to thee,
　　　While endless ages run.　Amen.

Latin, CHARLES COFFIN 1676–1749
Tr JOHN CHANDLER 1808–76†

420　O JESUS, I have promised
　　　To serve thee to the end;
　Be thou for ever near me,
　　　My Master and my Friend;
　I shall not fear the battle
　　　If thou art by my side,
　Nor wander from the pathway
　　　If thou wilt be my guide.

2 O let me hear thee speaking
   In accents clear and still,
Above the storms of passion,
   The murmurs of self-will;
O speak to reassure me,
   To hasten or control;
O speak, and make me listen,
   Thou guardian of my soul.

3 O Jesus, thou hast promised
   To all who follow thee,
That where thou art in glory
   There shall thy servant be;
And, Jesus, I have promised
   To serve thee to the end;
O give me grace to follow,
   My Master and my Friend.

4 O let me see thy footmarks,
   And in them plant mine own;
My hope to follow duly
   Is in thy strength alone;
O guide me, call me, draw me,
   Uphold me to the end;
And then in heaven receive me,
   My Saviour and my Friend.

JOHN BODE 1816–74

421   O KING enthroned on high,
Thou Comforter divine,
Blest Spirit of all truth, be nigh
And make us thine.

2   Thou art the Source of life,
Thou art our treasure-store;
Give us thy peace, and end our strife
For evermore.

3   Descend, O heavenly Dove,
Abide with us alway;
And in the fullness of thy love
Cleanse us, we pray.

Greek c 8th century
Tr JOHN BROWNLIE 1857–1925

422   O LORD of heaven, and earth, and sea,
To thee all praise and glory be;
How shall we show our love to thee,
Who givest all?

2   The golden sunshine, vernal air,
Sweet flowers and fruits, thy love declare;
Where harvests ripen, thou art there,
Who givest all.

3   For peaceful homes, and healthful days,
For all the blessings earth displays,
We owe thee thankfulness and praise,
Who givest all.

4 Thou didst not spare thine only Son,
But gav'st him for a world undone,
And freely with that blessèd One
        Thou givest all.

5 Thou giv'st the Spirit's blessèd dower,
Spirit of life, and love, and power,
And dost his sevenfold graces shower
        Upon us all.

6 For souls redeemed, for sins forgiven,
For means of grace and hopes of heaven,
Father, all praise to thee be given,
        Who givest all.

7 We lose what on ourselves we spend,
We have as treasure without end
Whatever, Lord, to thee we lend,
        Who givest all;

8 To thee, from whom we all derive
Our life, our gifts, our power to give:
O may we ever with thee live,
        Who givest all.

CHRISTOPHER WORDSWORTH 1807–85

423 O LORD of hosts, all heaven possessing,
        And hid in splendour all thine own,
In doubt and darkness dimly guessing,
        Men might thy glory half have known:
But now in Christ we see thy face,
Behold thy love, and know thy grace.

2 Illumine all thy chosen teachers
    The Spirit's wisdom to unfold;
From out the Scripture may thy preachers
    Bring forth its treasures new and old,
And oldest, youngest, find in thee
Of truth and love the boundless sea.

3 Let faith still light the lamp of science,
    And knowledge own thee Lord of truth;
Let age still find in thee reliance,
    Nor lose the primal awe of youth;
So better, wiser, may we grow,
As time's swift currents onward flow.

4 Preserve us here in mystic union
    With saints in heaven from sin set free,
And hold us in that blest communion
    Of all on earth who trust in thee;
So keep our souls, or there or here,
Within that love which casts out fear.

EDITORS, altered from verses
by EDWARD PLUMPTRE 1821–91

424 O LOVE divine, how sweet thou art!
When shall I find my longing heart
    All taken up by thee?
I thirst, I faint and die to prove
The greatness of redeeming love,
    The love of Christ to me.

2   Stronger his love than death or hell;
    Its riches are unsearchable:
        The first-born sons of light
    Desire in vain its depths to see;
    They cannot reach the mystery,
        The length and breadth and height.

3* God only knows the love of God;
    O that it now were shed abroad
        In this poor stony heart!
    For love I sigh, for love I pine;
    This only portion, Lord, be mine,
        Be mine this better part.

4   For ever would I take my seat
    With Mary at the Master's feet:
        Be this my happy choice;
    My only care, delight, and bliss,
    My joy, my heaven on earth, be this,
        To hear the Bridegroom's voice.

                        CHARLES WESLEY 1707–88†

425   *O amor quam ecstaticus*

    O LOVE, how deep, how broad, how high!
    How passing thought and fantasy
    That God, the Son of God, should take
    Our mortal form for mortals' sake.

2   He sent no angel to our race
    Of higher or of lower place,
    But wore the robe of human frame,
    And he himself to this world came.

3 For us baptized, for us he bore
His holy fast, and hungered sore;
For us temptations sharp he knew;
For us the tempter overthrew.

4 For us to wicked men betrayed,
Scourged, mocked, in crown of thorns arrayed;
For us he bore the cross's death;
For us at length gave up his breath.

5 For us he rose from death again,
For us he went on high to reign,
For us he sent his Spirit here
To guide, to strengthen, and to cheer.

6 All honour, laud, and glory be,
O Jesu, Virgin-born, to thee,
All glory, as is ever meet,
To Father and to Paraclete.   Amen.

Latin, 15th century
Tr BENJAMIN WEBB 1819–85‡

426 O PRAISE the Lord, ye servants of the Lord,
Into his courts your joyful homage bring,
Ye that within his holy temple stand
Lift up your hands, lift up your voice and sing:
So shall ye have the blessing from your King.

2 He that hath made all heaven and all the worlds,
Shall from that Sion where his saints adore
Look down with favour, sanctify his Church,
Bless them that tread his sanctuary floor,
And keep them in his ways for evermore.

3 All glory now to God the Father's name;
   Son everlasting, glory unto thee;
   And, Holy Spirit, glory thine the same;
   One God eternal, blessed Trinity,
   As ever was, and evermore shall be.   Amen.

                          From a 19th century pamphlet
                               at ST OSWALD'S, DURHAM

427   O PRAISE ye the Lord!
             Praise him in the height;
          Rejoice in his word,
             Ye angels of light;
          Ye heavens adore him
             By whom ye were made,
          And worship before him,
             In brightness arrayed.

2   O praise ye the Lord!
        Praise him upon earth,
     In tuneful accord,
        Ye sons of new birth;
     Praise him who has brought you
        His grace from above,
     Praise him who has taught you
        To sing of his love.

3   O praise ye the Lord!
        All things that give sound;
     Each jubilant chord,
        Re-echo around;
     Loud organs, his glory
        Forth tell in deep tone,
     And sweet harp, the story
        Of what he has done.

4 O praise ye the Lord!
    Thanksgiving and song
To him be outpoured
    All ages along:
For love in creation,
    For heaven restored,
For grace of salvation,
    O praise ye the Lord!   (Amen Amen).

H. W. BAKER 1821–77

428   *Suitable for the Gradual*

O SON of God, eternal Love,
Who came in mercy from above
To bring to men the Father's grace,
And sanctify a ransomed race.

2 Illumine every Christian mind,
And grant us through your Word to find
The truth that sets the bondsman free,
The service that is liberty.

3 To Christ whose blood for us was shed,
Who rose victorious from the dead,
Whose glory all the saints adore,
Be endless praise for evermore.

G. B. TIMMS b 1910

429   O THOU in all thy might so far,
    In all thy love so near,
Beyond the range of sun and star,
    And yet beside us here.

2 What heart can comprehend thy name,
     Or searching find thee out,
Who art within, a quickening flame,
     A presence round about?

3 Yet though I know thee but in part,
     I ask not, Lord, for more;
Enough for me to know thou art,
     To love thee and adore.

4 And dearer than all things I know
     Is childlike faith to me,
That makes the darkest way I go
     An open path to thee.

FREDERICK HOSMER 1840–1929

430 O THOU not made with hands,
     Not throned above the skies,
Nor walled with shining walls,
     Nor framed with stones of price,
More bright than gold or gem,
God's own Jerusalem!

2 Where'er the gentle heart
     Finds courage from above;
Where'er the heart forsook
     Warms with the breath of love;
Where faith bids fear depart,
City of God, thou art.

3   Thou art where'er the proud
      In humbleness melts down;
Where self itself yields up;
      Where martyrs win their crown;
Where faithful souls possess
Themselves in perfect peace;

4   Where in life's common ways
      With cheerful feet we go;
Where in his steps we tread,
      Who trod the way of woe;
Where he is in the heart,
City of God, thou art.

5   Not throned above the skies,
      Nor golden-walled afar,
But where Christ's two or three
      In his name gathered are,
Be in the midst of them,
God's own Jerusalem.

FRANCIS PALGRAVE 1824–97

431   O THOU who camest from above,
      The pure celestial fire to impart,
Kindle a flame of sacred love
      On the mean altar of my heart.

2   There let it for thy glory burn
      With inextinguishable blaze,
And trembling to its source return
      In humble prayer, and fervent praise.

3　Jesus, confirm my heart's desire
　　　To work, and speak, and think for thee;
　　Still let me guard the holy fire,
　　　And still stir up thy gift in me.

4　Ready for all thy perfect will,
　　　My acts of faith and love repeat,
　　Till death thy endless mercies seal,
　　　And make my sacrifice complete.

CHARLES WESLEY 1707–88

432　　　*O quanta qualia sunt illa sabbata*

O WHAT their joy and their glory must be,
Those endless sabbaths the blessèd ones see!
Crown for the valiant; to weary ones rest;
God shall be all, and in all ever blest.

2*　What are the Monarch, his court, and his
　　　　throne?
　　What are the peace and the joy that they own?
　　Tell us, ye blest ones, that in it have share,
　　If what ye feel ye can fully declare.

3　Truly Jerusalem name we that shore,
　　'Vision of peace,' that brings joy evermore!
　　Wish and fulfilment can severed be ne'er,
　　Nor the thing prayed for come short of the
　　　　prayer.

4　We, where no trouble distraction can bring,
　　Safely the anthems of Sion shall sing;
　　While for thy grace, Lord, their voices of
　　　　praise
　　Thy blessèd people shall evermore raise.

5* There dawns no sabbath, no sabbath is o'er,
  Those sabbath-keepers have one and no more;
  One and unending is that triumph-song
  Which to the angels and us shall belong.

6* Now in the meanwhile, with hearts raised on
      high,
  We for that country must yearn and must sigh,
  Seeking Jerusalem, dear native land,
  Through our long exile on Babylon's strand.

7 Low before him with our praises we fall,
  Of whom, and in whom, and through whom
      are all;
  Of whom, the Father; and through whom, the
      Son;
  In whom, the Spirit, with these ever One.
                                        Amen.

PETER ABELARD 1079–1142
Tr J. M. NEALE 1818–66

433   *Psalm 104*

  O WORSHIP the King
    All glorious above;
  O gratefully sing
    His power and his love:
  Our Shield and Defender,
    The Ancient of days,
  Pavilioned in splendour,
    And girded with praise.

2 O tell of his might,
 O sing of his grace,
Whose robe is the light,
 Whose canopy space.
His chariots of wrath
 The deep thunder-clouds form,
And dark is his path
 On the wings of the storm.

3 This earth, with its store
 Of wonders untold,
Almighty, thy power
 Hath founded of old:
Hath stablished it fast
 By a changeless decree,
And round it hath cast,
 Like a mantle, the sea.

4* Thy bountiful care
 What tongue can recite?
It breathes in the air,
 It shines in the light;
It streams from the hills,
 It descends to the plain,
And sweetly distils
 In the dew and the rain.

5* Frail children of dust,
 And feeble as frail,
In thee do we trust,
 Nor find thee to fail;
Thy mercies how tender!
 How firm to the end!
Our Maker, Defender,
 Redeemer, and Friend.

6 O measureless Might,
    Ineffable Love,
  While angels delight
    To hymn thee above,
  Thy humbler creation,
    Though feeble their lays,
  With true adoration
    Shall sing to thy praise.

ROBERT GRANT 1779–1838

434 OFT in danger, oft in woe,
  Onward, Christians, onward go;
  Bear the toil, maintain the strife,
  Strengthened with the Bread of Life.

2 Onward, Christians, onward go,
  Join the war, and face the foe;
  Will ye flee in danger's hour?
  Know ye not your Captain's power?

3 Let your drooping hearts be glad;
  March in heavenly armour clad;
  Fight, nor think the battle long,
  Victory soon shall tune your song.

4 Let not sorrow dim your eye,
  Soon shall every tear be dry;
  Let not fears your course impede,
  Great your strength, if great your need.

5 Onward then in battle move;
More than conquerors ye shall prove;
Though opposed by many a foe,
Christian soldiers, onward go.

HENRY KIRKE WHITE 1785–1806
and others

435 ONWARD, Christian soldiers,
Marching as to war,
With the Cross of Jesus
Going on before.
Christ the royal Master
Leads against the foe;
Forward into battle,
See, his banners go!
Onward, Christian soldiers,
Marching as to war,
With the Cross of Jesus
Going on before.

2* At the sign of triumph
Satan's legions flee;
On then, Christian soldiers,
On to victory.
Hell's foundations quiver
At the shout of praise;
Brothers, lift your voices,
Loud your anthems raise.

3* Like a mighty army
    Moves the Church of God;
Brothers, we are treading
    Where the saints have trod;
We are not divided,
    All one body we,
One in hope and doctrine,
    One in charity.

4 Crowns and thrones may perish,
    Kingdoms rise and wane,
But the Church of Jesus
    Constant will remain;
Gates of hell can never
    'Gainst that Church prevail;
We have Christ's own promise,
    And that cannot fail.

5 Onward, then, ye people,
    Join our happy throng,
Blend with ours your voices
    In the triumph song;
Glory, laud, and honour
    Unto Christ the King;
This through countless ages
    Men and angels sing.

S. BARING-GOULD 1834–1924

436
Psalm 103

PRAISE, my soul, the King of heaven;
    To his feet thy tribute bring.
Ransomed, healed, restored, forgiven,
    Who like me his praise should sing?
    Praise him! Praise him!
    Praise the everlasting King.

2 Praise him for his grace and favour
   To our fathers in distress;
 Praise him still the same for ever,
   Slow to chide, and swift to bless.
     Praise him! Praise him!
   Glorious in his faithfulness.

3 Father-like, he tends and spares us;
   Well our feeble frame he knows;
 In his hands he gently bears us,
   Rescues us from all our foes.
     Praise him! Praise him!
   Widely as his mercy flows.

4 Angels, help us to adore him;
   Ye behold him face to face;
 Sun and moon, bow down before him;
   Dwellers all in time and space.
     Praise him! Praise him!
   Praise with us the God of grace.

H. F. LYTE 1793–1847

437   *Psalm 148*

PRAISE the Lord! ye heavens, adore him;
   Praise him, angels, in the height;
 Sun and moon, rejoice before him,
   Praise him, all ye stars and light:
 Praise the Lord! for he has spoken,
   Worlds his mighty voice obeyed;
 Laws, which never shall be broken,
   For their guidance he has made.

2 Praise the Lord! for he is glorious;
  Never shall his promise fail;
 God has made his saints victorious,
  Sin and death shall not prevail.
 Praise the God of our salvation;
  Hosts on high, his power proclaim;
 Heaven and earth, and all creation,
  Laud and magnify his name!

3 Worship, honour, glory, blessing,
  Lord, we offer to thy name;
 Young and old, thy praise expressing,
  Join their Saviour to proclaim.
 As the saints in heaven adore thee,
  We would bow before thy throne;
 As thine angels serve before thee,
  So on earth thy will be done.

Verses 1, 2 Foundling Hospital Collection 1796
Verse 3 EDWARD OSLER 1798–1863

438 PRAISE to God whose word was spoken
  In the deed which made the earth;
 His the voice that called a nation,
  His the fires that tried her worth.
    God has spoken:
  Praise him for his saving word.

2 Praise to God whose word was written
  In the Scripture's sacred page,
 Record of the revelation
  Showing him to every age.
    God has spoken:
  Praise him for his saving word.

3 Praise to God whose Word incarnate
    Glorified the flesh of man,
Deeds and words and death and rising
    Tell the grace in heaven's plan.
        God has spoken:
    Praise him for his saving Word.

4 Praise to God who through his Spirit
    Ever speaks his word to man;
Spirit, dwelling deep within us,
    Show us all the Father's plan.
        God is speaking:
    Praise him for his saving word.

                  R. T. BROOKS 1918–85‡

439 PRAISE to the Holiest in the height,
    And in the depth be praise,
In all his words most wonderful,
    Most sure in all his ways.

2 O loving wisdom of our God!
    When all was sin and shame,
A second Adam to the fight
    And to the rescue came.

3* O wisest love! that flesh and blood,
    Which did in Adam fail,
Should strive afresh against their foe,
    Should strive and should prevail;

4* And that a higher gift than grace
    Should flesh and blood refine,
God's presence and his very self,
    And essence all-divine.

5 O generous love! that he who smote
    In Man for man the foe,
The double agony in Man
    For man should undergo;

6 And in the garden secretly,
    And on the cross on high,
Should teach his brethren, and inspire
    To suffer and to die.

7 Praise to the Holiest in the height,
    And in the depth be praise,
In all his words most wonderful,
    Most sure in all his ways.

JOHN HENRY NEWMAN 1801–90

440 PRAISE to the Lord, the Almighty, the King
    of creation;
O my soul, praise him, for he is thy health and
    salvation:
    Come ye who hear,
    Brothers and sisters draw near,
Praise him in glad adoration.

2 Praise to the Lord, who o'er all things so
    wondrously reigneth,
Shelters thee under his wings, yea, so gently
    sustaineth:
    Hast thou not seen
    All that is needful hath been
Granted in what he ordaineth?

3 Praise to the Lord, who doth prosper thy work,
        and defend thee;
   Surely his goodness and mercy here daily
        attend thee;
        Ponder anew
        All the Almighty can do,
     He who with love doth befriend thee.

4* Praise to the Lord, who, when tempests their
        warfare are waging,
   Who, when the elements madly around thee are
        raging,
        Biddeth them cease,
        Turneth their fury to peace,
     Whirlwinds and waters assuaging.

5* Praise to the Lord, who when darkness of sin
        is abounding,
   Who, when the godless do triumph, all virtue
        confounding,
        Sheddeth his light,
        Chaseth the horrors of night,
     Saints with his mercy surrounding.

6 Praise to the Lord! O let all that is in me adore
        him!
   All that hath life and breath come now with
        praises before him!
        Let the Amen
        Sound from his people again:
     Gladly for ay we adore him.

German, JOACHIM NEANDER 1650–80
Tr CATHERINE WINKWORTH 1827–78
and others

439

441   *Psalm 122*

PRAY that Jerusalem may have
 Peace and felicity:
Let them that love thee and thy peace
 Have still prosperity.

2 Therefore I wish that peace may still
 Within thy walls remain,
And ever may thy palaces
 Prosperity retain.

3 Now, for my friends' and brethren's sake,
 Peace be in thee, I'll say;
And for the house of God our Lord
 I'll seek thy good alway.

Scottish Psalter 1650

442   PRAYER is the soul's sincere desire,
 Uttered or unexpressed;
The motion of a hidden fire
 That trembles in the breast.

2 Prayer is the burden of a sigh,
 The falling of a tear,
The upward glancing of an eye
 When none but God is near.

3 Prayer is the simplest form of speech
 That infant lips can try;
Prayer the sublimest strains that reach
 The Majesty on high.

4 Prayer is the contrite sinner's voice,
   Returning from his ways,
While angels in their songs rejoice,
   And cry, 'Behold, he prays!'

5 Prayer is the Christian's vital breath,
   The Christian's native air,
His watchword at the gates of death:
   He enters heaven with prayer.

6 The saints in prayer appear as one
   In word, and deed, and mind,
While with the Father and the Son
   Sweet fellowship they find.

7 O thou by whom we come to God,
   The Life, the Truth, the Way,
The path of prayer thyself hast trod:
   Lord, teach us how to pray.

JAMES MONTGOMERY 1771–1854

443 REJOICE, the Lord is King,
   Your Lord and King adore;
Mortals, give thanks and sing,
   And triumph evermore:
      Lift up your heart, lift up your voice;
      Rejoice, again I say, rejoice.

2 Jesus, the Saviour, reigns,
   The God of truth and love;
When he had purged our stains,
   He took his seat above:

3 His kingdom cannot fail;
     He rules o'er earth and heaven;
  The keys of death and hell
     Are to our Jesus given:

4 He sits at God's right hand
     Till all his foes submit,
  And bow to his command,
     And fall beneath his feet:
       Lift up your heart, lift up your voice;
       Rejoice, again I say, rejoice.

CHARLES WESLEY 1707–88

444 REJOICE to-day with one accord,
     Sing out with exultation;
  Rejoice and praise our mighty Lord,
     Whose arm hath brought salvation.
      His works of love proclaim
      The greatness of his name;
      For he is God alone,
      Who hath his mercy shown:
     Let all his saints adore him!

2 When in distress to him we cried
     He heard our sad complaining;
  O trust in him, whate'er betide,
     His love is all-sustaining.
      Triumphant songs of praise
      To him our hearts shall raise;
      Now every voice shall say,
      O praise our God alway:
     Let all his saints adore him!

H. W. BAKER 1821–77

445   ROCK of ages, cleft for me,
Let me hide myself in thee;
Let the water and the blood,
From thy riven side which flowed,
Be of sin the double cure,
Cleanse me from its guilt and power.

2   Not the labours of my hands
Can fulfil thy law's demands;
Could my zeal no respite know,
Could my tears for ever flow,
All for sin could not atone;
Thou must save, and thou alone.

3   Nothing in my hand I bring,
Simply to thy cross I cling;
Naked, come to thee for dress;
Helpless, look to thee for grace;
Foul, I to the fountain fly;
Wash me, Saviour, or I die.

4   While I draw this fleeting breath,
When mine eyes are closed in death,
When I soar through tracts unknown,
See thee on thy judgement throne;
Rock of ages, cleft for me,
Let me hide myself in thee.

AUGUSTUS TOPLADY 1740–78†

446   SING Alleluya forth ye saints on high,
And let the Church on earth make glad reply:
To Christ the King, sing Alleluya!

2   To him who is both Word of God and Son,
Who, out of love, our nature did put on:

3 To him who, born of Mary, shared our life,
And in our manhood triumphed in the strife:

4 To him who did for all our sins atone,
In naked majesty on Calvary's throne:

5 To him who rose victorious from the dead,
And reigns on high, his people's Lord and Head:

6 To him who sent the Holy Spirit's grace,
To bear the Father's love to every race:

7 To him, the universal Saviour, now
Let every knee in adoration bow:
To Christ the King, sing Alleluya!

G. B. TIMMS b 1910

447 SING praise to God who reigns above,
The God of all creation,
The God of power, the God of love,
The God of our salvation;
With healing balm my soul he fills,
And every faithless murmur stills:
To God all praise and glory!

2 The angel host, O King of kings,
Thy praise for ever telling,
In earth and sky all living things
Beneath thy shadow dwelling,
Adore the wisdom which could span
And power which formed creation's plan:

3   What God's almighty power hath made
     His gracious mercy keepeth;
By morning glow or evening shade
     His watchful eye ne'er sleepeth:
Within the kingdom of his might
Lo! all is just, and all is right:

4*   Then all my gladsome way along
     I sing aloud thy praises,
That men may hear the grateful song
     My voice unwearied raises:
Be joyful in the Lord, my heart!
Both soul and body bear your part!

5   O ye who name Christ's holy name,
     Give God all praise and glory:
All ye who own his power, proclaim
     Aloud the wondrous story!
Cast each false idol from his throne,
The Lord is God, and he alone:

> German, JOHANN SCHUTZ 1640–90
> *Tr* FRANCES COX 1812–97

448   *Suitable for use in Procession*

SING, ye faithful, sing with gladness,
    Wake your noblest, sweetest strain,
With the praises of your Saviour
    Let his house resound again;
Him let all your music honour,
    And your songs exalt his reign.

2   Sing how he came forth from heaven,
     Bowed himself to Bethlehem's cave,
  Stooped to wear the servant's vesture,
     Bore the pain, the cross, the grave,
  Passed within the gates of darkness,
     Thence his banished ones to save.

3   So, he tasted death for all men,
     He, of all mankind the head,
  Sinless one, among the sinful,
     Prince of life, among the dead;
  Thus he wrought the full redemption,
     And the captor captive led.

4   Now on high, yet ever with us,
     From his Father's throne the Son
  Rules and guides the world he ransomed,
     Till the appointed work be done,
  Till he see, renewed and perfect,
     All things gathered into one.

5   Alleluya to the Father,
     Alleluya to the Son,
  Alleluya to the Spirit,
     Ever three and ever one,
  One in love and one in glory,
     While unending ages run.   Amen.

JOHN ELLERTON 1826–93

449   SOLDIERS of Christ, arise,
      And put your armour on,
  Strong in the strength which God supplies
      Through his eternal Son;

2 Strong in the Lord of Hosts,
   And in his mighty power:
Who in the strength of Jesus trusts
   Is more than conqueror.

3 Stand then in his great might,
   With all his strength endued;
And take, to arm you for the fight,
   The panoply of God.

4 Leave no unguarded place,
   No weakness of the soul:
Take every virtue, every grace,
   And fortify the whole.

5 From strength to strength go on,
   Wrestle and fight and pray;
Tread all the powers of darkness down
   And win the well-fought day.

6 That, having all things done,
   And all your conflicts past,
Ye may o'ercome through Christ alone,
   And stand entire at last.

CHARLES WESLEY 1707–88

450   *Pugnate, Christi milites*

SOLDIERS, who are Christ's below,
Strong in faith resist the foe;
Boundless is the pledged reward
Unto them who serve the Lord.

2 'Tis no palm of fading leaves
  That the conqueror's hand receives;
  Joys are his, serene and pure,
  Light that ever shall endure.

3 For the souls that overcome
  Waits the beauteous heavenly home,
  Where the blessèd evermore
  Tread on high the starry floor.

4 Passing soon and little worth
  Are the things that tempt on earth;
  Heavenward lift thy soul's regard;
  God himself is thy reward;

5 Father who the crown dost give,
  Saviour by whose death we live,
  Spirit who our hearts dost raise,
  Three in One, thy name we praise.   Amen.

Latin, 18th century
Tr JOHN CLARK 1839–88

451   SONGS of praise the angels sang,
          Heaven with alleluyas rang,
          When creation was begun,
          When God spake and it was done.

2 Songs of praise awoke the morn
  When the Prince of Peace was born;
  Songs of praise arose when he
  Captive led captivity.

3 Heaven and earth must pass away,
Songs of praise shall crown that day;
God will make new heavens and earth,
Songs of praise shall hail their birth.

4 And will man alone be dumb
Till that glorious kingdom come?
No, the Church delights to raise
Psalms and hymns and songs of praise.

5 Saints below, with heart and voice,
Still in songs of praise rejoice;
Learning here, by faith and love,
Songs of praise to sing above.

6 Hymns of glory, songs of praise,
Father, unto thee we raise;
Jesu, glory unto thee,
Ever with the Spirit be.   Amen.

JAMES MONTGOMERY 1771–1854†

452   STAND up, and bless the Lord,
Ye people of his choice;
Stand up, and bless the Lord your God
With heart and soul and voice.

2   Though high above all praise,
Above all blessing high,
Who would not fear his holy Name,
And praise and magnify?

3   O for the living flame
From his own altar brought,
To touch our lips, our minds inspire,
And wing to heaven our thought!

4   God is our strength and song,
And his salvation ours;
Then be his love in Christ proclaimed
With all our ransomed powers.

5   Stand up, and bless the Lord,
The Lord your God adore;
Stand up, and bless his glorious name
Henceforth for evermore.

JAMES MONTGOMERY 1771–185.

453   STAND up!—stand up for Jesus!
Ye soldiers of the Cross;
Lift high his royal banner,
It must not suffer loss.
From victory unto victory
His army he shall lead,
Till every foe is vanquished,
And Christ is Lord indeed.

2   Stand up!—stand up for Jesus!
The trumpet call obey,
Forth to the mighty conflict
In this his glorious day.
Ye that are men now serve him
Against unnumbered foes;
Let courage rise with danger,
And strength to strength oppose.

3 Stand up!—stand up for Jesus!
Stand in his strength alone;
The arm of flesh will fail you,
Ye dare not trust your own.
Put on the gospel armour,
Each piece put on with prayer;
Where duty calls or danger,
Be never wanting there!

4 Stand up!—stand up for Jesus!
The strife will not be long;
This day the noise of battle,
The next the victor's song.
To him that overcometh
A crown of life shall be;
He with the King of Glory
Shall reign eternally.

GEORGE DUFFIELD 1818–88

454 STILL throned in heaven, to men in unbelief
Christ spreads his hands all day;
They scan his claims, give judgement cold and
brief,
And fearless turn away.

2 Once more, O peerless mystery of grace,
Thy sweet appeal renew;
Light up dark minds, win souls to thine
embrace,
High forts of doubt subdue.

3 Speak, till the sons of men with hearts unseared,
    Led by that voice of thine,
Find thee each day more glorious, more
    endeared,
    Christ human, Christ divine.

WILLIAM BRIGHT 1824–1901†

455 STRONG Son of God, immortal Love,
    Whom we, that have not seen thy face,
    By faith, and faith alone, embrace,
Believing where we cannot prove:

2 Thou wilt not leave us in the dust;
    Thou madest man, he knows not why;
    He thinks he was not made to die:
And thou hast made him, thou art just.

3 Thou seemest human and divine,
    The highest, holiest manhood thou:
    Our wills are ours, we know not how;
Our wills are ours, to make them thine.

4 Our little systems have their day;
    They have their day and cease to be:
    They are but broken lights of thee,
And thou, O Lord, art more than they.

ALFRED TENNYSON 1809–92

456   TEACH me, my God and King,
In all things thee to see;
And what I do in anything
To do it as for thee!

2   A man that looks on glass,
On it may stay his eye;
Or if he pleaseth, through it pass,
And then the heaven espy.

3   All may of thee partake;
Nothing can be so mean,
Which with this tincture, 'for thy sake',
Will not grow bright and clean.

4   A servant with this clause
Makes drudgery divine;
Who sweeps a room, as for thy laws,
Makes that and the action fine.

5   This is the famous stone
That turneth all to gold;
For that which God doth touch and own
Cannot for less be told.

GEORGE HERBERT 1593-1633

457   *Psalm 23*

THE King of love my Shepherd is,
Whose goodness faileth never;
I nothing lack if I am his
And he is mine for ever.

2 Where streams of living water flow
　　My ransomed soul he leadeth,
And where the verdant pastures grow
　　With food celestial feedeth.

3 Perverse and foolish oft I strayed,
　　But yet in love he sought me,
And on his shoulder gently laid,
　　And home, rejoicing, brought me.

4 In death's dark vale I fear no ill
　　With thee, dear Lord, beside me;
Thy rod and staff my comfort still,
　　Thy cross before to guide me.

5 Thou spread'st a table in my sight;
　　Thy unction, grace bestoweth:
And O what transport of delight
　　From thy pure chalice floweth!

6 And so through all the length of days
　　Thy goodness faileth never;
Good Shepherd, may I sing thy praise
　　Within thy house for ever.

H. W. BAKER 1821–77

458 *Psalm 23*

THE Lord my pasture shall prepare,
And feed me with a shepherd's care;
His presence shall my wants supply,
And guard me with a watchful eye;
My noonday walks he shall attend,
And all my midnight hours defend.

2 When in the sultry glebe I faint,
   Or on the thirsty mountain pant,
   To fertile vales and dewy meads
   My weary wandering steps he leads,
   Where peaceful rivers, soft and slow,
   Amid the verdant landscape flow.

3 Though in a bare and rugged way
   Through devious lonely wilds I stray,
   Thy bounty shall my pains beguile;
   The barren wilderness shall smile
   With sudden green and herbage crowned,
   And streams shall murmur all around.

4 Though in the paths of death I tread,
   With gloomy horrors overspread,
   My steadfast heart shall fear no ill,
   For thou, O Lord, art with me still:
   Thy friendly staff shall give me aid,
   And guide me through the dreadful shade.

JOSEPH ADDISON 1672–1719

459   *Psalm 23*

THE Lord's my shepherd, I'll not want;
   He makes me down to lie
In pastures green; he leadeth me
   The quiet waters by.

2 My soul he doth restore again,
      And me to walk doth make
   Within the paths of righteousness,
      E'en for his own name's sake.

3 Yea, though I walk in death's dark vale,
   Yet will I fear no ill:
For thou art with me, and thy rod
   And staff me comfort still.

4 My table thou hast furnishèd
   In presence of my foes;
My head thou dost with oil anoint
   And my cup overflows.

5 Goodness and mercy all my life
   Shall surely follow me;
And in God's house for evermore
   My dwelling-place shall be.

Scottish Psalter 1650

For a further version of Psalm 23 see 77

460 THERE is a land of pure delight,
   Where saints immortal reign;
Infinite day excludes the night,
   And pleasures banish pain.

2 There everlasting spring abides,
   And never-withering flowers;
Death, like a narrow sea, divides
   This heavenly land from ours.

3 Sweet fields beyond the swelling flood
   Stand dressed in living green;
So to the Jews old Canaan stood,
   While Jordan rolled between.

4 But timorous mortals start and shrink
    To cross this narrow sea,
And linger shivering on the brink,
    And fear to launch away.

5 O could we make our doubts remove,
    These gloomy doubts that rise,
And see the Canaan that we love
    With unbeclouded eyes!

6 Could we but climb where Moses stood,
    And view the landscape o'er,
Not Jordan's stream, nor death's cold flood,
    Should fright us from the shore!

ISAAC WATTS 1674–1748

461 THERE's a wideness in God's mercy
    Like the wideness of the sea;
There's a kindness in his justice
    Which is more than liberty.

2 There is no place where earth's sorrows
    Are more felt than up in heaven;
There is no place where earth's failings
    Have such kindly judgement given.

3 For the love of God is broader
    Than the measure of man's mind;
And the heart of the Eternal
    Is most wonderfully kind.

4 But we make his love too narrow
   By false limits of our own;
And we magnify his strictness
   With a zeal he will not own.

5 There is plentiful redemption
   In the blood that has been shed;
There is joy for all the members
   In the sorrows of the Head.

6 There is grace enough for thousands
   Of new worlds as great as this;
There is room for fresh creations
   In that upper home of bliss.

7 If our love were but more simple,
   We should take him at his word;
And our lives would be all gladness
   In the joy of Christ our Lord.

F. W. FABER 1814–63†

462 THEY whose course on earth is o'er,
   Think they of their brethren more?
They before the throne who bow,
   Feel they for their brethren now?

2 We by enemies distrest,
   They in paradise at rest;
We the captives, they the freed;
   We and they are one indeed:

3 One in all we seek or shun,
   One, because our Lord is one;
One in home and one in love;
   We below, and they above.

4 They whom space on earth divides,
Mountains, rivers, ocean-tides;
Have they with each other part?
Have they fellowship in heart?

5 Each to each may be unknown,
Wide apart their lots be thrown;
Yet in sacrament and prayer
Each with other hath a share.

6 Saints departed, even thus
Hold communion still with us;
Still with us, beyond the veil,
Praising, pleading without fail.

7 So with them our hearts we raise,
Share their work and join their praise,
Rendering worship, thanks and love
To the Trinity above.

J. M. NEALE 1818–66‡

463 THINE for ever! God of love,
Hear us from thy throne above;
Thine for ever may we be
Here and in eternity.

2 Thine for ever! O, how blest
They who find in thee their rest!
Saviour, Guardian, heavenly Friend,
O defend us to the end.

3   Thine for ever! Lord of life,
    Shield us through our earthly strife;
    Thou the Life, the Truth, the Way,
    Guide us to the realms of day.

4   Thine for ever! thou our guide,
    All our wants by thee supplied,
    All our sins by thee forgiven,
    Led by thee from earth to heaven.

MARY MAUDE 1819–1913

464   THOU art the Way: by thee alone
          From sin and death we flee;
      And he who would the Father seek
          Must seek him, Lord, by thee.

2   Thou art the Truth: thy word alone
        True wisdom can impart;
    Thou only canst inform the mind
        And purify the heart.

3   Thou art the Life: the rending tomb
        Proclaims thy conquering arm;
    And those who put their trust in thee
        Nor death nor hell shall harm.

4   Thou art the Way, the Truth, the Life:
        Grant us that Way to know,
    That Truth to keep, that Life to win,
        Whose joys eternal flow.

GEORGE DOANE 1799–1859

465 THOU didst leave thy throne and thy kingly
crown
When thou camest to earth for me;
But in Bethlehem's home there was found no
room
For thy holy nativity:
O come to my heart, Lord Jesus;
There is room in my heart for thee.

2 Heaven's arches rang when the angels sang,
Proclaiming thy royal degree;
But in lowly birth didst thou come to earth,
And in great humility:

3 Thou camest, O Lord, with the living word
That should set thy people free;
But with mocking scorn and with crown of thorn
They bore thee to Calvary:

4 When all heaven shall ring, and her choirs shall
sing,
At thy coming to victory,
Let thy voice call me home, saying, Yet there is
room,
There is room at my side for thee:

EMILY ELLIOTT 1836–97

466 THOU whose almighty word
Chaos and darkness heard,
And took their flight;
Hear us, we humbly pray,
And where the gospel-day
Sheds not its glorious ray
Let there be light.

2 Thou who didst come to bring
  On thy redeeming wing
    Healing and sight,
  Health to the sick in mind,
  Sight to the inly blind,
  O now to all mankind
    Let there be light.

3 Spirit of truth and love,
  Life-giving, holy Dove,
    Speed forth thy flight;
  Move o'er the waters' face,
  Bearing the lamp of grace,
  And in earth's darkest place
    Let there be light.

4 Blessèd and holy Three,
  Glorious Trinity,
    Wisdom, Love, Might,
  Boundless as ocean's tide
  Rolling in fullest pride,
  Through the world far and wide
    Let there be light.

JOHN MARRIOTT 1780–1825

467   *Psalm 34*

THROUGH all the changing scenes of life,
  In trouble and in joy,
The praises of my God shall still
  My heart and tongue employ.

2 O magnify the Lord with me,
  With me exalt his name;
When in distress to him I called,
  He to my rescue came.

3 The hosts of God encamp around
  The dwellings of the just;
Deliverance he affords to all
  Who on his succour trust.

4 O make but trial of his love,
  Experience will decide
How blest are they, and only they,
  Who in his truth confide.

5 Fear him, ye saints, and you will then
  Have nothing else to fear;
Make you his service your delight,
  Your wants shall be his care.

6 To Father, Son, and Holy Ghost,
  The God whom we adore,
Be glory, as it was, is now,
  And shall be evermore.   Amen.

TATE and BRADY *New Version* 1696

468 THROUGH the night of doubt and sorrow
  Onward goes the pilgrim band,
Singing songs of expectation,
  Marching to the Promised Land.

2 Clear before us through the darkness
  Gleams and burns the guiding light;
Brother clasps the hand of brother,
  Stepping fearless through the night.

3   One the light of God's own presence
      O'er his ransomed people shed,
Chasing far the gloom and terror,
      Brightening all the path we tread;

4   One the object of our journey,
      One the faith which never tires,
One the earnest looking forward,
      One the hope our God inspires:

5   One the strain that lips of thousands
      Lift as from the heart of one;
One the conflict, one the peril,
      One the march in God begun;

6   One the gladness of rejoicing
      On the far eternal shore,
Where the One Almighty Father
      Reigns in love for evermore.

Danish, BERNHARDT INGEMANN 1789–1862
Tr S. BARING-GOULD 1834–1924

469   TO Mercy, Pity, Peace, and Love,
      All pray in their distress,
And to these virtues of delight
      Return their thankfulness.

2   For Mercy, Pity, Peace, and Love,
      Is God our Father dear;
And Mercy, Pity, Peace, and Love,
      Is Man, his child and care.

3 For Mercy has a human heart,
    Pity, a human face;
And Love, the human form divine,
    And Peace, the human dress.

4 Then every man, of every clime,
    That prays in his distress,
Prays to the human form divine:
    Love, Mercy, Pity, Peace.

WILLIAM BLAKE 1757–1827

470 *Suitable for use in Procession*

Gloriosi Salvatoris

TO the name that brings salvation
    Praise and honour let us pay,
Which for many a generation
    Hid in God's foreknowledge lay,
But to every tongue and nation
    Holy Church proclaims today.

2 Jesus—be that name our treasure,
    Name beyond that words can tell;
Name of gladness, name of pleasure,
    Ear and heart delighting well;
Name of sweetness, passing measure,
    Freeing souls from sin's dark spell.

3 Name that calls for adoration,
    Name that speaks of victory,
Name for grateful meditation
    In the vale of misery,
Name for loving veneration
    By the citizens on high.

4 Name that whosoever preaches
    Makes sweet music to the ear;
Who in prayer this name beseeches
    Finds divinest comfort near;
Joyful then the heart that reaches
    To embrace that name so dear.

5 Name by hard-won right exalted
    Over every other name;
And when man was sore assaulted
    Put the enemy to shame:
Strength to them that else had halted,
    Sight to blind, and health to lame.

6 Jesu, we thy name adoring,
    Long to see thee as thou art:
Of thy clemency imploring
    So to write it in our heart,
That hereafter, upward soaring,
    We with angels may have part.

7 Where thou reignest with the Father,
    Thou the everlasting Son,
Where with the eternal Spirit,
    Threefold God, yet ever One,
May our eyes behold thy splendour
    When our earthly course is done.

Latin c 15th century
Tr J. M. NEALE 1818–66
and EDITORS

The above hymn is specially suitable on feasts of our Lord and in churches bearing the title of Christ Church, St Saviour, etc.

471 WE love the place, O God,
 Wherein thine honour dwells;
The joy of thine abode
 All earthly joy excels.

2 We love the house of prayer,
 Wherein thy servants meet;
And thou, O Lord, art there
 Thy chosen flock to greet.

3 We love the sacred font,
 For there the holy Dove
To pour is ever wont
 His blessing from above.

4 We love thine altar, Lord;
 O, what on earth so dear!
For there, in faith adored,
 We find thy presence near.

5 We love the word of life,
 The word that tells of peace,
Of comfort in the strife,
 And joys that never cease.

6 We love to sing below
 For mercies freely given;
But O, we long to know
 The triumph-song of heaven!

7 Lord Jesus, give us grace
 On earth to love thee more,
In heaven to see thy face,
 And with thy saints adore.

WILLIAM BULLOCK 1798–1874
and H. W. BAKER 1821–77

472 WHEN all thy mercies, O my God,
　　My rising soul surveys,
Transported with the view, I'm lost
　　In wonder, love, and praise.

2　Unnumbered comforts to my soul
　　Thy tender care bestowed,
Before my infant heart conceived
　　From whom those comforts flowed.

3　When in the slippery paths of youth
　　With heedless steps I ran,
Thine arm unseen conveyed me safe,
　　And led me up to man.

4　When worn with sickness oft hast thou
　　With health renewed my face;
And when in sins and sorrows sunk,
　　Revived my soul with grace.

5　Through every period of my life
　　Thy goodness I'll pursue,
And after death in distant worlds
　　The glorious theme renew.

6　Through all eternity to thee
　　A joyful song I'll raise;
For O, eternity's too short
　　To utter all thy praise.

JOSEPH ADDISON 1672–1719

473 WHEN morning gilds the skies,
My heart awaking cries,
    May Jesus Christ be praised:
Alike at work and prayer
To Jesus I repair;
    May Jesus Christ be praised.

2* The sacred minster bell
It peals o'er hill and dell,
    May Jesus Christ be praised:
O hark to what it sings,
As joyously it rings,
    May Jesus Christ be praised.

3* My tongue shall never tire
Of chanting in the choir,
    May Jesus Christ be praised:
The fairest graces spring
In hearts that ever sing,
    May Jesus Christ be praised.

4* When sleep her balm denies,
My silent spirit sighs,
    May Jesus Christ be praised:
When evil thoughts molest,
With this I shield my breast,
    May Jesus Christ be praised.

5* Does sadness fill my mind?
A solace here I find,
    May Jesus Christ be praised:
Or fades my earthly bliss?
My comfort still is this,
    May Jesus Christ be praised.

6 The night becomes as day,
   When from the heart we say,
      May Jesus Christ be praised:
   The powers of darkness fear,
   When this sweet chant they hear,
      May Jesus Christ be praised.

7 In heaven's eternal bliss
   The loveliest strain is this,
      May Jesus Christ be praised:
   Let air, and sea, and sky
   From depth to height reply,
      May Jesus Christ be praised.

8 Be this, while life is mine,
   My canticle divine,
      May Jesus Christ be praised:
   Be this the eternal song
   Through all the ages on,
      May Jesus Christ be praised.

German, 19th century
Tr EDWARD CASWALL 1814–78

474 WHO is this so weak and helpless,
   Child of lowly Hebrew maid,
Rudely in a stable sheltered,
   Coldly in a manger laid?
'Tis the Lord of all creation,
   Who this wondrous path hath trod;
He is God from everlasting,
   And to everlasting God.

2   Who is this—a Man of Sorrows,
    Walking sadly life's hard way,
Homeless, weary, sighing, weeping
    Over sin and Satan's sway?
'Tis our God, our glorious Saviour,
    Who above the starry sky
Now for us a place prepareth
    Where no tear can dim the eye.

3*   Who is this—behold him raining
    Drops of blood upon the ground?
Who is this—despised, rejected,
    Mocked, insulted, beaten, bound?
'Tis our God, who gifts and graces
    On his Church now poureth down;
Who shall smite in holy vengeance
    All his foes beneath his throne.

4   Who is this that hangeth dying,
    With the thieves on either side?
Nails his hands and feet are tearing,
    And the spear hath pierced his side.
'Tis the God who ever liveth
    'Mid the shining ones on high,
In the glorious golden city
    Reigning everlastingly.

W. WALSHAM HOW 1823–97

475 YE holy angels bright,
Who wait at God's right hand,
Or through the realms of light
Fly at your Lord's command,
Assist our song,
For else the theme
Too high doth seem
For mortal tongue.

2 Ye blessèd souls at rest,
Who ran this earthly race,
And now, from sin released,
Behold the Saviour's face,
God's praises sound,
As in his sight
With sweet delight
Ye do abound.

3 Ye saints, who toil below,
Adore your heavenly King,
And onward as ye go
Some joyful anthem sing;
Take what he gives
And praise him still,
Through good or ill,
Who ever lives!

4 My soul, bear thou thy part,
Triumph in God above:
And with a well-tuned heart
Sing thou the songs of love!
Let all thy days
Till life shall end,
Whate'er he send,
Be filled with praise.

RICHARD BAXTER 1615–91 and others

476
YE servants of God, your Master proclaim,
And publish abroad his wonderful name:
The name all-victorious of Jesus extol:
His kingdom is glorious, and rules over all.

2 God ruleth on high, almighty to save;
And still he is nigh, his presence we have:
The great congregation his triumph shall sing,
Ascribing salvation to Jesus our King.

3 Salvation to God who sits on the throne!
Let all cry aloud, and honour the Son:
The praises of Jesus the angels proclaim,
Fall down on their faces, and worship the Lamb.

4 Then let us adore, and give him his right:
All glory and power, all wisdom and might,
All honour and blessing, with angels above,
And thanks never-ceasing, and infinite love.

CHARLES WESLEY 1707–88

477
YE that know the Lord is gracious,
Ye for whom a Corner-stone
Stands, of God elect and precious,
Laid that ye may build thereon,
See that on that sure foundation
Ye a living temple raise,
Towers that may tell forth salvation,
Walls that may re-echo praise.

2 Living stones, by God appointed
    Each to his allotted place,
Kings and priests, by God anointed,
    Shall ye not declare his grace?
Ye, a royal generation,
    Tell the tidings of your birth,
Tidings of a new creation
    To an old and weary earth.

3 Tell the praise of him who called you
    Out of darkness into light,
Broke the fetters that enthralled you,
    Gave you freedom, peace and sight:
Tell the tale of sins forgiven,
    Strength renewed and hope restored,
Till the earth, in tune with heaven,
    Praise and magnify the Lord.

C. A. ALINGTON 1872–1955

478 YE watchers and ye holy ones,
Bright Seraphs, Cherubim and Thrones,
    Raise the glad strain, Alleluya!
Cry out Dominions, Princedoms, Powers,
Virtues, Archangels, Angels' choirs,
    Alleluya, Alleluya, Alleluya, Alleluya,
        Alleluya!

2 O higher than the Cherubim,
More glorious than the Seraphim,
    Lead their praises, Alleluya!
Thou Bearer of the eternal Word,
Most gracious, magnify the Lord,
    Alleluya, Alleluya, Alleluya, Alleluya,
        Alleluya!

3 Respond, ye souls in endless rest,
　Ye Patriarchs and Prophets blest,
　　Alleluya, Alleluya!
　Ye holy Twelve, ye Martyrs strong,
　All Saints triumphant, raise the song
　　Alleluya, Alleluya, Alleluya, Alleluya,
　　　Alleluya!

4 O friends, in gladness let us sing,
　Supernal anthems echoing,
　　Alleluya, Alleluya!
　To God the Father, God the Son,
　And God the Spirit, Three in One,
　　Alleluya, Alleluya, Alleluya, Alleluya,
　　　Alleluya!

ATHELSTAN RILEY 1858–1945

Verse 2 refers to the Mother of Jesus.

PART V

CHURCH AND PEOPLE

479 FAITH of our fathers, taught of old
By faithful shepherds of the fold,
　　The hallowing of our nation;
Thou wast through many a wealthy year,
Through many a darkened day of fear,
　　The rock of our salvation.
Arise, arise, good Christian men,
Your glorious standard raise again,
　　The Cross of Christ who calls you;
Who bids you live and bids you die
For his great cause, and stands on high
　　To witness what befalls you.

2* Our fathers heard the trumpet call
Through lowly cot and kingly hall
　　From oversea resounding;
They bowed their stubborn wills to learn
The truths that live, the thoughts that burn,
　　With new resolve abounding.
Arise, arise, good Christian men,
Your glorious standard raise again,
　　The Cross of Christ who guides you;
Whose arm is bared to join the fray,
Who marshals you in stern array,
　　Fearless, whate'er betides you.

3 Our fathers held the faith received,
   By saints declared, by saints believed,
     By saints in death defended;
   Through pain of doubt and bitterness,
   Through pain of treason and distress,
     They for the right contended.
   Arise, arise, good Christian men,
   Your glorious standard raise again,
     The Cross of Christ who bought you;
   Who leads you forth in this new age
   With long-enduring hearts to wage
     The warfare he has taught you.

4* Though frequent be the loud alarms,
   Though still we march by ambushed arms
     Of death and hell surrounded,
   With Christ for Chief we fear no foe,
   Nor force nor craft can overthrow
     The Church that he has founded.
   Arise, arise, good Christian men,
   Your glorious standard raise again,
     The Cross wherewith he signed you;
   The King himself shall lead you on,
   Shall watch you till the strife be done,
     Then near his throne shall find you.

T. A. LACEY 1853–1931

480 IN Christ there is no East or West,
    In him no South or North,
   But one great fellowship of love
    Throughout the whole wide earth.

2   Join hands, then, brothers of the faith,
     Whate'er your race may be;
  Who serves my Father as a son
     Is surely kin to me.

3   In Christ now meet both East and West,
     In him meet South and North,
  All Christlike souls are one in him,
     Throughout the whole wide earth.

JOHN OXENHAM 1852–1941†

481   JESUS, Lord, we look to thee,
     Let us in thy name agree,
     Show thyself the Prince of peace,
     Bid all strife for ever cease.

2   Make us of one heart and mind,
     Courteous, pitiful and kind;
     To thy Church the pattern give,
     Show how true believers live.

3   Free from anger and from pride,
     Let us thus in thee abide;
     All the depths of love express,
     All the heights of holiness.

4   Love, all hatreds has destroyed,
     Rendered all distinctions void;
     Colour, race, and factions fall:
     Thou, O Christ, art all in all.

CHARLES WESLEY 1707–88
and EDITORS

482 SPREAD, O spread, thou mighty word,
Spread the kingdom of the Lord,
Wheresoe'er his breath has given
Life to beings meant for heaven.

2 Tell them how the Father's will
Made the world, and makes it still,
How he sent his Son to save,
How Christ conquered o'er the grave.

3 Tell of our Redeemer's love,
Who for ever doth remove
By his holy sacrifice
All the guilt that on us lies.

4 Tell them of the Spirit given
Now to guide us on to heaven,
Strong and holy, just and true,
Working both to will and do.

5 Word of life, most pure and strong,
Lo, for thee the nations long;
Spread, till from its dreary night
All the world awakes to light!

German, JONATHAN BAHNMAIER 1774–1841
Tr CATHERINE WINKWORTH 1827–78†

483 THE Church of God a kingdom is,
Where Christ in power doth reign,
Where spirits yearn till seen in bliss
Their Lord shall come again.

2　Glad companies of saints possess
　　　This Church below, above;
　And God's perpetual calm doth bless
　　　Their paradise of love.

3　An altar stands within the shrine
　　　Whereon, once sacrificed,
　Is set, immaculate, divine,
　　　The Lamb of God, the Christ.

4　There rich and poor, from countless lands,
　　　Praise Christ on mystic rood;
　There nations reach forth holy hands
　　　To take God's holy food.

5　There pure life-giving streams o'erflow
　　　The sower's garden-ground;
　And faith and hope fair blossoms show,
　　　And fruits of love abound.

6　O King, O Christ, this endless grace
　　　To us and all men bring,
　To see the vision of thy face
　　　In joy, O Christ, our King.

LIONEL MUIRHEAD 1845–1925

484　THE Church's one foundation
　　　Is Jesus Christ, her Lord;
　She is his new creation
　　　By water and the word:
　From heaven he came and sought her
　　　To be his holy Bride,
　With his own blood he bought her,
　　　And for her life he died.

2 Elect from every nation,
    Yet one o'er all the earth,
Her charter of salvation
    One Lord, one faith, one birth;
One holy name she blesses,
    Partakes one holy food,
And to one hope she presses
    With every grace endued.

3* Though with a scornful wonder
    Men see her sore opprest,
By schisms rent asunder,
    By heresies distrest,
Yet saints their watch are keeping,
    Their cry goes up, 'How long?'
And soon the night of weeping
    Shall be the morn of song.

4 'Mid toil, and tribulation,
    And tumult of her war,
She waits the consummation
    Of peace for evermore;
Till with the vision glorious
    Her longing eyes are blest,
And the great Church victorious
    Shall be the Church at rest.

5 Yet she on earth hath union
    With God the Three in One,
And mystic sweet communion
    With those whose rest is won:
O happy ones and holy!
    Lord, give us grace that we
Like them, the meek and lowly,
    On high may dwell with thee.

SAMUEL STONE 1839–1900

481

485 THY hand, O God, has guided
  Thy flock, from age to age;
The wondrous tale is written,
  Full clear, on every page;
Our fathers owned thy goodness,
  And we their deeds record;
And both of this bear witness:
  One Church, one Faith, one Lord.

2 Thy heralds brought glad tidings
  To greatest, as to least;
They bade men rise, and hasten
  To share the great King's feast;
And this was all their teaching,
  In every deed and word,
To all alike proclaiming
  One Church, one Faith, one Lord.

3 Through many a day of darkness,
  Through many a scene of strife,
The faithful few fought bravely
  To guard the nation's life.
Their gospel of redemption,
  Sin pardoned, man restored,
Was all in this enfolded,
  One Church, one Faith, one Lord.

4 And we, shall we be faithless?
  Shall hearts fail, hands hang down?
Shall we evade the conflict,
  And cast away our crown?
Not so: in God's deep counsels
  Some better thing is stored;
We will maintain, unflinching,
  One Church, one Faith, one Lord.

5 Thy mercy will not fail us,
   Nor leave thy work undone;
With thy right hand to help us,
   The victory shall be won;
And then, by men and angels,
   Thy name shall be adored,
And this shall be their anthem,
   One Church, one Faith, one Lord.

EDWARD PLUMPTRE 1821–91

486 WE have a gospel to proclaim,
   Good news for men in all the earth,
The gospel of a Saviour's name:
   We sing his glory, tell his worth.

2 Tell of his birth at Bethlehem,
   Not in a royal house or hall,
But in a stable dark and dim:
   The Word made flesh, a light for all.

3 Tell of his death at Calvary,
   Hated by those he came to save,
In lonely suffering on the cross:
   For all he loved, his life he gave.

4 Tell of that glorious Easter morn,
   Empty the tomb, for he was free:
He broke the power of death and hell
   That we might share his victory.

5 Tell of his reign at God's right hand,
   By all creation glorified:
He sends his Spirit on his Church,
   To live for him, the Lamb who died.

6 Now we rejoice to name him King:
    Jesus is Lord of all the earth.
This gospel message we proclaim;
    We sing his glory, tell his worth.

EDWARD BURNS b 1938

487   *The Head of the Church*

YOU, living Christ, our eyes behold
    Amid your Church appearing,
All girt about your breast with gold
    And bright apparel wearing;
Your countenance is burning bright,
A sun resplendent in its might:
    Lord Christ, we see your glory.

2 Your glorious feet have sought and found
    Your sons of every nation;
With everlasting voice you sound
    The call of our salvation;
Your eyes of flame still search and scan
The whole outspreading realm of man:
    Lord Christ, we see your glory.

3 O risen Christ, today alive,
    Amid your Church abiding,
Who now your risen body give,
    New life and strength providing,
We join in heavenly company
To sing your praise triumphantly,
    For we have seen your glory.

EDMUND MORGAN 1888–1979
based on Revelation 1. 12–16

See also

302 O thou who at thy Eucharist didst pray
355 Eternal Ruler of the ceaseless round
441 Pray that Jerusalem may have

NATIONAL

488   AND did those feet in ancient time
            Walk upon England's mountains green?
        And was the holy Lamb of God
            On England's pleasant pastures seen?
        And did the countenance divine
            Shine forth upon our clouded hills?
        And was Jerusalem builded here
            Among those dark satanic mills?

2   Bring me my bow of burning gold!
            Bring me my arrows of desire!
        Bring me my spear! O clouds, unfold!
            Bring me my chariot of fire!
        I will not cease from mental fight,
            Nor shall my sword sleep in my hand,
        Till we have built Jerusalem
            In England's green and pleasant land.

WILLIAM BLAKE 1757–1827

489   *National Anthem*

GOD save our gracious Queen,
Long live our noble Queen,
  God save the Queen!
Send her victorious,
Happy and glorious,
Long to reign over us,
  God save the Queen!

2 Thy choicest gifts in store
On her be pleased to pour,
  Long may she reign:
May she defend our laws,
And ever give us cause
To sing with heart and voice
  God save the Queen!

3* Nor on this land alone,
But be God's mercies known
  From shore to shore:
Lord, make the nations see
That men should brothers be,
And form one family
  The wide world o'er.

Verses 1 and 2 ANONYMOUS
Verse 3 W. E. HICKSON 1803–70

490 JUDGE eternal, throned in splendour,
    Lord of lords and King of kings,
With thy living fire of judgement
    Purge this realm of bitter things:
Solace all its wide dominion
    With the healing of thy wings.

2   Still the weary folk are pining
    For the hour that brings release:
And the city's crowded clangour
    Cries aloud for sin to cease;
And the homesteads and the woodlands
    Plead in silence for their peace.

3   Crown, O God, thine own endeavour;
    Cleave our darkness with thy sword;
Feed the faithless and the hungry
    With the richness of thy word:
Cleanse the body of this nation
    Through the glory of the Lord.

HENRY SCOTT HOLLAND 1847–1918†

491 LORD, while for all mankind we pray
    Of every clime and coast,
O hear us for our native land,
    The land we love the most.

2   O guard our shores from every foe;
    With peace our borders bless;
With prosperous times our cities crown,
    Our fields with plenteousness.

3   Unite us in the sacred love
        Of knowledge, truth, and thee;
    And let our hills and valleys shout
        The songs of liberty.

4   Lord of the nations, thus to thee
        Our country we commend;
    Be thou her refuge and her trust,
        Her everlasting Friend.

JOHN WREFORD 1800–81

492   O GOD of earth and altar,
        Bow down and hear our cry,
    Our earthly rulers falter,
        Our people drift and die;
    The walls of gold entomb us,
        The swords of scorn divide,
    Take not thy thunder from us,
        But take away our pride.

2   From all that terror teaches,
        From lies of tongue and pen,
    From all the easy speeches
        That comfort cruel men,
    From sale and profanation
        Of honour and the sword,
    From sleep and from damnation,
        Deliver us, good Lord!

3　Tie in a living tether
　　The prince and priest and thrall,
Bind all our lives together,
　　Smite us and save us all;
In ire and exultation
　　Aflame with faith, and free,
Lift up a living nation,
　　A single sword to thee.

G. K. CHESTERTON 1874–1936

493　REJOICE, O land, in God thy might,
His will obey, him serve aright;
For thee the Saints uplift their voice:
Fear not, O land, in God rejoice.

2　Glad shalt thou be, with blessing crowned,
With joy and peace thou shalt abound;
Yea, love with thee shall make his home
Until thou see God's kingdom come.

3　He shall forgive thy sins untold:
Remember thou his love of old;
Walk in his way, his word adore,
And keep his truth for evermore.

ROBERT BRIDGES 1844–1930

See also

417　O God, our help in ages past

THE KINGDOM OF GOD

494   CHRIST is the world's true Light,
Its Captain of salvation,
The Daystar shining bright
To every man and nation;
New life, new hope awakes,
Where'er men own his sway:
Freedom her bondage breaks,
And night is turned to day.

2   In Christ all races meet,
Their ancient feuds forgetting,
The whole round world complete,
From sunrise to its setting:
When Christ is throned as Lord,
Men shall forsake their fear,
To ploughshare beat the sword,
To pruning-hook the spear.

3   One Lord, in one great name
Unite us all who own thee;
Cast out our pride and shame
That hinder to enthrone thee;
The world has waited long,
Has travailed long in pain;
To heal its ancient wrong,
Come, Prince of Peace, and reign.

G. W. BRIGGS 1875–1959

495 GOD is working his purpose out as year
      succeeds to year,
God is working his purpose out and the time is
      drawing near;
Nearer and nearer draws the time, the time
      that shall surely be,
When the earth shall be filled with the glory of
      God as the waters cover the sea.

2 From utmost east to utmost west where'er
      man's foot hath trod,
By the mouth of many messengers goes forth
      the voice of God,
'Give ear to me, ye continents, ye isles, give
      ear to me,
That the earth may be filled with the glory of
      God as the waters cover the sea.'

3 What can we do to work God's work, to
      prosper and increase
The brotherhood of all mankind, the reign of
      the Prince of Peace?
What can we do to hasten the time, the time
      that shall surely be,
When the earth shall be filled with the glory of
      God as the waters cover the sea?

4 March we forth in the strength of God with the
    banner of Christ unfurled,
That the light of the glorious gospel of truth
    may shine throughout the world;
Fight we the fight with sorrow and sin, to set
    their captives free,
That the earth may be filled with the glory of
    God as the waters cover the sea.

5 All we can do is nothing worth unless God
    blesses the deed;
Vainly we hope for the harvest-tide till God
    gives life to the seed;
Yet nearer and nearer draws the time, the time
    that shall surely be,
When the earth shall be filled with the glory of
    God as the waters cover the sea.

A. C. AINGER 1841–1919

496 O CHRIST the Lord, O Christ the King,
Who wide the gates of death didst fling,
Whose place upon creation's throne
By Easter triumph was made known,
Rule now on earth from realms above,
Subdue the nations by thy love.

2 Lord, vindicate against men's greed
The weak, whose tears thy justice plead;
Thy pity, Lord, on men who lie
Broken by war and tyranny;
Show them the cross which thou didst bear,
Give them the power that conquered there.

3 Let those whose pride usurps thy throne
Acknowledge thou art Lord alone;
Cause those whose lust torments mankind
Thy wrath to know, thy mercy find;
Make all the rebel world proclaim
The mighty power of thy blest name.

4 So shall creation's bondage cease,
Its pangs of woe give birth to peace;
And all the earth, redeemed by thee,
Shall know a glorious liberty:
O haste the time, make short the days,
Till all our cries dissolve in praise.

R. T. BROOKS 1918–85‡

497 O LORD our God, arise!
The cause of truth maintain,
And wide o'er all the peopled world
Extend her blessed reign.

2 Thou Prince of life, arise!
Nor let thy glory cease;
Far spread the conquests of thy grace,
And bless the earth with peace.

3   O Holy Ghost, arise!
      Spread forth thy quickening wing,
  And o'er a dark and ruined world
    Let light and order spring.

4   All on the earth, arise!
      To God the Saviour sing;
  From shore to shore, from earth to heaven
    Let echoing anthems ring.

RALPH WARDLOW 1779–1853

498 SON of God, eternal Saviour,
    Source of life and truth and grace,
Son of Man, whose birth among us
    Hallows all our human race,
Thou, our Head, who, throned in glory,
    For thine own dost ever plead,
Fill us with thy love and pity,
    Heal our wrongs, and help our need.

2 As thou, Lord, hast lived for others,
    So may we for others live;
Freely have thy gifts been granted,
    Freely may thy servants give.
Thine the gold and thine the silver,
    Thine the wealth of land and sea,
We but stewards of thy bounty,
    Held in solemn trust for thee.

3 Come, O Christ, and reign among us,
   King of love, and Prince of peace,
Hush the storm of strife and passion,
   Bid its cruel discords cease;
By thy patient years of toiling,
   By thy silent hours of pain,
Quench our fevered thirst of pleasure,
   Shame our selfish greed of gain.

4* Dark the path that lies behind us,
   Strewn with wrecks and stained with blood;
But before us gleams the vision
   Of the coming brotherhood.
See the Christlike host advancing,
   High and lowly, great and small,
Linked in bonds of common service
   For the common Lord of all.

5 Son of God, eternal Saviour,
   Source of life and truth and grace,
Son of Man, whose birth among us
   Hallows all our human race.
Thou who prayedst, thou who willest
   That thy people should be one,
Grant, O grant our hope's fruition:
   Here on earth thy will be done.

SOMERSET LOWRY 1855–1932

499   THY kingdom come, O God,
    Thy rule, O Christ, begin;
  Break with thy iron rod
    The tyrannies of sin.

2   Where is thy reign of peace
    And purity and love?
  When shall all hatred cease,
    As in the realms above?

3   When comes the promised time
    That war shall be no more,
  And lust, oppression, crime,
    Shall flee thy face before?

4   We pray thee Lord, arise,
    And come in thy great might;
  Revive our longing eyes,
    Which languish for thy sight.

5   O'er lands both near and far
    Thick darkness broodeth yet:
  Arise, O morning Star,
    Arise, and never set.

LEWIS HENSLEY 1824–1905†

500 THY kingdom come! on bended knee
The passing ages pray;
And faithful souls have yearned to see
On earth that kingdom's day.

2 But the slow watches of the night
Not less to God belong;
And for the everlasting right
The silent stars are strong.

3 And lo, already on the hills
The flags of dawn appear;
Gird up your loins, ye prophet souls,
Proclaim the day is near:

4 The day in whose clear-shining light
All wrong shall stand revealed,
When justice shall be throned in might,
And every hurt be healed;

5 When knowledge, hand in hand with peace,
Shall walk the earth abroad:
The day of perfect righteousness,
The promised day of God.

FREDERICK HOSMER 1840–1929

See also

3 Come, thou long expected Jesus
7 Hills of the north, rejoice
15 The Lord will come and not be slow
469 To Mercy, Pity, Peace, and Love

LITURGICAL SECTION

ADVENT

   501 The Advent Prose

   502 The Advent Sequence: *Salus aeterna*

   503 The Great Advent Antiphons

   504 Magnificat (Tone II 1)

CHRISTMAS

   505 The Christmas Sequence: *Laetabundus*

CANDLEMAS

   506 Nunc Dimittis with Antiphon (Tone VIII 1)

LENT

   507 The Lent Prose

PALM SUNDAY

   508 The Introits

   509 All glory, laud and honour

   510 The Prophetic Anthem

   511 Ride on! ride on in majesty

MAUNDY THURSDAY

   512 Hymn at the Blessing of Oils

   513 At the Washing of Feet: *Ubi Caritas*

   514 At the Communion: *Sancti, venite*

   515 At the Stripping: Psalm 22 with Antiphon

GOOD FRIDAY

   516 The Reproaches

   517 Faithful Cross! above all other

EASTER EVE

   518 Psalms for the Vigil with Antiphons

EASTER

   519 The Sequence: *Victimae Paschali*

PENTECOST

   520 The Sequence: *Veni, sancte Spiritus*

PART VI

LITURGICAL SECTION

AN ADVENT PROSE

501 RORATE. *Drop down, ye heavens, from above, and let the skies pour down righteousness.*

1 Be not wroth very sore, O Lord, neither remember iniquity for ever : thy holy cities are a wilderness, Sion is a wilderness, Jerusalem a desolation : our holy and our beautiful house, where our fathers praised thee.

2 We have sinned, and are as an unclean thing, and we all do fade as a leaf : and our iniquities, like the wind, have taken us away; thou hast hid thy face from us : and hast consumed us, because of our iniquities.

3 Ye are my witnesses, saith the Lord, and my servant whom I have chosen; that ye may know me and believe me : I, even I, am the Lord, and beside me there is no Saviour : and there is none that can deliver out of my hand.

4 Comfort ye, comfort ye my people; my salvation shall not tarry : I have blotted out as a thick cloud thy transgressions : Fear not, for I will save thee : for I am the Lord thy God, the Holy One of Israel, thy Redeemer.

502 *Salus aeterna*

1 SAVIOUR eternal!
   Health and life of the world unfailing,

2 Light everlasting!
   And in verity our redemption,

3 Grieving that the ages of men must perish
   Through the tempter's subtlety,

4 Still in heaven abiding, thou camest earthward
   Of thine own great clemency:

5 Then freely and graciously
   Deigning to assume humanity,

6 To lost ones and perishing
   Gavest thou thy free deliverance,
      Filling all the world with joy.

7 O Christ, our souls and bodies cleanse
   By thy perfect sacrifice;

8 That we as temples pure and bright
   Fit for thine abode may be.

9 By thy former advent justify,

10 By thy second grant us liberty:

11 That when in the might of glory
    Thou descendest, Judge of all,

12 We in raiment undefilèd,
    Bright may shine, and ever follow,
    Lord, thy footsteps blest, where'er they lead us.

Latin, before 11th century
Tr MAXWELL BLACKER 1822–88

THE GREAT ADVENT
ANTIPHONS

503 *O Sapientia.* O Wisdom, which camest out of the mouth of the Most High, and reachest from one end to another, mightily and sweetly ordering all things : Come and teach us the way of prudence.

O Adonai. O Adonai, and Leader of the house of Israel, who appearedst in the bush to Moses in a flame of fire, and gavest him the Law in Sinai : Come and deliver us with an outstretched arm.

O Radix Jesse. O Root of Jesse, which standest for an ensign of the people, at whom kings shall shut their mouths, to whom the Gentiles shall seek : Come and deliver us, and tarry not.

O Clavis David. O Key of David, and Sceptre of the house of Israel; that openest, and no man shutteth, and shuttest, and no man openeth : Come and bring the prisoner out of the prison-house, and him that sitteth in darkness and the shadow of death.

O Oriens. O Day-spring, Brightness of Light Everlasting, and Sun of Righteousness : Come and enlighten him that sitteth in darkness and the shadow of death.

O Rex gentium. O King of the Nations, and their desire; the Corner-stone, who makest both one : Come and save mankind, whom thou formedst of clay.

O Emmanuel. O Emmanuel, our King and Lawgiver, the Desire of all nations, and their Salvation : Come and save us, O Lord our God.

O Virgo virginum. O Virgin of virgins, how shall this be? For neither before thee was any like thee, nor shall there be after. Daughters of Jerusalem, why marvel ye at me? The thing which ye behold is a divine mystery.

504   *Magnificat*

The antiphons at 503 are sung before and after this canticle: the intonation is sung in every verse.

Tone II (1)

1 My soul doth magnify the *Lord*: and my spirit hath rejoiced in God *my* Sav-iour.

2 For he hath re-*gard*-ed: the lowliness of his *hand*-maid-en.

3 For behold from *hence*-forth: all generations shall call *me* bless-ed.

4 For he that is mighty hath magnified *me*: and ho-*ly* is his name.

5 And his mercy is on them that *fear* him: through-out all ge-*ne*-ra-tions.

6 He hath shewed strength with his *arm*: he hath scattered the proud | in the imagina-*tion* of their hearts.

7 He hath put down the mighty from their *seat*: and hath exalted the hum-*ble* and meek.

8 He hath filled the hungry with good *things*: and
the rich he hath sent emp-*ty* a-way.

9 He, remembering his mercy, hath holpen his
servant *Is*-ra͡el: as he promised to our fore-
fathers | Abraham and his seed *for* e-ver.

Glory be to the Father and to the *Son*: and to *the*
Ho͡ly Ghost.

As it was in the beginning, is now, and ever *shall*
be: world without *end*. A-men.

CHRISTMAS SEQUENCE

505   *Laetabundus*

1   COME rejoicing,
Faithful men, with rapture singing
Alleluya!

2   Monarchs' Monarch,
From a holy maiden springing,
Mighty wonder!

3   Angel of the Counsel here,
Sun from star, he doth appear,
Born of maiden:

4   He a sun who knows no night,
She a star whose paler light
Fadeth never.

5   As a star its kindred ray,
Mary doth her Child display,
Like in nature;

504

6 Still undimmed the star shines on,
And the maiden bears a Son,
    Pure as ever.

7 Lebanon his cedar tall
To the hyssop on the wall
    Lowly bendeth;

8 From the highest, him we name
Word of God, to human frame
    Now descendeth.

9 Yet the synagogue denied
What Esaias had descried:
Blindness fell upon the guide,
    Proud, unheeding.

10 If her prophets speak in vain,
Let her heed a Gentile strain,
And, from mystic Sibyl, gain
    Light and leading.

11 No longer then delay,
Hear what the Scriptures say,
Why be cast away
    A race forlorn?

12 Turn and this Child behold,
That very Son, of old
In God's writ foretold,
    A maid hath borne.

Latin c 11th century
Tr By various hands

THE PRESENTATION OF CHRIST
IN THE TEMPLE

506   The Candlemas Ceremony

During the lighting of the candles, or at the beginning of the procession, this antiphon may be sung

A light to lighten the Gentiles, and the glory of thy people Israel.

It may be followed by the canticle Nunc Dimittis, the antiphon being repeated by all after each verse, or if preferred, repeated once only at the end of the canticle.

Tone VIII (1)

1 Lord, now lettest thou thy servant depart in *peace*: ac-*cord*-ing to thy word.

2 For mine eyes have *seen:* – *thy* sal-va-tion.

3 Which thou hast pre-*par*-ed: before the face of *äll* people.

4 To be a light to lighten the *Gen*-tiles: and to be the glory of thy *peo*-ple Is-ra-el.

Glory be to the Father and to the *Son*: and *to* the Ho-ly Ghost.

As it was in the beginning, is now, and ever *shall* be: world with-*out* end. Amen.

For the procession the following hymns are suitable

33 Of the Father's heart begotten
157 Hail to the Lord who comes

At the close of the procession the following may be said or sung

V Your light is come, O Jerusalem.
R And the glory of the Lord is risen upon you.

O Lord Christ, yourself the temple of the heavenly city, and its light, and its surpassing splendour: Grant that we who in this earthly house offer to you our worship, may be brought in peace to the vision of your glory in heaven; where, with the Father and the Holy Spirit you live and reign, one God, now and for ever. *Amen.*

A LENT PROSE

507 ATTENDE. *Hear us, O Lord, have mercy upon us: for we have sinned against thee.*

1 To thee, Redeemer, on thy throne of glory: lift we our weeping eyes in holy pleadings : listen, O Jesu, to our supplications.

2 O thou chief Corner-stone, Right Hand of the Father : Way of Salvation, Gate of Life Celestial : cleanse thou our sinful souls from all defilement.

3 God, we implore thee, in thy glory seated : bow down and hearken to thy weeping children : pity and pardon all our grievous trespasses.

4 Sins oft committed now we lay before thee : with true contrition, now no more we veil them : grant us, Redeemer, loving absolution.

5 Innocent, captive, taken unresisting : falsely accused, and for us sinners sentenced, save us, we pray thee, Jesu our Redeemer.

PALM SUNDAY

The Palm Procession

508   *Before the Blessing of Palms may be sung or said*

The children of the Hebrews, carrying palms
and olive branches, went forth to meet the Lord,
crying out and saying, Hosanna in the highest!

and/or this

Hosanna to the Son of David! Blessed is he who
comes in the name of the Lord! Hosanna in the
highest!

509   *For the Procession*

> *ALL glory, laud and honour*
> *To thee, Redeemer, King,*
> *To whom the lips of children*
> *Made sweet hosannas ring.*

2   Thou art the King of Israel,
    Thou David's royal Son,
Who in the Lord's name comest,
    The King and blessèd One.

3   The company of angels
    Are praising thee on high,
And mortal men and all things
    Created make reply.

4   The people of the Hebrews
    With palms before thee went;
Our praise and prayer and anthems
    Before thee we present.

5 To thee before thy passion
　　They sang their hymns of praise;
To thee, now high exalted,
　　Our melody we raise.

6 Thou didst accept their praises,
　　Accept the prayers we bring,
Who in all good delightest,
　　Thou good and gracious King.

7* Do thou direct our footsteps
　　Upon our earthly way,
And bring us by thy mercy
　　To heaven's eternal day.

8* Within that blessèd City
　　Thy praises may we sing,
And ever raise hosannas
　　To our most loving King.

St Theodulph of Orleans d 821
Tr J. M. Neale 1818–66‡

510　THE PROPHETIC ANTHEM

*At the entrance to the sanctuary this
anthem may be sung*

O JERUSALEM, look toward the east, and
behold: lift up thine eyes, O Jerusalem, and
behold the power of thy King!

Sarum Processional

Suitable as the Introit

511 RIDE on, ride on in majesty!
Hark, all the tribes hosanna cry,
Thy humble beast pursues his road
With palms and scattered garments strowed.

2 Ride on, ride on in majesty!
In lowly pomp ride on to die:
O Christ, thy triumphs now begin
O'er captive death and conquered sin.

3 Ride on, ride on in majesty!
The wingèd squadrons of the sky
Look down with sad and wondering eyes
To see the approaching sacrifice.

4 Ride on, ride on in majesty!
Thy last and fiercest strife is nigh;
The Father on his sapphire throne
Awaits his own anointed Son.

5 Ride on, ride on in majesty!
In lowly pomp ride on to die;
Bow thy meek head to mortal pain,
Then take, O God, thy power, and reign.

HENRY MILMAN 1791–1868

The theme of the Eucharist which follows is that of the Passion.

512   At the Blessing of the Oils

BLEST by the sun, the olive tree
  Brought clusters of fair fruit to birth,
Whose ripeness now we bring with prayer,
  Lord Christ, redeemer of the earth.

2 Eternal King, look down and bless
    The oil your servants offer here,
  And may it be a lively sign
    Which all the powers of darkness fear.

3 From those washed in the sacred font
    Let Satan's influence depart,
  And when this oil the brow shall seal,
    Transforming grace invade the heart.

4 Our wounded nature thus be healed
    By your anointing grace, O Lord;
  In men and women so renewed
    Shall God's own image be restored.

5 Lord Christ, the Father's only Son,
    Who took our flesh in Mary's womb,
  Give light to your anointed ones,
    And break the power of death's dark tomb.

6 So may this joyous paschal feast,
    The time when saving grace is given,
  Fill every Christian soul with praise,
    And raise our minds from earth to heaven.

From an early Latin hymn
Tr RICHARD RUTT b 1925

At the Washing of Feet

513 *Suitable also for general use*

Ubi caritas

God is love, and where true love is, God himself is there.

1 HERE in Christ, we gather, love of Christ our calling;
Christ, our love, is with us, gladness be his greeting;
Let us all revere and love him, God eternal:
Loving him, let each love Christ in all his brothers.
God is love, etc.

2 When we Christians gather, members of one Body,
Let there be in us no discord, but one spirit;
Banished now be anger, strife and every quarrel:
Christ our God be present always here among us.
God is love, etc.

3 Grant us love's fulfilment, joy with all the blessed
When we see your face, O Saviour, in its glory;
Shine on us, O purest Light of all creation,
Be our bliss while endless ages sing your praises.
God is love, etc.

From the Latin liturgy of
Maundy Thursday
Tr JAMES QUINN b 1919

At the Communion

514 *Suitable also for general use*

Sancti, venite

1 *COME, Christ's beloved, feed on his body true,*
   Drink your salvation in his precious blood.

2 Saved by his body, hallowed by his blood,
   Here in God's banquet, let us thank our Lord.

3 *Christ, in this myst'ry gives us his flesh and blood,*
   Guiding us safely through death's shade to light.

4 Son of the Father, King of all the world,
   Christ is our Saviour, by his cross and blood.

5 *Christ, priest and victim, offers himself for all,*
   At once the giver, and the gift divine.

6 Priests of the old law, offering blood outpoured,
   Did but foreshadow Christ, the victim-priest.

7 *Christ our redeemer, Christ now the light of men,*
   Does thus enrich us by his grace sublime.

8 Bring to this banquet faithful hearts sincere;
   Take hence the promise of eternal life.

9 *Come, Christ's beloved, feed on his body true,*
   Drink your salvation in his precious blood.

> Latin, freely adapted from the
> 7th century *Antiphonary of
> Bennchar*

The verses in italic are sung by all

The Ceremonies after Communion

515 *For the Procession to the Altar of Repose see 268*

At the Stripping of the Altars Psalm 22 (*without Gloria*) *may be said or sung, with this antiphon before and after:*

They part my garments among them, and cast lots upon my vesture.

Tone II (1)

1 My God, my God, look upon me; | why hast thou for-*sa*-ken⌒me: and art so far from my health, and from the words *of* my⌒complaint?

2 O my God, I cry in the day-time, but thou hearest *not* : and in the night-season also *I* take⌒no rest.

3 And thou continuest *ho*-ly : O thou worship *of* Is⌒ra-el.

4 Our fathers hoped in *thee* : they trusted in thee, and thou didst *de*-liv⌒er them.

5 They called upon thee, and were *hol*-pen : they put their trust in thee, and were not *con*-found-ed.

6 But as for me, I am a worm and no *man* : a very scorn of men, and the outcast of *the* peo-ple.

7 All they that see me laugh me to *scorn* : they shoot out their lips, and shake their⌒hëads, say-ing,

8 He trusted in God that he would de-*liv*-er⌒him : let him deliver him, if he *will* have him.

9 But thou art he that took me out of my mother's

womb : thou wast my hope, when I hanged yet upon *my* moˆther's breasts.

10 I have been left unto thee ever since I was *born* : thou art my God, even from *my* moˆther's womb.

11 O go not from me, for trouble is hard at *hand* : and there is none *to* help me.

12 Many oxen are come a-*bout* me : fat bulls of Basan close me in *on* evˆ'ry side.

13 They gape upon me with their *mouths* : as it were a ramping and a roar-*ing* li-on.

14 I am poured out like water, | and all my bones are out of *joint* : my heart also in the midst of my body is even *like* meltˆing wax.

15 My strength is dried up like a potsherd, | and my tongue cleaveth to my *gums* : and thou shalt bring me into *the* dustˆof death.

16 For many dogs are come a-*bout* me : and the council of the wicked layeth siege *a*-gainst me.

17 They pierced my hands and my feet ; I may tell all my *bones* : they stand staring and looking *up*-on me.

18 They part my garments a-*mong* them : and cast lots upon *my* ves-ture.

19 But be not thou far from me, O *Lord* : thou art my succour, haste thee *to* help me.

20 Deliver my soul from the *sword* : my darling from the pow-*er* ofˆthe dog.

21 Save me from the lion's *mouth* : thou hast heard me also from among the horns of *the* unˆi-corns.

22 I will declare thy Name unto my *bre*-thren : in the midst of the congregation will *I* praise thee.

23 O praise the Lord, ye that *fear* him : magnify him, all ye of the seed of Jacob, | and fear him, all ye seed *of* Is⌃ra-el.

24 For he hath not despised nor abhorred the low estate of the *poor* : he hath not hid his face from him, | but when he called unto him *he* heard him.

25 My praise is of thee in the great congre-*ga*-tion : my vows will I perform in the sight of them *that* fear him.

26 The poor shall eat, and be *sat*-is⌐fied : they that seek after the Lord shall praise him ; your heart shall live *for* ev-er.

27 All the ends of the world shall remember themselves, and be turned unto the *Lord* : and all the kindreds of the nations shall worship *be*-fore him.

28 For the kingdom is the *Lord's* : and he is the Governor among *the* peo-ple.

29 All such as be fat upon *earth* : have eaten, *and* wor-shipped.

30 All they that go down into the dust shall kneel be-*fore* him: and no man hath quickened *his* own soul.

31 My seed shall *serve* him : they shall be counted unto the Lord for a ge-*ne*-ra-tion.

32 They shall come, and the heavens shall declare his *righ*-teous⌃ness : unto a people that shall be born, whom *the* Lord⌃hath made.

The Veneration of the Cross

516 *During the unveiling of the Cross the following versicle and response, which may be twice repeated, is said or sung.*

BEHOLD the wood of the Cross, whereon was hung the Saviour of the world.

R O come, let us worship.

The Reproaches

The Veneration begins, while the Reproaches are sung or said, followed by the hymn 'Faithful Cross!'.

O MY people, what have I done to thee, or wherein have I wearied thee? Answer me. Because I brought thee out of the land of Egypt, thou hast prepared a cross for thy Saviour.

Holy God, holy and mighty, holy and immortal, have mercy upon us.

Because I led thee through the desert forty years, and fed thee with manna, and brought thee into a land exceeding good, thou hast prepared a cross for thy Saviour.

Holy God, etc.

What could I do more for thee that I have not done? I planted thee, my choicest vine, and thou hast become exceeding bitter unto me; for when I was thirsty thou gavest me to drink vinegar mingled with gall, and pierced with a spear the side of thy Saviour.

Holy God, etc.

We venerate thy Cross, O Lord, and praise and glorify thy holy Resurrection: for by virtue of the Cross, joy has come to the whole world.

517 *During the Veneration this hymn (or such part of it as is required) may be sung instead of, or in addition to the Reproaches at 516. It begins with the refrain 'Faithful Cross', which is repeated after each verse.*

> *Faithful Cross! above all other,*
> *One and only noble tree!*
> *None in foliage, none in blossom,*
> *None in fruit thy peer may be;*
> *Sweetest wood and sweetest iron,*
> *Sweetest weight is hung on thee.*

SING, my tongue, the glorious battle,
    Sing the ending of the fray,
O'er the Cross, the victor's trophy,
    Sound the loud triumphant lay:
Tell how Christ, the world's Redeemer,
    As a Victim won the day.

2 God in pity saw man fallen,
    Shamed and sunk in misery,
When he fell on death by tasting
    Fruit of the forbidden tree:
Then another tree was chosen
    Which the world from death should free.

3   Therefore when the appointed fulness
        Of the holy time was come,
    He was sent who maketh all things
        Forth from God's eternal home:
    Thus he came to earth, incarnate,
        Offspring of a maiden's womb.

4   Thirty years among us dwelling,
        Now at length his hour fulfilled,
    Born for this, he meets his Passion,
        For that this he freely willed,
    On the Cross the Lamb is lifted,
        Where his life-blood shall be spilled.

5   Bend thy boughs, O Tree of Glory,
        Thy too rigid sinews bend;
    For awhile the ancient rigour
        That thy birth bestowed, suspend,
    And the King of heavenly beauty
        On thy bosom gently tend.

6   Thou alone wast counted worthy
        This world's Ransom to sustain,
    That a shipwrecked race might ever
        Thus a port of refuge gain,
    With the sacred blood anointed
        From the Lamb for sinners slain.

7   He endured the nails, the spitting,
        Vinegar and spear and reed;
    From that holy Body piercèd
        Blood and water forth proceed:
    Earth and stars and sky and ocean
        By that flood from stain are freed.

8 To the Trinity be glory,
To the Father and the Son,
With the co-eternal Spirit,
Ever Three and ever One,
One in love and one in splendour,
While unending ages run. Amen.

Latin, *Venantius Fortunatus* 530–609
Tr PERCY DEARMER 1867–1936 and
J. M. NEALE 1818–66†

THE EASTER VIGIL

518   *The following psalms with their antiphons are suitable for use after the lessons at the Easter Vigil. The first should be sung after the account of Creation, the second after the account of the Crossing of the Red Sea, the third and fourth after any of the readings from the prophets.*
Alternatively see 537, 535, 529, 530 from the responsorial psalms.

I   Tone III (2)   *from Psalm 104*

Antiphon Send forth thy Spirit, O Lord, and renew the face of the earth.

1 Praise the Lord, *O* my ( ) soul : O Lord my God, thou art become exceeding glorious | thou art clothed with majes-*ty* and honour.

2 Thou has laid the foun-*da*-tions^of the earth: that it never should *move* at a-ny^time.

3 Thou coveredst it with the deep like as *with* garment : the waters *stand* in the hills.

4 Thou sendest the springs in-*to* the riv-ers : which *run* a-mong the^hills.

5 Beside them shall the fowls of the air have their *ha*-bi-ta-tions : and sing a-*mong* the branch-es.

6 Thou waterest the *hills* from a-bove : the earth is filled with the *fruit* of thy works.

7 Thou bringest forth *grass* for the cat-tle: and green herb for the *ser*-vice of men.

II   Tone II (1)   *from Exodus 15*

Antiphon I will sing unto the Lord, for he has triumphed gloriously.

1 I will sing unto the Lord, for he has triumphed *glo*-rious ly : the horse and his rider he has thrown *in*-to the sea.

2 The Lord is my strength and my song, and he has become my sal-*va*-tion : this is my God and I will praise him | my father's God, and I will *ex*-alt him.

3 The Lord is a man of *war* : the Lord *is* his name.

4 Pharaoh's chariots and his host he has cast into the *sea* : and his chosen officers are sunk in *the* Red Sea.

5 The floods *co*-ver them : they went down into the depths *like* a stone.

6 Thy right hand, O Lord, is glorious in *pow*-er : thy right hand, O Lord, shatters *the* e ne-my.

7 Thou wilt bring in thy people | and plant them on thine own *moun*-tain : the place O Lord which thou hast made for thine abode | the sanctuary O Lord which thy hands have *es*-tab-lished.

8 The Lord will *reign* : for ever *and* e-ver.

III   Tone VIII (2)   *from Isaiah 12*

Antiphon With joy you will draw water, from the wells of salvation.

1   Behold, God is my sal-*va*-tion : I will trust and *will* not be a fraid.

2   For the Lord God is my strength and my *song* : and he has become *my* sal-va-tion.

3   With joy you will draw *wa*-ter : from the wells *of* sal-va-tion.

4   And you will say in that *day* : Give thanks to the Lord | *call* up-on his name.

5   Make known his deeds among the *na*-tions : proclaim that his name *is* ex-alt-ed.

6   Sing praises to the Lord, for he has done *glo*-rious ly : let this be *known* in all the earth.

7   Shout and sing for joy, O inhabitant of *Si*-on : for great in your midst is the Holy *One* of Is-ra el.

IV   Tone III (4)   *from Psalms 42, 43*

Antiphon My soul is athirst for God, yea even for the living God.

1   Like as the hart de-*sir*-eth the wat-er brooks : so longeth my soul af-*ter* thee O God.

2   My soul is athirst for God yea even *for* the liv-ing God : when shall I come to appear before the pre-*sence* of God?

3   Now when I think thereupon | I pour out my *heart* by my-self : for I went with the multitude | and brought them forth into *the* house of God.

4 In the voice of praise *and* thanks-giv-ing: among such as *keep* ho'ly day.

5 O send out thy light and thy truth that *they* may lead me : and bring me unto thy holy hill, and to *thy* dwell-ing.

6 And that I may go unto the altar of God | even unto the God of my *joy* and glad-ness : and upon the harp will I give thanks unto thee, *O* God'my God.

EASTER SEQUENCE

519   *Victimae Paschali*

I CHRISTIANS, to the Paschal Victim
Offer your thankful praises!

2 A Lamb the sheep redeemeth:
Christ, who only is sinless,
Reconcileth sinners to the Father;

3 Death and life have contended
In that combat stupendous:
The Prince of Life, who died, reigns immortal.

4 Speak Mary, declaring
What thou sawest wayfaring:

5 'The Tomb of Christ, who is living,
The glory of Jesu's Resurrection:

6 Bright angels attesting,
The shroud and napkin resting.

7 Yea, Christ my hope is arisen:
To Galilee he goes before you.'

8 Happy they who hear the witness, Mary's word
believing
Above the tales of doubt and deceiving.

9 Christ indeed from death is risen, our new life
obtaining.
Have mercy, victor King, ever reigning!

Latin, c. 11th century
Tr cento

WHITSUNDAY SEQUENCE

The Golden Sequence

520   *Veni, sancte Spiritus*

1 COME, thou Holy Spirit, come,
And from thy celestial home
Shed thy light and brilliancy:
Father of the poor, draw near,
Giver of all gifts, be here,
Come, the soul's true radiancy.

2 Come, of comforters the best,
Of the soul the sweetest guest,
Come in toil refreshingly:
Thou in labour rest most sweet,
Thou art shadow from the heat,
Comfort in adversity.

3 O thou Light most pure and blest,
Shine within the inmost breast
Of thy faithful company:

Where thou art not, man has nought;
Every holy deed and thought
   Comes from thy divinity.

4 Sinful hearts do thou make whole,
Bring to life the arid soul,
   Guide the feet that go astray.
Make the stubborn heart unbend,
To the faint, new hope extend,
   Wounded souls, their hurt allay.

5 Fill the faithful, who confide
In thy power to guard and guide,
   With thy sevenfold mystery:
Here thy grace and virtue send,
Grant salvation in the end,
   And in heaven felicity.

Latin, STEPHEN LANGTON d 1228
Tr J. M. NEALE 1818–66
and EDITORS

This hymn, set to other melodies, is also given at 139

CORPUS CHRISTI SEQUENCE

Part 1

521   *Lauda, Sion, Salvatorem*

1 LAUD, O Sion, thy salvation,
Laud with hymns of exultation
   Christ, thy King and Shepherd true:
Spend thyself, his honour raising,
Who surpasseth all thy praising;
   Never canst thou reach his due.

2 Sing to-day, the mystery showing
   Of the living, life-bestowing
     Bread from heaven before thee set;
   E'en the same of old provided,
   Where the Twelve, divinely guided,
     At the holy Table met.

3 Full and clear ring out thy chanting,
   Joy nor sweetest grace be wanting
     To thy heart and soul to-day;
   When we gather up the measure
   Of that Supper and its treasure,
     Keeping feast in glad array.

4 Lo, the new King's Table gracing,
   This new Passover of blessing
     Hath fulfilled the elder rite:
   Now the new the old effaceth,
   Truth revealed the shadow chaseth,
     Day is breaking on the night.

5 What he did at Supper seated,
   Christ ordained to be repeated,
     His memorial ne'er to cease:
   And, his word for guidance taking,
   Bread and wine we hallow, making
     Thus our Sacrifice of peace.

6 This the truth to Christians given—
   Bread becomes his Flesh from heaven,
     Wine becomes his holy Blood.
   Doth it pass thy comprehending?
   Yet by faith, thy sight transcending,
     Wondrous things are understood.

7   Yea, beneath these signs are hidden
    Glorious things to sight forbidden:
        Look not on the outward sign.
    Wine is poured and Bread is broken,
    But in either sacred token
        Christ is here by power divine.

8   Whoso of this Food partaketh,
    Christ divideth not nor breaketh,
        He is whole to all that taste.
    Whether one this bread receiveth
    Or a thousand, still he giveth
        One same Food that cannot waste.

9   Good and evil men are sharing
    One repast, an end preparing
        Varied as the heart of man;
    Life or death shall be awarded,
    As their days have been recorded
        Which from their beginning ran.

10 When the Sacrament is broken,
    Doubt not in each severed token,
    Hallowed by the word once spoken,
        Resteth all the true content:
    Nought the precious Gift divideth,
    Breaking but the sign betideth,
    He himself the same abideth,
        Nothing of his fullness spent.

Part 2

Ecce! Panis Angelorum

11 Lo! the Angels' Food is given
To the pilgrim who hath striven;
See the children's Bread from heaven,
    Which to dogs may not be cast;

Truth the ancient types fulfilling,
Isaac bound, a victim willing,
Paschal lamb, its life-blood spilling,
    Manna sent in ages past.

Part 3

Bone Pastor, Panis vere

12 O true Bread, good Shepherd, tend us,
Jesu, of thy love befriend us,
Thou refresh us, thou defend us,
Thine eternal goodness send us
    In the land of life to see;
Thou who all things canst and knowest,
Who on earth such Food bestowest,
Grant us with thy saints, though lowest,
Where the heavenly Feast thou showest,
    Fellow-heirs and guests to be.

ST THOMAS AQUINAS 1227–74
Tr cento

522   *Jerusalem et Sion filiae*

1 SION'S daughters, sons of Jerusalem,
   All ye hosts of heavenly chivalry,
   Lift your voices, singing right merrily
            Alleluya!

2 Christ our Saviour weds on this festival
   Holy Church, the pattern of righteousness,
   Whom from depths of uttermost misery
            He hath rescued.

3 Now the bride receiveth his benison,
   Tasteth now the joys of the Paraclete,
   Kings and queens with jubilant melody
            Call her blessèd,

4 Mother meet for sinful humanity,
   Life's sure haven, rest for the sorrowful,
   Strong protectress, born in a mystery
            Ever wondrous.

5 Not more bright the sun in his majesty,
   Not more fair the moon in her loveliness,
   Radiant as the stars in the firmament,
            Perfect as the dawn:

6 So the Church shines forth on her pilgrimage,
   Cleansed in Jordan's waters of penitence,
   Drawn to hear the wisdom of Solomon
            From the world's end.

7 So, foretold in figures and prophecies,
  Clothed in nuptial vesture of charity,
  Joined to Christ, o'er heaven's glad citizens
      Now she reigneth.

8 Welcome, feast of light and felicity,
  Bride to Bridegroom wedded in unity,
  In her mystic marriage is typified
      Our salvation.

9 Christ, whose joys we joyfully celebrate,
  Grant us all a place with thy chosen ones,
  True delights, ineffable happiness,
      Rest eternal.

Latin, 12th century
Tr GABRIEL GILLETT 1873–1948†

This hymn, set to another melody, is also given at 212

SEQUENCE FOR ALL SAINTS

523   *Sponsa Christi*

1 SPOUSE of Christ, whose earthly conflict
    Here below doth never cease,
  Lift thy voice and tell the triumphs
    Of the blessèd ones at peace.

2 Joyful be this day of gladness,
    Feast of all the saints on high;
  Let our songs, 'mid heaven's rejoicing,
    Sound in sweetest harmony.

3 There, the ever-Virgin Mother,
     Reunited with her Son,
  Leads the praise of all the ransomed
     Who that heavenly realm have won.

4 There, the angels and archangels,
     Circling round the throne on high,
  Hymn the Lord of all creation
     In divinest minstrelsy.

5 John, the herald and forerunner,
     Heads the great prophetic throng,
  While the patriarchs in chorus
     Join to swell the angels' song.

6 Near to Christ, the Twelve apostles,
     Chosen as foundation stones,
  Now behold the City's splendour,
     Seated on celestial thrones.

7 There the martyrs, robed in crimson,
     Sign of life-blood freely spent,
  Now enjoy the life eternal.
     In the Saviour's love content.

8 Virgins, to the Lamb devoted,
     Following in steadfast love,
  Bring the bridal garlands with them
     To the marriage-feast above.

9 There, confessors are rewarded,
     And each holy, humble soul,
  Who on earth left no memorial,
     Now make up the saintly whole.

10   All the blest adore for ever
      God's surpassing majesty,
  Threefold anthems ever raising
      To the all-holy Trinity.

11   In your heavenly habitation,
      That eternal home on high,
  Hear, ye saints, our prayer and pleading,
      As to God we lift our cry.

12   By your heavenly intercession
      Help your fellow-Christians here,
  That in love of Christ our Saviour
      We through grace may persevere.

13   So may God our Father grant us
      Here to serve in holiness,
  And at length by his good mercy
      Share that heaven which ye possess.

EDITORS and others, based on the
Latin of Jean Baptiste de Contes
1601–79

SEQUENCE FOR ALL SOULS

524   *Dies irae, dies illa*

1   DAY of wrath and doom impending,
    David's word with Sibyl's blending!
    Heaven and earth in ashes ending!

2   O, what fear man's bosom rendeth,
    When from heaven the Judge descendeth,
    On whose sentence all dependeth!

3 Wondrous sound the trumpet flingeth,
Through earth's sepulchres it ringeth,
All before the throne it bringeth.

4 Death is struck, and nature quaking,
All creation is awaking,
To its Judge an answer making.

5 Lo! the book exactly worded,
Wherein all hath been recorded;
Thence shall judgement be awarded.

6 When the Judge his seat attaineth,
And each hidden deed arraigneth,
Nothing undisclosed remaineth.

7 What shall I, frail man, be pleading?
Who for me be interceding,
When the just are mercy needing?

8 King of majesty tremendous,
Who dost free salvation send us,
Fount of pity, then befriend us!

9 Think, kind Jesu!—my salvation
Caused thy wondrous Incarnation;
Leave me not to reprobation.

10 Faint and weary thou hast sought me,
On the Cross of suffering bought me;
Shall such grace be vainly brought me?

11 Righteous Judge! for sin's pollution
Grant thy gift of absolution,
Ere that day of retribution.

12   Guilty, now I pour my moaning,
All my shame with anguish owning;
Spare, O God, thy suppliant groaning!

13   Through the sinful woman shriven,
Through the dying thief forgiven,
Thou to me a hope hast given.

14   Worthless are my prayers and sighing,
Yet, good Lord, in grace complying,
Rescue me from night undying.

15   With thy sheep a place provide me,
From the goats afar divide me,
To thy right hand do thou guide me.

16   When the wicked are confounded,
Doomed to shame and loss unbounded
Call me, with thy saints surrounded.

17   Low I kneel, with heart's submission;
See, like ashes my contrition!
Help me in my last condition!

18   Ah! that day of tears and mourning!
From the dust of earth returning,
Man for judgement must prepare him;
Spare, O God, in mercy spare him!
Lord, all-pitying, Jesu blest,
Grant them thine eternal rest.

THOMAS OF CELANO 13th century
Tr W. J. IRONS 1812–83‡

INTROIT   Tone VI

525   *Requiem aeternam*

Ant. Rest eternal grant unto them, O Lord : and may light perpetual shine upon them.

Ps. Thou, O God, art praised in *Si*-on : and unto thee shall the vow be performed *in* Je-ru-sa˘lem.

Thou that hearest *the* prayer : unto *thee* shall all flesh˘come.

Ant. Rest eternal grant unto them, O Lord : and may light perpetual shine upon them.

The Sequence for All Souls 524 may be used.
See also 326–330 and other hymns noted there.

THE RUSSIAN CONTAKION
OF THE DEPARTED

526   GIVE rest, O Christ, to thy servant with thy saints, where sorrow and pain ˙are no more, neither sighing, but life everlasting.

Thou only art immortal, the Creator and Maker of man; and we are mortal, formed of the earth, and unto earth shall we return; for so thou didst ordain when thou createdst me, saying: Dust thou art, and unto dust shalt thou return. All we go down to the dust, and, weeping o'er the grave, we make our song: Alleluya, alleluya, alleluya.

Give rest, O Christ, to thy servant with thy
saints, where sorrow and pain are no more,
neither sighing, but life everlasting.

Tr W. J. BIRKBECK
1869–1916

PROCESSIONS

*Hymns suitable for a procession are noted after the
office hymns in the various sections of this book.
Processions have a value in marking the high days
of the liturgical year. One form which the procession can take is as a festival entrance before the
Eucharist. When so used, it is a token pilgrimage to
the holy place, and should not begin at the altar,
but at some other point in the church where the
ministers and singers can assemble. So it becomes
the means of arriving at the sanctuary.*

527 *It is sometimes appropriate that at the close of a
procession a versicle, response and collect should be
said or sung. For that purpose the following
suggestions are given. The collects could equally
well be used as an additional post-communion
prayer on festivals.*

CHRISTMAS

V The Word was made flesh.
R And dwelt among us.

Almighty Father, whose only-begotten Son,
Jesus Christ, became incarnate for our salvation:
Grant that we may be made partakers of his
eternal life who stooped to share our mortal life:

who with you and the Holy Spirit, lives and
reigns one God, now and for ever. *Amen.*

EPIPHANY

V Nations shall come to your light.
R And kings to the brightness of your rising.

O God, who by the guiding of a star revealed
your only-begotten Son to the Gentiles: Grant
that we, who know you now by faith, may after
this life enjoy the vision of your heavenly glory;
through Jesus Christ our Lord. *Amen.*

EASTER

V The Lord is risen from the dead, Alleluya.
R Who for our sake hung upon the tree,
Alleluya.

Eternal Father, by whose almighty power your
Son, our Saviour, rose victorious from the tomb:
Grant that we, who were baptised into his death
and were raised to new life in him, may ever live
to his glory; through Jesus Christ our Lord.
Amen.

ASCENSION

V Christ has gone up on high, Alleluya.
R And has led captivity captive, Alleluya.

Almighty Father, who raised your Son Jesus
Christ to your own right hand in glory: Grant
that we, doing his will upon earth, may be
brought to behold his face in heaven; where with
you, O Father, and the Holy Spirit, he lives and
reigns, now and for ever. *Amen.*

PENTECOST

V Let your loving Spirit lead me forth, Alleluya.
R Into the land of righteousness, Alleluya.

Holy Father, who poured down your Spirit upon the waiting Church, that the good news of your love might be heard in all the earth: Grant that we, who have been named the disciples of your Son, may obey his command to proclaim the gospel of salvation; who lives and reigns, with you and the Holy Spirit, one God, now and for ever. *Amen.*

TRINITY SUNDAY

V Let us bless the Father, the Son, and the Holy Spirit.
R Let us praise and exalt him for ever.

Almighty God, Father, Son, and Holy Spirit: Grant that we, who ever trust in your loving-kindness, may always adore your glory and majesty; who are one eternal Trinity in Unity, God over all, blessed for ever. *Amen.*

THE BLESSED VIRGIN MARY

V Hail, Mary, full of grace, the Lord is with you.
R You will bring forth a son, and call his name Jesus.

Most loving Father, who by the obedience of Mary did repair the sin of Eve: Grant that we who venerate the Virgin Mother of the Lord may follow her in faithfulness, and at length attain the company of your saints in heaven; through Jesus Christ our Lord. *Amen.*

THE SAINTS

V The righteous shall be had in everlasting remembrance.
R The memory of the just is blessed.

O God, whose glory the redeemed in heaven eternally adore: Grant that we who rejoice in the festival of (Saint *N*) (all your saints), may be brought to praise you in life everlasting; through Jesus Christ our Lord. *Amen.*

DEDICATION FESTIVAL

V Let your priests be clothed with righteousness.
R And your people sing with joyfulness.

Grant, O heavenly Father, that we who with joy commemorate the building of this earthly temple, may at length be found worthy, with all the redeemed, to worship you in that Jerusalem which is above; through Jesus Christ our Lord. *Amen.*

RESPONSORIAL PSALMS

These are primarily for use between the first and second readings of scripture at the eucharist. The choir, or a cantor, sings the response, which is then repeated by the congregation. The verses follow, sung in free rhythm to the set tone. After each verse the congregation sings the response. The mark | in the verse indicates the point at which the tone's reciting note is left for the remaining three notes of each phrase. The final stressed syllable of each line should coincide with the last of these notes, and any remaining syllables be lightly sung on the same note.

The following psalms are suitable for the season or feast indicated:

The musical settings of the psalm tones and responses are by Dom Gregory Murray, (1905–92)

528   Psalm 25

To you, O Lord, I lift up my soul.

1   Show me your | ways, O Lord,
    And teach | me your paths.
    Lead me forth | in your truth,
    For you are | God my Saviour.   *R*

2 Good and righteous | is the Lord,
He brings back | those who stray,
He guides the meek | in his ways,
And shows his paths | to the lowly. *R*

3 All his ways are mer | cy and truth,
For those who are faithful | to his word.
To those who love him, he re | veals his mind,
And shows them | all his will. *R*

529   Psalm 33

O taste and see that the Lord is good.

1 Let the righteous rejoice | in the Lord:
It is good to give him | thanks and praise.
For the word of the | Lord is true,
And in all his deeds | he is faithful. *R*

2 By his word were the | heavens made,
And all the stars by the breath | of his mouth.
He spoke the word and | it was done;
He commanded and it | came to pass. *R*

3 The eyes of the Lord are ov | er the righteous,
And his ear is open | to their cry,
To deliver their | souls from death,
And to feed them in the | time of dearth. *R*

4 We patiently wait | on the Lord,
For he is our help | and our shield.
Let your steadfast love guard and keep | us, O
Lord,
For our hope | is in you. *R*

530 Psalm 42/43

As the running deer seeks the flowing brook, even so my soul longs for you, my God.

1   My soul is a | thirst for God,
    Even for the | living God:
    But when shall | I attain
    The vision | of his face? *R*

2   O send your | light and truth,
    And let them | be my guide,
    To reach your | holy hill,
    The place of | your abode. *R*

3   Why so heavy | O my soul?
    Why so disquiet | ed within me?
    O put your | trust in God,
    My helper | and my God. *R*

4   To God's altar | will I go,
    To God my | chiefest joy:
    On the strings | of the harp
    I will offer | him my praise. *R*

531 Psalm 47

Jesus reigns, our Lord and King.

1   Let all nations | clap their hands,
    Sing to God with | hymns of praise,
    For the Lord is high and to | be adored,
    The great King over | all the earth. *R*

2 He is gone up with | shouts of joy,
  The trumpet sounds as the | Lord ascends:
  O sing praises | to our God,
  Sing praises | to our King. *R*

3 For God is King of | all the earth,
  His mighty acts shall | be proclaimed:
  The Lord is King over | all the world,
  He reigns in glory | on his throne. *R*

532 Psalm 51

Have mercy on us, Lord, for we have sinned.

1 Have mercy upon me, O God, in | your great love,
  In your compassion blot out | my offences:
  Wash me throughly | from my guilt,
  And cleanse me | from my sin. *R*

2 To you I con | fess my faults,
  For they ever stare me | in the face:
  Against you it is that | I have sinned,
  And done evil | in your sight. *R*

3 Make me a clean | heart, O God,
  And renew a right spir | it within me:
  Cast me not out | of your sight,
  Nor take your holy | spirit from me. *R*

4 Uphold me | with your might,
  And strengthen me with | perseverance:
  Open my | lips, O Lord,
  And my mouth shall de | clare your praise. *R*

533 Psalm 63

O God, you are my God, for you my soul is athirst.

1 O God, my God, for | you I long,
   For you my soul | is athirst,
   All my being | pines for you,
   As thirsty | land for rain. *R*

2 In the sanctuary I | come to you,
   To behold your glo | ry and might:
   To know your love is better than | life itself,
   Therefore my lips shall | praise your name. *R*

3 So will I bless you | all my days,
   And lift my | hands in prayer:
   My soul shall feast up | on your love,
   My heart exults in | you, my God. *R*

4 For you, O God, have | been my help,
   Beneath your wings I | dwell secure:
   My soul shall ever | cling to you,
   And your right hand shall | hold me fast. *R*

534 Psalm 84

How lovely is your dwelling place.

1 How lovely is your | dwelling place,
   O | Lord of hosts!
   My soul longs to enter | in your courts,
   To rejoice in the | living God. *R*

2 Blessèd are those who dwell | in your house,
   They will never | cease your praise:
   For one day | in your courts
   Is better than a | thousand days. *R*

3 Blessèd is the man whose strength | is in you,
   In whose heart are | all your ways:
   O Lord | God of hosts,
   Happy the man who | trusts in you. *R*

535   Psalm 98

*All the ends of the earth have seen the salvation of
our God.*

1 Sing to the Lord | a new song,
   For he has done mar | vellous things:
   With his own right hand and with his | holy arm,
   He has brought de | liverance. *R*

2 The Lord has made known his | righteous love,
   In the sight of | all mankind,
   And his faithful | ness and truth
   Toward the house of | Is-ra-el. *R*

3 All the ends of the | earth have seen,
   The salvation | of our God:
   Let all the world be | glad in him,
   Sing, rejoice and | give him thanks. *R*

4 Let music sound up | on the harp,
   Let psalms be offered | to his praise:
   With trumpets and with | songs of joy
   Shout the praise of | God our King. *R*

536 Psalm 103

The Lord is compassion and love.

1 O my soul | bless the Lord,
And all my being, bless his | holy name:
O my soul | bless the Lord,
And forget not | all his love. *R*

2 He forgives you | all your guilt,
And heals your | every ill,
Redeems your life | from the grave,
Crowns you with friend | ship and love. *R*

3 The Lord is full of compas | sion and love,
Slow to anger | rich in grace:
He has not dealt with us af | ter our sins,
Nor repaid us for | all our faults. *R*

4 As far as east is | from the west,
So far does he re | move our sins:
As a father has pity | on his sons,
So the Lord has mercy | on his own. *R*

537 Psalm 104

*Send forth your spirit, O Lord,
and renew the face of the earth.*

1 Praise the Lord | O my soul,
O Lord God, your glor | y is great:
How manifold | are your works,
In wisdom you have | made them all. *R*

2 All creatures | look to you,
    To give them their | food to eat:
    When you open your hand, they are | filled with good,
    When you hide your face, they | pine away. *R*

3 When you take away their | breath, they die,
    And return to the earth | whence they came:
    When you send forth your spirit, all things | spring to life,
    And the face of the earth | is renewed. *R*

4 The glory of the Lord shall | never cease,
    The Lord shall rejoice in | all his works:
    I will sing to the Lord as long | as I live,
    I will praise my God while my | breath remains. *R*

538   Psalm 116

To God the Lord raise hymns of praise,
and with your lips proclaim his name.

1 I will love the Lord, who | heard my prayer,
    Who inclined his ear to my | supplication:
    For he delivered my soul | from the grave,
    And wiped a | way my tears. *R*

2 The Lord preserves the | meek of heart;
    I was brought low, | but he saved me.
    Return to your rest | O my soul,
    For the Lord has blest you | with his grace. *R*

3 What shall I render | to the Lord
   For all his | loving kindness?
   I will take to my lips sal | vation's cup,
   And call up | on his name. *R*

4 I will pay to the Lord our | God my vows
   In the presence | of his people;
   I will offer the sacri | fice of praise,
   And call up | on his name. *R*

539   Psalm 118

        This is the day of the Lord:
        We rejoice and are glad.

1 O give thanks to the Lord for | he is good,
   And his loving mercy | never fails:
   Let every son of Is | ra-el say
   That his love en | dures for ever. *R*

2 Victorious is the | Lord's right hand,
   The Lord's right hand has | raised me up:
   I shall not | die, but live,
   And declare the works | of the Lord. *R*

3 The stone which the build | ers refused,
   Has become the chief | corner-stone:
   This is the | Lord's own work,
   And it is marvellous | in our eyes. *R*

540   Psalm 145

*I will bless your name for ever,
my God and King.*

1   Great is the Lord, and worthy | of all praise,
    His glory is past | searching out:
    Men shall recount the might | of your deeds,
    And proclaim your | majesty.   *R*

2   The Lord loves all that | he has made,
    His mercy is over | all his works:
    All your works | speak your praise,
    And your people | give you thanks.   *R*

3   Your right hand raises | those that fall,
    And those bowed down are | lifted up:
    All creatures wait on | you for food,
    And from your hand their | wants are filled.   *R*

4   The Lord is near to | those who call,
    He hears their cry and | brings them help:
    My mouth shall tell the | praise of God,
    And let all flesh his | name adore.   *R*

541 THE ORDER FOR HOLY COMMUNION RITE A

A New English Folk Mass

To be sung freely and flowingly, after the manner of good speech. The melody should clothe the words, and the note-values are not meant to be treated rigidly.

KYRIE ELEISON

Lord,— have— mer - cy. Lord,— have— mer - cy.

Christ,— have— mer - cy. Christ,— have— mer - cy.

Lord,— have— mer - cy. Lord,— have— mer - cy.

GLORIA IN EXCELSIS

Glo - ry to God in the high - est,

and peace to his peo - ple on earth.

Lord God, heavenly King,

al-migh-ty God and Fa-ther, we wor-ship you,

we give you thanks, we praise you for your glo - ry.

Lord— Je-sus Christ, on-ly son of the Fa-ther,

Lord God, Lamb of God, you take a-way the sin of the world:

have mer-cy on us; you are seat-ed

at the right hand of the Fa-ther: re-ceive our prayer.—

For you a - lone are the Ho-ly One,

RITE A

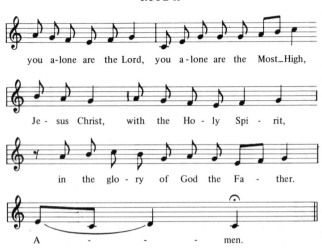

you a-lone are the Lord, you a-lone are the Most High,

Je - sus Christ, with the Ho - ly Spi - rit,

in the glo - ry of God the Fa - ther.

A - - - men.

GOSPEL READING

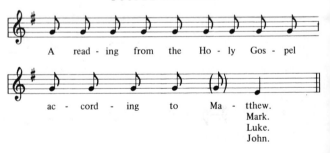

A read - ing from the Ho - ly Gos - pel

ac - cord - ing to Ma - tthew.
Mark.
Luke.
John.

R. Glo - ry to Christ our Sa - viour.

RITE A

This is the Gos - pel of Christ.

R. Praise to Christ our Lord.

or this:-

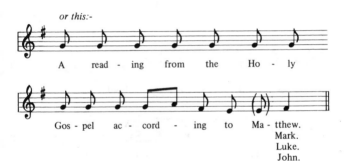

A read - ing from the Ho - ly

Gos - pel ac - cord - ing to Ma - tthew.
Mark.
Luke.
John.

R. Glo - ry to Christ___ our Sav - iour.

This is the Gos - pel of Christ.

R. Praise to Christ___ our Lord.

THE SURSUM CORDA

Either

The— Lord— be with you.

R. And— al - so with you.

Or

The— Lord— is here.

R. His— Spi- rit is with us.

Lift up your_____ hearts._____

R. We lift them to_____ the Lord._____

Let us give thanks— to_____ the Lord— our God

R. It is right to give him thanks— and praise._____

THE SANCTUS

and

BENEDICTUS

Priest .... say - ing: Ho - ly, ho - ly, ho - ly Lord,

God of power and might, hea-ven and earth are full of your glo - ry.

Ho - san - na in the high - est.

Bles - sed is he who comes in the name of the Lord.

Ho - san - na in the high - est.

555

RITE A

THE ACCLAMATION

Priest

Let us proclaim the mys - te - ry of faith:

With vigour

Christ has died: Christ is risen: Christ will come a - gain.

DOXOLOGY

for use with Eucharistic Prayer I

Bless - ing and hon - our and glo - ry and power
be yours for ev - er and ev - er. A - men.

AGNUS DEI

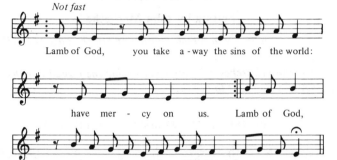

Not fast

Lamb of God, you take a - way the sins of the world:

have mer - cy on us. Lamb of God,

you take a - way the sins of the world: grant_ us peace.

or this version

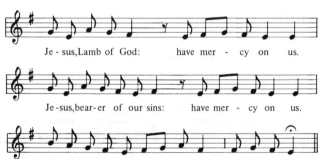

Je - sus, Lamb of God: have mer - cy on us.

Je - sus, bear - er of our sins: have mer - cy on us.

Je - sus, re - deem - er of___ the world: give us your peace.

THE ORDER FOR
HOLY COMMUNION RITE B

Setting by John Merbecke

To be sung freely in speech-rhythm and at the pace of good reading.

In many churches it is better not to sing the Creed *nor the* Our Father, *but to say them.*

RESPONSE TO THE SUMMARY OF THE LAW

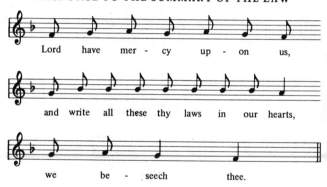

Lord have mer - cy up - on us,

and write all these thy laws in our hearts,

we be - seech thee.

KYRIE ELEISON

Lord,— have— mer - cy, Lord,— have— mer - cy.

Ky - ri - e e - lei - son, Ky - ri - e e - lei - son,

Christ,— have— mer - cy, Christ,— have— mer - cy.

Chris - te e - lei - son, Chris - te e - lei - son,

RITE B

GLORIA IN EXCELSIS
(often omitted in Advent and Lent)

559

God the Fa - ther al - migh - ty.

O Lord the on - ly be - got - ten Son, Je - sus Christ,

O Lord God, Lamb of God, Son of the Fa - ther,

that ta - kest a - way the sins of the world,

have mer - cy up - on us.

Thou that ta - kest a - way the sins of the world,

re - ceive our prayer.

Thou that sit-test at the right hand of God the Fa-ther, have mer-cy up-on us. For thou on-ly art ho-ly; thou on-ly art the Lord; thou on-ly, O Christ, with the Ho-ly Ghost, art the Most High in the glo-ry of God the Fa-ther. A-men.

THE NICENE CREED

Priest   *People*

I be-lieve in one God, the Fa-ther al-migh-ty,

ma-ker of heav'n and earth, and of all things vi - si - ble

and in - vi - si - ble. And in one Lord Je - sus Christ,

the on - ly be - got - ten Son of God,

be - got - ten of his Fa - ther be - fore all worlds.

God of God; Light of Light;

ve - ry God of ve - ry God, be - got - ten not made,

being of one substance with the Father,

by whom all things were made;

who for us men and for our salvation came down from heav'n,

and was incarnate by the Holy Ghost of the Virgin Mary

and was made man, and was crucified also for us

under Pontius Pilate. He suffered and was buried,

and the third day He rose again,

according to the scriptures,

and as - cend - ed in - to heav'n,

and sit - teth on the right hand of the Fa - ther.

And He shall come a - gain with glo - ry to

judge both the quick and the dead:

whose king - dom shall have no end.

And I be - lieve in the Ho - ly Ghost,

the Lord, the Giv - er of life,

who pro - ceed - eth from the Fa - ther and the Son.

Who with the Fa - ther and the Son

to - ge - ther is wor-shipped and glo - ri - fied,

who spake by the pro - phets.

And I be - lieve one ho - ly,

ca - tho - lic and ap - o - sto - lic Church.

I ack - now - ledge one bap - tism

for the re - mis - sion of sins.

And I look for the re - sur - rec - tion of the dead;

and the life of the world to come. A - men.

RITE B

THE SURSUM CORDA

The Lord be with you: And with thy spirit.

Lift up your hearts: We lift them up unto

the Lord. Let us give thanks unto the Lord our God:

It is meet and right so to do.

(Priest ending)

... ev-er-more prais-ing thee and say-ing:

RITE B

SANCTUS

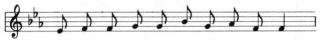

Ho - ly, Ho - ly, Ho - ly Lord God of hosts.

Hea - ven and earth are full of thy glo - ry.

Glo - ry be to Thee O Lord most high.

BENEDICTUS

Bles-sed is he that co-meth in the name of the Lord.

Ho - san - na in the high - est.

THE LORD'S PRAYER

Priest As our Saviour has taught us, so we pray.

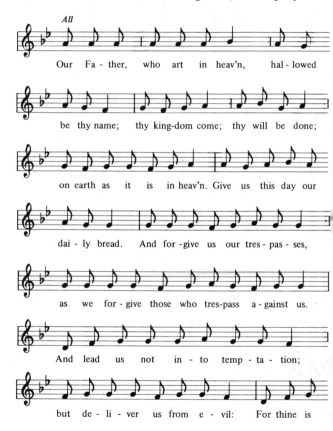

All

Our Fa - ther, who art in heav'n, hal - lowed

be thy name; thy king-dom come; thy will be done;

on earth as it is in heav'n. Give us this day our

dai - ly bread. And for -give us our tres - pas - ses,

as we for - give those who tres-pass a - gainst us.

And lead us not in - to temp - ta - tion;

but de - li - ver us from e - vil: For thine is

RITE B

the king - dom, the power and the glo - ry, for ev - er and ev - er. A - men.

AGNUS DEI

O Lamb of God, that ta - kest a - way the sins of the world, have mer - cy up - on us.

O Lamb of God, that ta - kest a - way the sins of the world, have mer - cy up - on us.

O Lamb of God, that ta - kest a - way the sins of the world, grant us thy peace.

INDEXES

HYMNS SUGGESTED FOR SUNDAYS AND SOME HOLY DAYS ACCORDING TO THE NEW LECTIONARY

In selecting the hymns an effort has been made to give variety of style, metre and key within a single service. The first list for the day provides hymns for the Eucharist, in this order: Introit, after the Epistle, Offertory, Communion, Postcommunion. A procession is suggested on major festivals, but if no procession takes place, the hymn might be substituted for that given for the introit. The hymns usually follow the general theme of the lessons, though occasionally the link with a particular lesson is so close that an alternative should be chosen if the lesson is not read in that year.

The second list, separated by an asterisk, gives hymns which could be substituted for those in the first list, or from which hymns could be selected for a second service. It should be noted that the ASB lectionary often makes use of the eucharistic lessons in one year at Morning and Evening Prayer in the other year, and selection can be made accordingly. On certain Sundays it is appropriate to use both at the Eucharist and at Evensong hymns which are particularly associated with the theme of the day—for example, 'On Jordan's bank' on Advent 3. The second list contains many general hymns unrelated to any lectionary, the use of which will enable a congregation to enjoy a large and varied selection during the course of a year.

---

9 before Christmas
(*5 before Advent*) (Office Hymns 149, 150)
466 Thou whose almighty word
349 Come let us join our cheerful songs
263 All creatures of our God and King
274 Author of life divine
265 Lord of beauty
*
237 Morning has broken

433 O worship the King
399 Light of the lonely pilgrim's heart
285 For the beauty of the earth
240 When all the world to life is waking
253 The duteous day now closeth
and hymns 264 to 267

8 before Christmas
(*4 before Advent*) (Office Hymns 149, 150)

255 Most glorious Lord of life (or 358)
342 Breathe on me, breath of God
332 All hail the power of Jesu's name
 83 Glory be to Jesus
439 Praise to the holiest

*

358 Father of heaven, whose love profound
294 Just as I am
364 God is love: let heaven adore him
341 Blest are the pure in heart
401 Light's abode, celestial Salem
490 Judge eternal, throned in splendour
354 Eternal Father, strong to save

7 before Christmas
(3 before Advent) (Office Hymns 149, 150)
416 O God of Bethel (or 417 if Remembrance Sunday)
370 Help us O Lord
148 The God of Abraham praise
281 Draw nigh and take the Body of the Lord
394 Let all the world in every corner sing

*

418 O happy band of pilgrims
357 Father hear the prayer we offer
362 Glorious things of thee are spoken
495 God is working his purpose out
431 O thou who camest from above
383 Jesu lover of my soul

251 Sun of my soul, thou Saviour dear

6 before Christmas
(2 before Advent) (Office Hymns, 149, 150)
416 O God of Bethel (or 417 if Remembrance Sunday)
315 Word of the Father
333 All my hope on God is founded (or 468)
300 O food of men wayfaring
368 Guide me O thou great Redeemer

*

418 O happy band of pilgrims
460 There is a land of pure delight
362 Glorious things of thee are spoken
116 O praise our great and glorious God
296 Lord enthroned in heavenly splendour
435 Onward Christian soldiers
372 He who would valiant be
468 Through the night of doubt and sorrow

5 before Christmas
(Sunday next before Advent) (Office Hymns 149, 150)
467 Through all the changing scenes of life (or 345)
344 Children of the heavenly King
447 Sing praise to God who reigns above (or 352)
284 Father, we thank thee, who hast planted
499 Thy kingdom come O God

*

15 The Lord will come and not be slow
388 Jesus shall reign
353 Dear Lord and Father of mankind (esp Yr 1)
393 Lead us, heavenly Father
434 Oft in danger
18 Ye servants of the Lord
404 Lord of our life and God of our salvation
252 The day thou gavest, Lord, is ended

Advent 1
(Office Hymns 1, 2)
14 The Advent of our God (or 501)
5 Hark, the glad sound (or 502)
16 Wake, O Wake (Yr 1) or 9 Lo, he comes (Yr 2)
13 O quickly come
286 From glory to glory

*

449 Soldiers of Christ arise
388 Jesus shall reign
18 Ye servants of the Lord
16 Wake, O Wake (Yr 2)
9 Lo, he comes (Yr 1)
3 Come thou long expected Jesus
501 Drop down ye heavens from above

Advent 2 (Office Hymns 1, 2)
15 The Lord will come and not be slow (or 501)
2 O heavenly word of God on high (or 502)
438 Praise to God whose word was spoken (or 9)
303 O word immortal

8 Lift up your heads, ye mighty gates

*

407 Lord thy word abideth
315 Word of the Father
388 Jesus shall reign (Yr 2)
13 O quickly come
7 Hills of the north, rejoice
466 Thou whose almighty word

Advent 3 (Office Hymns 1, 2)
12 On Jordan's bank (or 501)
6 Hark a herald voice is calling (or 502)
7 Hills of the north, rejoice
275 Blessed Jesu, Mary's son
500 Thy kingdom come, on bended knee

*

322 Pour out thy spirit
483 The Church of God a kingdom is
443 Rejoice the Lord is King (Yr 2)
170 Lo, in the wilderness
499 Thy kingdom come O God
11 O come, O come, Emmanuel

Advent 4 (Office Hymns 1, 2)
11 O Come, O come, Emmanuel (or 1, or 501)
180 Hail O star that pointest (Yr 1 only) or
181 The Lord whom earth (Yr 2 only) (or 502)
10 Long ago, prophets knew (or 16)
17 When came in flesh the incarnate word

xxi

3 Come thou long expected Jesus

*

4 Gabriel's message does away
9 Lo, he comes
268 Of the glorious body telling
443 Rejoice the Lord is King
6 Hark the glad sound
501 Drop down ye heavens from above

Christmas Midnight Mass
(Procession 33 or 30 if not used below)

23 Behold the great creator makes
42 While shepherds watched (or 505)
32 O little town of Bethlehem
465 Thou didst leave thy throne (or 28, 30 or 35)
26 Hark the herald angels sing

*

29 It came upon the midnight clear
31 O little one sweet
19 Come thou redeemer of the earth (esp as Introit or Procession)
38 The maker of the sun and moon
295 Let all mortal flesh keep silence

Christmas Day (Office Hymns 19, 20)
(Procession 30 or 24)

42 While shepherds watched
39 Unto us a boy is born (or 505)
34 Once in royal David's city (or 24)

22 Away in a manger
26 Hark the herald angels sing

*

20 From east to west
36 The first Nowell
25 God rest you merry
295 Let all mortal flesh keep silence
27 How brightly shines the morning star

Christmas 1 (Office Hymns 19, 20)

21 A great and mighty wonder
44 Faithful vigil ended (esp Yr 2) (or 505)
37 The great God of heaven
41 Where is this stupendous stranger
25 God rest you merry (or 23)

*

157 Hail to the Lord who comes (Yr 2)
43 Child of the stable's secret birth
27 How brightly shines
35 Silent night
28 In the bleak mid-winter
23 Behold the great creator makes
258 O Christ the same

Christmas 2 (Office Hymns 19, 20)

20 From east to west
45 The growing limbs of God the Son (or 505)
36 The first Nowell (or 34)
40 What child is this
39 Unto us a boy is born

*

22 Away in a manger

43 Child of the stable's secret birth
38 The maker of the sun and moon
34 Once in royal David's city
21 A great and mighty wonder
239 Lord of all hopefulness
258 O Christ the same
203 When Christ was born in Bethlehem (Yr 2)

Epiphany of Our Lord (Office Hymn 46)
(Procession 50)
51 Hail thou source of every blessing
49 Brightest and best
47 As with gladness
295 Let all mortal flesh keep silence
48 Bethlehem of noblest cities

*
52 O worship the Lord
23 Behold the great creator makes
43 Child of the stable's secret birth
40 What child is this
36 The first Nowell

Epiphany 1 (Office Hymn 46)
46 Why impious Herod
58 The sinless one to Jordan came
52 O worship the Lord
425 O love how deep, how broad, how high
352 Crown him with many crowns

*
47 As with gladness

49 Brightest and best
48 Bethlehem of noblest cities
23 Behold the great creator makes
470 To the name that brings salvation
55 Hail to the Lord's anointed

Epiphany 2 (Office Hymns 53, 54)
55 Hail to the Lord's anointed
57 The race that long in darkness pined
353 Dear Lord and Father of mankind
302 O thou who at thy Eucharist (in Unity week) otherwise 41
393 Lead us heavenly Father

*
200 Jesus calls us
214 Let the round world with songs
216 Disposer supreme
390 Jesus where'er thy people meet
420 O Jesus I have promised
366 God of mercy, God of grace

Epiphany 3 (Office Hymns 53, 54)
451 Songs of praise the angels sang
366 God of mercy, God of grace
56 Songs of thankfulness and praise
41 Where is this stupendous stranger (or in Unity Week 302)
483 The Church of God a kingdom is

*
274 Author of life divine

276 Bread of heaven
300 O food of men wayfaring
298 May the grace of Christ our Saviour
284 Father we thank thee
425 O love how deep, how broad, how high
360 Firmly I believe and truly
361 Forth in the peace of Christ we go

Epiphany 4 (Office Hymns 53, 54)
426 O praise thy Lord ye servants
206 Christ is our cornerstone
430 O thou not made with hands
299 My spirit longs for thee
362 Glorious things of thee are spoken

*

 52 O worship the Lord
209 Lo! God is here
207 Eternal power whose high abode
257 This is the day the Lord has made
249 Round me falls the night
312 Where the appointed sacrifice

Epiphany 5 (Office Hymns 53, 54)
 53 This day the first of days (or 256)
365 God moves in a mysterious way
377 Immortal, invisible, God only wise
373 How shall I sing that majesty
235 Forth in thy name O Lord I go

*

347 Come gracious Spirit, heavenly Dove

340 Beyond all mortal praise
339 Be thou my vision
405 Lord of the boundless curves of space
495 God is working his purpose out
466 Thou whose almighty word
267 The spacious firmament on high

Epiphany 6 (Office Hymns 53, 54)
232 Awake my soul
369 Happy are they, they that love God
470 To the name that brings salvation
305 Soul of my Saviour (or 275)
372 He who would valiant be

*

342 Breathe on me, breath of God
341 Blest are the pure in heart
335 All praise to thee
459 The Lord's my shepherd
425 O love, how deep, how broad, how high
245 God that madest earth and heaven

9 before Easter (Office Hymns 53, 54)
254 Come let us with our Lord arise
341 Blest are the pure in heart (esp Yr 1)
433 O worship the King
464 Thou art the way
359 Fight the good fight

*

267 The spacious firmament on high

265 Lord of beauty, thine the splendour
365 God moves in a mysterious way (Yr 2)
337 As pants the hart
387 Jesus, good above all other
253 The duteous day now closeth

8 before Easter (Office Hymns 53, 54)

436 Praise my soul, the king of heaven
324 Thine arm O Lord (Yr 1 only) or
415 O for a thousand tongues (Yr 2 only)
401 Lights abode, celestial Salem
294 Just as I am (or 385)
463 Thine for ever, God of love

*

139 Come thou Holy Spirit, come
102 A brighter dawn is breaking
391 King of glory, King of peace
378 Immortal love for ever full
325 Thou to whom the sick and dying
243 At even when the sun was set

7 before Easter (Office Hymns 53, 54)

358 Father of heaven, whose love profound
391 King of glory, King of peace
440 Praise to the Lord, the Almighty
384 Jesu my Lord, my God, my all (or 294)
424 O Love divine, how sweet thou art

*

404 Lord of our life and God of our salvation
376 I heard the voice of Jesus say
383 Jesu lover of my soul
436 Praise my soul, the king of heaven
66 Forgive our sins as we forgive
84 It is a thing most wonderful
85 Jesu meek and lowly
250 Saviour, again, to thy dear name we raise

Ash Wednesday (Office Hymns 59, 60)

59 Now is the healing time (or 60 or 507)
71 Maker of earth to thee alone
67 Forty days and forty nights
70 Lord Jesus, think on me
74 O for a heart to praise my God

*

61 O Christ, who art the light and day
66 Forgive our sins as we forgive
75 O thou who dost accord us
382 Jesu, grant me this I pray
84 It is a thing most wonderful
63 All ye who seek a comfort sure

Lent 1 (Office Hymns 59, 60)

63 All ye who seek a comfort sure (or 507)
67 Forty days and forty nights
68 Jesu, Lord of life and glory
83 Glory be to Jesus
64 Be thou my guardian and my guide

*

61 O Christ who art the light and day

65 Christian dost thou see them

75 O thou who dost accord us

299 My spirit longs for thee

333 All my hope on God is founded

445 Rock of ages, cleft for me

507 Hear us O Lord

Lent 2 (Office Hymns 59, 60)

66 Forgive our sins as we forgive (or 507)

73 My God, I love thee

65 Christian dost thou see them

62 Ah, Holy Jesu, how hast thou offended

450 Soldiers who are Christ's below

*

61 O Christ who art the light and day

72 My faith looks up to thee

350 Come O thou traveller unknown

449 Soldiers of Christ arise

453 Stand up, Stand up for Jesus!

382 Jesu, grant me this I pray

337 As pants the hart for cooling streams

Lent 3 (Office Hymns 59, 60)

369 Happy are they (or 59, 60 or 507)

414 O for a closer walk with God (or 81)

76 Take up thy cross the Saviour said

69 Lord in this thy mercy's day (or 72)

379 In the Cross of Christ I glory

*

61 O Christ who art the light and day

81 Dost thou truly seek renown

71 Maker of earth, to thee alone

374 How sweet the name of Jesus sounds

474 Who is this so weak and helpless

439 Praise to the holiest in the height

172 Thou art the Christ (Yr 2)

376 I heard the voice of Jesus say

434 Oft in danger, oft in woe

Lent 4 (Office Hymns 59, 60)

77 The God of love my shepherd is

178 'Tis good Lord to be here

75 O thou who dost accord us

389 Jesus these eyes have never seen (or 308)

286 From glory to glory

*

61 O Christ who art the light and day

234 Christ whose glory fills the skies

247 O gladsome light, O grace

176 O vision blest of heavenly light

177 Christ upon the mountain peak

399 Light of the lonely pilgrim's heart

408 Love Divine, all loves excelling

Lent 5 (Office Hymns 78, 79 or 59, 60)

94 We sing the praise of him who died

91 Sweet the moments, rich in blessing (or 92)
90 O sacred head, sore wounded
85 Jesu, meek and lowly (or 89)
79 The royal banners (to a modern tune)

*

80 Servant of God, remember
82 Drop, drop slow tears
84 It is a thing most wonderful
92 There is a green hill
93 Were you there when they crucified
242 As now the sun's declining rays
439 Praise to the holiest in the height

Palm Sunday (Office Hymns 78, 79)
(Procession etc 508 to 510)
511 Ride on, Ride on in majesty!
87 Nature with open volume stands (or 88)
86 My song is love unknown
88 Now, my soul, thy voice upraising (or 89)
95 When I survey the wondrous cross

*

80 Servant of God, remember
82 Drop, drop slow tears
83 Glory be to Jesus
90 O sacred head, sore wounded
92 There is a green hill
96 O thou who through this holy week
474 Who is this so weak and helpless

Maundy Thursday (No Office Hymns)
280 Deck thyself, my soul, with gladness (or 311)
269 The heavenly word proceeding forth (or 304)
310 We hail thy presence glorious
270 According to thy gracious word
268 Of the glorious body telling
See also nos 513 to 515

*

281 Draw nigh, and take the body of the Lord
293 Jesus, our Master, on the night that they came
297 Lord Jesus Christ
302 O thou who at thy Eucharist didst pray
304 Once, only once, and once for all

Easter Eve (No Office Hymns)
(Vigil see 518)
317 With Christ we share (to tune 124)
296 Lord enthroned in heavenly splendour
102 A brighter dawn is breaking
119 The strife is o'er

*

100 The day draws on with golden light
101 The Lamb's high banquet we await
104 At the Lamb's high feast we sing
106 Come ye faithful, raise the strain
114 Now is eternal life

116 O praise our great and glorious Lord
120 Thine be the glory

Easter Day (Office Hymns 100, 101)
(Procession 109)
120 Thine be the glory (or 119)
111 Jesus Christ is risen (or 519)
104 At the Lamb's high feast we sing (or 106)
122 Thou hallowed chosen morn of praise
110 Jesus Christ is risen today

*

102 A brighter dawn is breaking
115 Now the green blade riseth
117 The day of resurrection
123 Walking in a garden
125 Ye sons and daughters (Evening Procession)
119 The strife is o'er
113 Love's redeeming work is done

Easter 1 (Office Hymns 100, 101)
106 Come ye faithful raise the strain
117 The day of resurrection (or 519)
116 O praise our great (or 101)
276 Bread of heaven (or 284, 300)
105 Christ the Lord is risen again

*

103 Alleluya, Alleluya!
107 Good Christian men, rejoice and sing
108 Hail Easter bright, in glory dight
112 Jesus lives!
118 The Lord is risen indeed

119 The strife is o'er
121 This joyful Eastertide
124 Ye choirs of new Jerusalem

Easter 2 (Office Hymns 100, 101)
101 The Lamb's high banquet we await (or 108)
118 The Lord is risen indeed
112 Jesus lives! (or 400 Year 1)
282 Faithful shepherd, feed me
120 Thine be the glory

*

105 Christ the Lord is risen again
114 Now is eternal life
446 Sing alleluya forth
457 The king of love my shepherd is (Yr 2)
458 The Lord my pasture shall prepare (Yr 2)
459 The Lord's my shepherd (Yr 2)
400 Light of the minds that know thee (Year 1)

Easter 3 (Office Hymns 100, 101)
124 Ye choirs of new Jerusalem
114 Now is eternal life (or 112)
103 Alleluya, alleluya!
121 This joyful Eastertide
113 Love's redeeming work is done

*

112 Jesus lives!
317 With Christ we share a mystic grave
363 Glory in the highest
375 I danced in the morning
345 Christ is the King
280 Deck thyself, my soul, with gladness

279 Come risen Lord, and deign to be our guest

Easter 4 (Office Hymns 100, 101)
107 Good Christian men, rejoice and sing
463 Thine for ever (Yr 1 only) or 347
464 Thou art the way (Yr 2 only) or 347
296 Lord enthroned in heavenly splendour
102 A brighter dawn is breaking (or 308)
437 Praise the Lord, ye heavens adore him

*

374 How sweet the name of Jesus sounds
376 I heard the voice of Jesus say (Yr 1)
347 Come gracious Spirit, heavenly Dove
442 Prayer is the soul's sincere desire
448 Sing ye faithful, sing with gladness
478 Ye watchers and ye holy ones
486 We have a gospel to proclaim

Easter 5 (Office Hymns 100, 101)
126 Lord, in thy name thy servants plead
416 O God of Bethel
351 Come, ye faithful, raise the anthem
274 Author of life divine
112 Jesus lives!

*

127 To thee our God we fly
114 Now is eternal life

262 We plough the fields
267 The spacious firmament on high
285 For the beauty of the earth
493 Rejoice, O land, in God thy might
490 Judge eternal, throned in splendour
487 You, living Christ, our eyes behold

Ascension Day (Office Hymn 128)
(Procession 130 or 109)
133 The eternal gates lift up their heads
128 Eternal Monarch, King most high
132 See the conqueror mounts in triumph
135 The Lord ascendeth up on high (or 129)
134 The head that once was crowned with thorns

*

109 Hail the day that sees him rise
129 O Christ our hope
and some of the hymns for the Sunday after Ascension

Sunday After Ascension (*Easter 6*)
(Office Hymn 128)
134 The head that once was crowned with thorns
131 O King most high of earth and sky
338 At the Name of Jesus
129 O Christ our hope (or 135)
271 Alleluya, sing to Jesus

*

135 The Lord ascendeth up on high

332 All hail the power of Jesu's name
375 I danced in the morning
443 Rejoice the Lord is King
446 Sing alleluya forth
448 Sing ye faithful, sing with gladness
476 Ye servants of God, your master proclaim
486 We have a gospel to proclaim
483 The Church of God a kingdom is

Whitsunday or Pentecost (Office Hymn 136)

(Procession 142 or 139)

143 Spirit of mercy, truth and love
139 Come thou Holy Spirit, come (or 138)
137 Come down, O Love divine
141 Holy Spirit, ever dwelling (or 140)
431 O thou who camest from above

*

138 Come Holy Ghost, our souls inspire
140 Holy Spirit, come confirm us
342 Breathe on me, Breath of God
347 Come gracious Spirit, heavenly Dove
348 Come Holy Ghost, our hearts inspire
367 Gracious Spirit, Holy Ghost
409 Love of the Father, Love of God the Son
419 O Holy Spirit, Lord of grace
421 O King enthroned on high

Trinity Sunday (Pentecost 1) (Office Hymn 144)

146 Holy, Holy, Holy!
144 Father most holy, merciful and tender
148 The God of Abraham praise (or 159)
147 Most ancient of all mysteries (or 145)
343 Bright the vision that delighted (or 444)

*

159 I bind unto myself today
295 Let all mortal flesh keep silence
298 May the grace of Christ our Saviour
356 Father eternal, Lord of the ages
358 Father of heaven, whose love profound
373 How shall I sing that majesty
433 O worship the King
246 Holy Father, cheer our way

Pentecost 2 (Trinity 1) (Office Hymns 149, 150)

334 All people that on earth do dwell
206 Christ is our cornerstone (Yr 1) or
480 In Christ there is no east or west (Yr 2)
484 The Church's one foundation (or 345)
287 Glory, love and praise and honour
450 Soldiers who are Christ's below

*

483 The Church of God a kingdom is

513 God is love, and where true love is

355 Eternal ruler of the ceaseless round

302 O thou who at thy Eucharist didst pray

345 Christ is the King!

477 Ye that know the Lord is gracious

481 Jesus, Lord, we look to thee

251 Sun of my Soul

Pentecost 3 (Trinity 2) (Office Hymns 149, 150)

256 On this day the first of days (or 255)

317 With Christ we share (Yr 1) or

374 How sweet the name (or 206) (Yr 2)

470 To the name that brings salvation

290 Holy God, we show forth here

434 Oft in danger, oft in woe

*

272 All for Jesus

333 All my hope on God is founded

429 O thou in all thy might so far

378 Immortal love for ever full

476 Ye servants of God, your master proclaim

486 We have a gospel to proclaim

243 At even when the sun was set

Pentecost 4 (Trinity 3) (Office Hymns 149, 150)

233 Glory to thee, who safe hast kept

428 O Son of God, eternal love

461 There's a wideness in God's mercy (Yr 2) (or 436 in both)

303 O word immortal

391 King of glory, King of peace

*

63 All ye who seek a comfort sure (Yr 2)

418 O happy band of pilgrims

239 Lord of all hopefulness

376 I heard the voice of Jesus say

487 You living Christ our eyes behold

331 Abide with me

Pentecost 5 (Trinity 4) (Office Hymns 149, 150)

390 Jesus where'er thy people meet

370 Help us Lord to learn (or 348) (Yr only) or

482 Spread, O spread thou mighty word (Yr 2)

485 Thy hand, O God, has guided

314 With solemn faith we offer up

472 When all thy mercies, O my God

*

494 Christ is the world's true light

495 God is working his purpose out

292 Jesu, thou joy of loving hearts

377 Immortal, invisible, God only wise

426 O praise the Lord, ye servants of the Lord

252 The day thou gavest, Lord, is ended

Pentecost 6 (Trinity 5) (Office Hymns 149, 150)

403 Lord of all being, throned afar (or 388)
414 O for a closer walk with God (or 349)
340 Beyond all mortal praise
294 Just as I am, without one plea
393 Lead us heavenly Father, lead us

*

461 There's a wideness in God's mercy (Yr 1)
423 O Lord of hosts, all heaven possessing
140 Holy Spirit come confirm us
349 Come let us join our cheerful songs (Yr 1)
342 Breathe on me, Breath of God
348 Come Holy Ghost, our hearts inspire

Pentecost 7 (Trinity 6) (Office Hymns 149, 150)

409 Love of the Father (or 138)
367 Gracious Spirit, Holy Ghost (Yr 1)
419 O Holy Spirit, Lord of grace (esp Yr 2)
448 Sing ye faithful, sing with gladness
386 O Jesu, thou King most wonderful
456 Teach me, my God and King

*

74 O for a heart to praise my God
408 Love Divine, all loves excelling
401 Lights abode, celestial Salem

469 To mercy, pity, peace and love
513 God is love, and where true love is
424 O Love divine, how sweet thou art

Pentecost 8 (Trinity 7) (Office Hymns 149, 150)

254 Come let us with our Lord arise
421 O King enthroned on high (or 143)
355 Eternal ruler of the ceaseless round
301 O most merciful (or 273)
394 Let all the world in every corner sing

*

347 Come gracious Spirit, heavenly Dove
346 City of God, how broad and far
139 Come, thou Holy Spirit, come
369 Happy are they, they that love God
371 He wants not friends that hath thy love
399 Light of the lonely pilgrim's heart
245 God that madest earth and heaven

Pentecost 9 (Trinity 8) (Office Hymns 149, 150)

449 Soldiers of Christ arise
359 Fight the good fight
433 O worship the King
305 Soul of my Saviour (or 304)

362 Glorious things of thee are spoken

*

324 Thine arm, O Lord, in days of old
453 Stand up, stand up for Jesus
435 Onward Christian soldiers
434 Oft in danger, oft in woe
364 God is love, let heaven adore him
383 Jesu lover of my soul
244 Glory to thee, my God, this night

Pentecost 10 (Trinity 9) (Office Hymns 149, 150)

238 New every morning is the love
341 Blest are the pure in heart
335 All praise to thee (or 338)
275 Blessed Jesu, Mary's Son
475 Ye holy angels bright

*

338 At the name of Jesus
 64 Be thou my guardian and my guide
365 God moves in a mysterious way
350 Come O thou traveller unknown
357 Father, hear the prayer we offer
240 When all the world to life is waking

Pentecost 11 (Trinity 10) (Office Hymns 149, 150)

234 Christ whose glory fills the skies
405 Lord of the boundless curves of space

498 Son of God, eternal Saviour
309 Victim divine, thy grace we claim
306 Strengthen for service, Lord, the hands

*

473 When morning gilds the skies
372 He who would valiant be
398 Lift up your hearts!
478 Ye watchers and ye holy ones
455 Strong Son of God, immortal love
456 Teach me, my God and King
387 Jesus good above all other

Pentecost 12 (Trinity 11) (Office Hymns 149, 150)

430 O thou not made with hands (or 346)
186 Tell out my soul
273 And now, O Father, mindful of the love (or 333)
307 Sweet Sacrament divine (or 308)
361 Forth in the peace of Christ we go

*

237 Morning has broken
373 How shall I sing that majesty
400 Light of the minds that know thee
415 O for a thousand tongues to sing
438 Praise to God whose word was spoken
458 The Lord my pasture shall prepare
494 Christ is the world's true light
248 O strength and stay

Pentecost 13 (*Trinity 12*) (Office Hymns 149, 150)

149 Father we praise thee (or 232)
379 In the cross of Christ I glory
 76 Take up thy cross the Saviour said
312 Where'er the appointed sacrifice
427 O praise ye the Lord

*

 63 All ye who seek a comfort sure
382 Jesu grant me this I pray
209 Lo, God is here! let us adore
499 Thy kingdom come, O God
402 Lord it belongs not to my care
404 Lord of our life and God of our salvation
239 Lord of all hopefulness

Pentecost 14 (*Trinity 13*) (Office Hymns 149, 150)

369 Happy are they, they that love God
419 O Holy Spirit, Lord of grace
381 Jerusalem the golden
297 Lord Jesus Christ (or 289)
500 Thy kingdom come, on bended knee

*

396 Let saints on earth in concert sing
406 Lord teach us how to pray aright (Yr 2)
298 May the grace of Christ our Saviour
285 For the beauty of the earth
236 Lord as I wake I turn to you
371 He wants not friends that hath thy love

436 Praise, my soul, the king of heaven

Pentecost 15 (*Trinity 14*) (Office Hymns 149, 150)

492 O God of earth and altar
441 Pray that Jerusalem may have (or 497)
401 Lights abode, celestial Salem
299 My spirit longs for thee (or 278)
490 Judge eternal, throned in splendour

*

362 Glorious things of thee are spoken
498 Son of God, eternal Saviour
346 City of God, how broad and far
491 Lord, while for all mankind we pray
493 Rejoice, O Land, in God thy might
499 Thy kingdom come, O God
265 Lord of beauty, thine the splendour
247 O gladsome light, O grace

Pentecost 16 (*Trinity 15*) (Office Hymns 149, 150)

358 Father of heaven, whose love profound
481 Jesus, Lord, we look to thee
271 Alleluya, sing to Jesus
283 Father, see thy children
477 Ye that know the Lord is gracious

*

479 Faith of our Fathers, taught of old

306 Strengthen for service, Lord, the hands

425 O Love, how deep, how broad, how high

480 In Christ there is no east or west

266 The Lord reigns clothed in strength

249 Round me falls the night

Pentecost 17 (Trinity 16) (Office Hymns 149, 150)

360 Firmly I believe and truly

257 This is the day the Lord has made

310 We hail thy presence glorious (or 280)

270 According to thy gracious word (or 290)

439 Praise to the holiest in the height

*

353 Dear Lord and Father of mankind

339 Be thou my vision

363 Glory in the highest

365 God moves in a mysterious way

474 Who is this so weak and helpless

351 Come, ye faithful, raise the anthem

251 Sun of my soul, thou Saviour dear

Pentecost 18 (Trinity 17) (Office Hymns 149, 150)

336 Angel-voices ever singing

318 My God, accept my heart this day

420 O Jesus I have promised

385 Jesu, the very thought of thee

235 Forth in thy name, O Lord I go

*

397 Let us with a gladsome mind

306 Strengthen for service, Lord, the hands

368 Guide me O thou great redeemer

354 Eternal Father, strong to save

462 They whose course on earth is o'er

471 We love the place, O God

431 O thou who camest from above

246 Holy Father, cheer our way

Pentecost 19 (Trinity 18) (Office Hymns 149, 150)

52 O worship the Lord

455 Strong Son of God, immortal love (or 454)

383 Jesu, lover of my soul

277 Bread of the world in mercy broken (or 445)

427 O praise ye the Lord

*

209 Lo, God is here! let us adore

374 How sweet the name of Jesus sounds

429 O thou in all thy might so far

454 Still throned in heaven

389 Jesus, these eyes have never seen

252 The day thou gavest, Lord, is ended

Pentecost 20 (Trinity 19) (Office Hymns 149, 150)

149 Father we praise thee (or 236)

399 Light of the lonely (Yr 1 only)
or
359 Fight the good fight (Yr 2 only)
473 When morning gilds the skies
288 God everlasting, wonderful and holy
388 Jesus shall reign wher'er the sun

*

450 Soldiers who are Christ's below
364 God is Love: let heaven adore him
380 It is finished
384 Jesu, my Lord, my God, my All
423 O Lord of hosts, all heaven possessing
418 O happy band of pilgrims
236 Lord, as I wake I turn to you

Pentecost 21 (Trinity 20) (Office Hymns 149, 150)
334 All people that on earth do dwell
428 O Son of God, eternal love
479 Faith of our Fathers (or 351)
411 My Lord, my Life, my Love
437 Praise the Lord, ye heavens adore him

*

385 Jesu, the very thought of thee
392 Lead, kindly light
424 O Love divine, how sweet thou art
468 Through the night of doubt and sorrow
445 Rock of ages, cleft for me
472 When all thy mercies, O my God

264 All things bright and beautiful
250 Saviour, again, to thy dear name

Pentecost 22 (Trinity 21) (Office Hymns 149, 150)
403 Lord of all being, throned afar
452 Stand up and bless the Lord
418 O happy band of pilgrims (or 448)
313 Wherefore O Father
443 Rejoice, the Lord is King

*

395 Let bells peal forth
442 Prayer is the soul's sincere desire
459 The Lord's my shepherd
422 O Lord of heaven and earth and sea
237 Morning has Broken
244 Glory to thee, my God, this night

Last Sunday After Pentecost (Office Hymns 149, 150)
345 Christ is the king (or 467)
198 The Church triumphant in thy love
432 O what their joy and their glory must be
291 Jesu the very thought is sweet (or 308)
410 My God, how wonderful thou art

*

412 My soul, there is a country
229 Joy and triumph everlasting
381 Jerusalem the golden
478 Ye watchers and ye holy ones

476 Ye servants of God
499 Thy kingdom come, O God

Dedication Festival (Office Hymn 204)
(Procession 210 or 205)
207 Eternal Power, whose high abode
211 O Word of God above (or 212)
205 Christ is made the sure foundation (or 479)
209 Lo! God is here! (or 208)
413 Now thank we all our God

*

206 Christ is our cornerstone
479 Faith of our Fathers (Procession)
483 The Church of God a kingdom is
485 Thy hand, O God, has guided
441 Pray that Jerusalem may have
471 We love the place, O God

Harvest Thanksgiving (Office Hymns 149, 150)
259 Come ye thankful people come
260 Fair waved the golden corn
261 To thee, O Lord, our hearts we raise
300 O food of men wayfaring (or 274, 276)
262 We plough the fields

*

See also the list after Hymn 262

All Saints (Office Hymn 196)
(Procession 197)
224 For all thy Saints, O Lord (or 196)
230 Palms of glory, raiment bright (or 523)
231 Who are these, like stars appearing
227 How bright these glorious spirits shine
198 The Church triumphant in thy love

*

225 Give me the wings of faith
226 Hark, the sound of holy voices
229 Joy and triumph everlasting
381 Jerusalem the golden
478 Ye watchers and ye holy ones
432 O what their joy and their glory must be

All Souls (No Office Hymns)
396 Let saints on earth in concert sing (or 525)
330 What sweet of life endureth (or 524)
327 Christ enthroned in highest heaven (or 326)
329 Jesu, Son of Mary (or 328)
114 Now is eternal life (or 112)

*

See also the list after Hymn 330

INDEX OF FIRST LINES

xliv